Boynton's Guide to
Compulsory Purchase and Compensation

Boynton's Guide to

Compulsory Purchase and Compensation

Sixth edition

David J Hawkins, *LLB*
Solicitor, Partner in Nabarro Nathanson

Consultant Editor

Sir John Boynton, *MC, LLB, PRTPI*
*Solicitor, formerly Chief Executive of
Cheshire County Council*

© Longman Group UK Ltd 1990

ISBN 0851216145

Published by
Longman Law, Tax and Finance
Longman Group UK Ltd
21-27 Lamb's Conduit Street, London WC1N 3NJ

Associated offices
Australia, Hong Kong, Malaysia, Singapore, USA

First published	1964
Second edition	1968
Third edition	1974
Fourth edition	1977
Fifth edition	1983
Sixth edition	1990

A CIP catalogue record for this book is available from
the British Library.

Printed in Great Britain by Biddles Ltd, Guildford, Surrey.

Contents

Part II: Injurious Effects and Displacement

Preface

When the publishers asked for the production of a new edition of this book, I felt that no one could better undertake this than David Hawkins who had collaborated with me on the fifth edition.

He is actively engaged for both private and public clients on many difficult issues in the field of compulsory purchase and compensation. I believe that his new edition continues the tradition of providing practical and readable advice in a complex area of law.

Nabarro Nathanson   JOHN BOYNTON
50 Stratton Street
London W1
1 June 1990

Foreword

It is now more than a quarter of a century since Sir John Boynton wrote the first edition of this Guide. Over the years the book has grown with the ever-increasing body of law and practice. Compulsory purchase powers are available in a wide variety of circumstances to numerous organisations and also arise through the use of private legislation. With the increase in land values over the years, compensation has become a more important feature in any site assembly exercise.

I hope that this edition will maintain the tradition established by Sir John of producing a useful and practical volume for those involved in advising on compulsory purchase, whether it be from the point of view of the acquiring authority, the landowner or others who might be affected.

Whilst there have been no fundamental alterations to the law since the previous edition, nevertheless many changes have occurred as a result of cases in the courts and new legislation. For example, the courts have reviewed the tests to be applied when considering confirmation of a compulsory purchase order. Another change is the need for authorities now to consider the value added tax position in site assembly.

In general the law is stated as at the end of January 1990 but it has been possible to incorporate some later changes, including in particular the Inquiries Procedure Rules 1990, the new prescribed forms for compulsory purchase orders, and the changes in blight notice and other procedures necessitated by the new rating system.

Nabarro Nathanson
50 Stratton Street
London W1
May 1990

DAVID HAWKINS

xvii

Table of Cases

Table of Statutes

Table of Statutory Instruments

Part I

Compulsory Purchase

Chapter 1

Powers of Compulsory Acquisition

Traditionally any book on compulsory purchase must start with a chapter on the acquisition of powers of compulsory purchase. There is, however, probably no branch of the law which causes less practical difficulty than the question whether or not compulsory powers of purchase exist in a particular case. When problems arise, they usually do so because the acquiring authority have changed their mind in mid-flight: a purchase conceived for one purpose is intended to be used for another, and the question of ultra vires may then arise: see, for example, *Capital Investments* v *Wednesfield Urban District Council* [1965] Ch 774.

This is not to say that every purpose of a public or local authority carries with it the power to acquire land compulsorily. There are some exceptional cases in which land can only be acquired by agreement. In a work of this size it is impossible to summarise all the powers that exist but the principal powers under which compulsory acquisitions are initiated are set out in Appendix 1, including in Pt II all the main highway powers.

Powers of compulsory acquisition are enjoyed by Government departments, local authorities, statutory undertakers, various semi-governmental agencies, new town corporations, urban development corporations, former nationalised industries which have been privatised and exceptionally by private companies.

If the reported proceedings of the Lands Tribunal are examined, it will be seen that most cases arise from a local authority acquisition, with the Department of Transport involved in many of the rest.

Compulsory powers can be given in a variety of ways as follows:

(1) By Acts of Parliament conferring direct power to purchase specific lands. The most usual example is a private Act promoted by a local or public authority for some specific purpose, eg, the construction of a railway. The promoters of

1

the Bill must deposit plans showing the extent of the land to be acquired, and the owners can object by petitioning in Parliament against the Bill. After the Royal Assent, the promoters are usually given a limited time to exercise their powers of acquisition, eg, three years, and if notice to treat is not served in that time, the powers lapse, unless extended by a further Act.

Early private acts incorporated the Lands Clauses Consolidation Act 1845 which provided a comprehensive code of procedure and also dealt with compensation. This was particularly valuable for the railway companies in the nineteenth century and much of the law concerning compulsory purchase arises from decisions under the 1845 Act. Although largely superseded by the equivalent provisions in the Compulsory Purchase Act 1965, it is necessary to remember first that the principles under the 1845 Act are still relevant and secondly that there is a substantial amount of private legislation each year and in some cases the 1845 Act still applies. For example, the London Docklands Railway Act 1985 incorporates, with certain modifications, the 1845 Act rather than the 1965 Act.

(2) By Acts of Parliament conferring general powers to acquire lands without further authorisation. Most of the examples under this heading relate to the defence of the realm, under which the only requirement may be that the lands be marked out and surveyed: the exercise of these powers is rare in peace-time.

(3) By Acts of Parliament which authorise the taking of lands compulsorily but require some further procedure to be adopted, ie, a specific scheme of purchase submitted for confirmation to some confirming authority.

Provisional orders were historically the first procedural device to control the use of general compulsory powers. The machinery was cumbersome and involved the confirmation by Parliament of orders made provisionally by the Local Government Board.

Compulsory purchase orders took the place of provisional orders increasingly from about 1909 onwards. A great advance in uniformity of procedure took place in 1946 with the passing of the Acquisition of Land (Authorisation Procedure) Act which has been re-enacted in the Acquisition of Land Act 1981. This lays down a standard procedure for purchases of land under existing public general Acts by local authorities and by the Minister of Transport in relation to trunk roads, where he is himself the highway authority. In practice most compulsory acquisitions today will be governed procedurally by the provisions of the Acquisition of Land Act 1981. An important exception until April 1990 was that the procedure for clearance areas was governed by s 579 of and Sched 22 to the Housing Act 1985. Other exceptional cases where the 1981 Act either does not apply or is modified include most of the Defence Acts; the Pipe-lines Act 1962; the Forestry Act 1967; the Development of Rural Wales Act 1976; the New Towns Act 1981 and the Water Act 1989.

Designation of land as a subject to compulsory purchase was introduced in the Town and Country Planning Act 1947. It was a procedure developed from the clearance area procedure in the Housing Acts and the declaratory order procedure in the Town and Country Planning Act 1944 (designed largely to deal with areas of war damage). Designation in a development plan was only an important preliminary step; the actual purchase still required the making of a compulsory purchase order, though a procedure existed for designation and compulsory purchase proceedings to be taken simultaneously (s 86 of the Town and Country Planning Act 1962, and the Town and Country Planning General Regulations 1964). A development plan prepared under the Town and Country Planning Act of 1947 or of 1962 might declare as subject to compulsory acquisition:

(*a*) land allocated by the plan for the functions of a Minister, local authority or statutory undertaker;

(*b*) land defined as an area of comprehensive development; or

(*c*) any other land which the authority considered should be designated to secure its use in the manner proposed by the plan.

The procedure survived until 1 April 1969, when the existing provisions (at that time to be found in s 67 of the Town and Country Planning Act 1962) were repealed by the Town and Country Planning Act 1968. This repeal was motivated by the fact that designation, as a procedure had not worked well in practice. Instead of designation, the Act of 1968 gave a wide general power to all local authorities to acquire land compulsorily:

(*a*) if required to secure the treatment of an area as a whole by development, redevelopment or improvement (or required in the public interest to be held together with land so required);

(*b*) if required for development or redevelopment as a whole to relocate population or industry, or to replace open space in the course of redevelopment or improvement of another area as a whole;

(c) if required immediately in the interests of the proper planning of the area.

These powers were re-enacted in ss 112 and 113 of the Town and Country Planning Act 1971, but the wording was simplified and amended by the Local Government, Planning and Land Act 1980, s 91. The power as now expressed is to acquire compulsorily:

(a) any land suitable and required for development, redevelopment or improvement;

(b) any land required for a purpose which it is necessary to achieve in the interests of the proper planning of the area.

The power extends to adjoining land needed for the execution of works to facilitate the development or use. Further, the power is available where the local authority intend to carry out the development through an agent and not themselves.

The tests of 'suitability' for development include reference to the development plan, any planning permission in force for the land and the considerations which would be material in determining any planning application for development on the land, and see *Company Developments (Property) Ltd* v *Secretary of State for the Environment* [1978] JPL 107—the word 'required' in the 1971 Act's provisions did not mean 'essential'.

The Community Land Act 1975 occupied a significant part of the fourth edition of this book. It was repealed by the Local Government, Planning and Land Act 1980. Some of its powers of acquisition were, however, reproduced in the Act of 1980, as were the provisions relating to the Land Authority for Wales.

Chapter 2

Prior Proceedings Settling the Principle of Acquisition

In recent years there has been a growth in the number of statutory procedures which, in effect, settle the principle that land is to be acquired by a public or local authority, but which do not involve individual notice to the owners concerned.

When consulted by someone who has received formal notice of the making of a compulsory purchase order (or merely a letter indicating the desire of the acquiring authority to buy the land) one of the first points to clear is whether the principle of acquisition has been virtually settled by one of these prior proceedings. If it has, it may be found that any powers of objection have in practice been much diminished. The examples given below are not meant to be exhaustive: they are merely intended to draw attention to the need for vigilance, and a close study of local newspapers.

1 New towns

An order may be made by the Secretary of State for the Environment designating the site of a new town under the New Towns Act 1981. The development corporation may then be authorised by means of a compulsory purchase order submitted in accordance with the provisions of Pt I of Sched 4 to the Act to acquire any land designated as the site of the new town whether or not it is proposed to develop or redevelop the land. Section 10 of the 1981 Act also contains provisions for the acquisition of land lying outside the boundary of the designated area.

It is worth noting that a development corporation does not have to serve notice of the making of a compulsory purchase order of land in the designated area upon individual owners, lessees and occupiers. A copy of the notice must, however, be fixed on some conspicuous object on the land and published in the *London Gazette* and a local newspaper for two successive weeks.

The normal right of an owner to have his objection considered at a local inquiry does not apply in the case of acquisitions by development corporations in new towns. The owner may get a private hearing at the Secretary of State's discretion, but may have to rely on written representations to him. The aim of Sched 4 to the Act is to expedite purchases and to restrict public local inquiries to cases where the Secretary of State in his discretion thinks that the matters to which the objection relates are such as to require investigation by public inquiry.

2 Development plans

One of the commonest ways in which the use of land will be settled is through the medium of a development plan prepared under the Town and Country Planning Act 1971. Whilst public notice has to be given of the making of a development plan, individual notice to owners is not required.

If the development plan completes the statutory process and comes into force, an owner who wishes later to object to a compulsory purchase order founded upon the provisions of the plans may find his rights of objection curtailed.

Section 132 of the Town and Country Planning Act 1971 provides that where the proposed purchase is under the general power of acquisition for planning purposes given in ss 112 or 113 of the Act, the confirming authority may disregard any objection to the compulsory purchase order which in his opinion 'amounts in substance to an objection to the provisions of the development plan defining the proposed use of that or any other land'. Note that this discretion to disregard an objection only arises where the purchase is founded upon the powers to acquire land under the powers in the Town and Country Planning Act 1971 (as amended) summarised in Chapter 1. If the land were defined as a housing site in the development plan and a compulsory purchase order were later made under the Housing Acts, then s 132 would not be applicable. In fact, the section is a carry-over from the designation procedure which has been abolished since 1969 (see Chapter 1).

Even if an objection to compulsory purchase cannot legally be disregarded under s 132 of the Act of 1971, it is obvious that an owner will be prejudiced in his objection to purchase if a development plan has virtually settled the proposed use of his land. The owner will be under a practical disability in this sort of case as opposed to the legal disability inherent in s 132.

3 Old-style development plans

The Town and Country Planning Act 1947 introduced the concept of a detailed development plan which would define precisely the uses to which land in the area of the authority would be put. These were shown on maps for towns and counties, the former being obviously the more detailed of the two.

A development plan prepared under the Act of 1947 or its successor the Act of 1962 could define the sites of proposed roads, public and other buildings and works and sites to be used for other purposes. As has already been emphasised, if land were defined in an approved plan as the site of, for example, a school or open space, the owner's ability to object to acquisition for the purpose indicated in the plan would be reduced.

This first generation of development plans was found to have a number of defects mainly arising from the degree of precision attempted. The Report of the Planning Advisory Group in 1966 recommended drastic changes. Their recommendations were embodied in the Town and Country Planning Act 1968, and the new system introduced then was re-enacted in the Act of 1971. Further amendments were made by the Local Government Act 1972, the Town and Country Planning (Amendment) Act 1972, the Local Government, Planning and Land Act 1980, the Local Government Act 1985 and the Housing and Planning Act 1986.

4 Structure and local plans

The new-style development plan consists of a structure plan and a series of local plans. In metropolitan areas unitary plans will also have to be considered.

The *structure plan* made by the county council does not define precise uses for particular areas of land. It is a broad-brush type of plan, consisting of a written statement setting out the planning authorities' policies and general proposals. But it must be accompanied by a key diagram illustrating the policies and general proposals and must also must be accompanied by an explanatory memorandum summarising the reasoned justification for each and every policy and general proposal. This may also contain such illustrative material as the local planning authority think appropriate. The structure plan has to be approved by the Secretary of State for the Environment. Whilst there are rights of objection following advertisement of the submission of the plan, objectors do not have a

right to be heard at the examination in public, since it is for the
Secretary of State to select the topics to be considered and the persons
who might take part (s 9 of the 1971 Act). There is a non-statutory
code of procedure and guidance is given in Circular No 22/84.

Structure plans have now been prepared for every county and
alternative/replacement plans are being prepared as circumstances
change. It follows from the nature of the structure plan that failure to
object to its provisions is less likely to impair an owner's chances of
successful objection to a compulsory purchase order than would have
been the case under the old-style definitive type of development plan.

Local planning authorities (normally district councils or London
Borough Councils) have a duty to prepare such *local plans* for their
area as they think desirable. They may be of three kinds: district
plans, subject plans or action area plans. Objections to local plans are
determined by the plan-making authority not the Secretary of State,
and there are careful provisions for prior publicity (s 12 of the Town
and Country Planning Act 1971). Clearly all local plans must be
scrutinised with care, for it is these plans which define sites, and may
indicate areas for comprehensive development or redevelopment. It is
the local plan which is most likely to bring into play s 132 of the Act
of 1971, and to be a prior proceeding settling the principle of
acquisition. Particular regard should be paid to 'action area' plans.
These are prepared for areas selected for comprehensive treatment by
development, redevelopment or improvement to commence within ten
years from the date of deposit of the plan (s 11 (5) of the 1971 Act
and reg 14 of the Town and Country Planning (Structure and Local
Plans) Regulations 1982 (SI No 555 as amended by SI 1987 No
1760). They are therefore the most likely type of local plan to involve
compulsory powers of acquisition under s 112 of the Town and
Country Planning Act 1971.

Until the passing of the Local Government, Planning and Land Act
1980, action areas were identified in the structure plan for the area
and there was a duty on the local planning authority to prepare a local
plan for each such area. The local planning authority may now
prepare an action area plan without any designation in the structure
plan and the former duty has been removed except in relation to
structure plans approved before 13 November 1980. (See Sched 14,
para 8 (2) to the Act of 1980.)

The Housing and Planning Act 1986 introduced (except in Greater
London, where the old procedures continue pending the introduction
of unitary plans) revised procedures for making, altering, repealing or
replacing local plans (see s 41 and Pt I of Sched 10). These can result

in reduced publicity and consultation where it appears to the local planning authority that the issues involved are not of sufficient importance to warrant the full procedure. It will therefore be important for those affected to pay particular attention to the opportunities to object.

5 Unitary plans

In Greater London (where the structure plan is the Greater London Development Plan approved in 1976) and in the metropolitan areas affected by the Local Government Act 1985, the local plans systems has been replaced by the concept of a unitary plan, which will be a mixture of structure and local plan (see Pt 1 of Sched 1 to the Local Government Act 1985). Expedited procedures for altering unitary plans are included in the Housing and Planning Act 1986 (s 41 and Pt II of Sched 10). Again, unitary plans and proposals to amend them will have to be scrutinised with care as they will contain site specific proposals.

6 Timetable for implementation

Development plans, comprising county maps and town maps in the old style, were prepared for most of England and Wales but no further reviews and amendments may be prepared. They remain in force, however, until revoked either automatically following the adoption of a local plan for the area (para 5A of Sched 7 to the Act of 1971, inserted by the Local Government, Planning and Land Act 1980) or by order of the Secretary of State (para 6 of Sched 7). The Secretary of State may direct by order that any of the provisions of the old development plan shall continue in force in the area of the local plan (para 5B of Sched 7).

The problems which can arise in the field of assessing compensation as a result of the transition from old- to new-style development plans are mentioned at p 199.

7 Designation maps in the transition period

As we have seen in Chapter 1, designation of land as subject to compulsory purchase was abolished in the case of any development plan submitted for approval after 1 April 1969. Designation maps will therefore only be found in development plans submitted before that date: but there may still be such plans in existence and operative.

What, therefore, is the effect of a designation map in an approved development plan? The fact of designation can no longer confer upon a local authority (or other public body) a right to acquire the land because the power of confirmation of compulsory purchase orders submitted under the old provisions only applied to orders submitted before 1 April 1969. Any such order submitted for confirmation after 1 April 1969 will have to be founded upon the new wider power of acquisition already referred to and contained in s 112 of the Town and Country Planning Act 1971. However, that fact that there is an approved designation proposal may be evidence to satisfy the confirming Minister that the requirements of s 112 of the Act of 1971 are met. It is also possible that s 132 of the Act 1971 would apply, so that the owner may find it difficult to object to the compulsory purchase order because his objection is likely to be in substance an objection to the provisions of the development plan (which will incorporate the designation map). However, with the passage of time such considerations are less likely to be conclusive.

Eventually approved designation maps will be revoked by orders made under s 105 (3) of the Town and Country Planning Act 1968. Such orders, as we have seen, will be made as a tidying up operation when the old-style development plan has been in whole or in part overtaken by material submitted under the present system. A designation map might, for example, be superseded by a local plan setting out proposals to deal with the area as an 'action area'.

Circular No 15/69 of the Ministry of Housing and Local Government and No 8/81 of the Department of the Environment give general guidance on the acquisition and disposal of land by local authorities under planning powers. The former also deals with the position arising from the abolition of the designation procedure.

8 Highways

The line of a new road can be settled in various ways, none involving individual notice to owners. However, the strict statutory procedure described in the subsequent paragraphs has been substantially modified in practice by government acceptance of procedures for public participation and consultation. These are set out in Department of Environment Circular No 30/73. The steps and timetable in the consultation process (normally involving a public exhibition of plans) will be publicly advertised. Basically the object is to allow the public to express a preference as between alternatives, whether alternative corridors, or alternatives within a chosen corridor, for a proposed new road.

The most common procedure for establishing the line of a new road is the making of a scheme under s 16 of the Highways Act 1980. This allows a highway authority to provide, 'along a route prescribed by the scheme, a special road for the use of traffic of any class prescribed thereby'. Most motorways, ie, roads restricted to use by certain only of the classes of traffic set out in the Fourth Schedule to the Act, are established by means of schemes made under this section.

A motorway scheme is published in draft with plans of the route and a period of not less than six weeks is allowed for objections. Paragraph 17 of Sched 1 to the Highways Act 1980 gives the highway authority the power to take steps to secure that publicity is given in the area affected by the proposed road scheme, additional to the publicity afforded by the statutory notices. Circular No 34/72 requires extensive arrangements for notifying persons affected either directly or because their properties lie within about 100 yards of the proposed works. Objectors to the scheme must state the grounds of their objection or they may be disregarded (para 18 of Sched 1 to the Highways Act 1980). A public inquiry is held if there are objections from local authorities, navigation authorities, or water authorities, or otherwise at the Secretary of State's discretion. When the line is established, detailed planning of the side road alterations, etc, is completed and a draft order under s 18 of the 1980 Act is published. Again, there is a minimum of six weeks allowed for objections and a public inquiry may be held. The confirming authority can disregard an objection to the side road, etc, order if satisfied that it amounts in substance to an objection to the main scheme under s 16 (Highways Act 1980, Sched 1, para 21).

Once the schemes have been made, the special road authority will set about acquiring the land by means of a compulsory purchase order. The special road authority will usually be the Secretary of State but it may be any other highway authority, eg, a county council. Where the special road authority is the Secretary of State, he will make the compulsory purchase order in draft under the Acquisition of Land Act 1981. If objections are made, the Secretary of State must consider them and, unless he decides not to proceed, will make the order with or without modifications. The confirming authority may also confirm the scheme as to part of the proposals and defer consideration of the remaining part for a specific period (Highways Act 1980, s 259).

On the other hand, if the special road authority is a local authority, the order will be made and submitted for confirmation to the Secretary of State in the normal way.

It follows from all this that where an order or scheme is made for the construction of a new road or improvements to the road system, an objection must be entered at the stage when an order or scheme is published under the Highways Act 1980.

It does not need further elaboration to realise the limited field which is in practice open to an owner who objects when the compulsory purchase order is made following approval of a scheme under s 16 or s 18 of the Highways Act 1980. The Secretary of State will listen carefully to the objection as he is bound to do, particularly if no public inquiry was held into the scheme itself. The most an owner can hope for in a case where the scheme has been approved is to try to secure detailed modifications in his own interest.

It is also worth noting the statutory limitation placed upon an objection to a development plan which incorporates the provisions of a statutory scheme or order made under the Highways Act 1980. Section 16 of the Town and Country Planning Act 1971, as amended by the Highways Act 1980, Sched 24, provides that an objection to a structure or local plan can be disregarded if it is in substance an objection with regard to things done or proposed to be done in pursuance of an order or scheme under ss 10, 14, 16, 18, 106 (1), 106 (3) or 108 (1) of the Highways Act 1980 (trunk road orders, special road schemes, orders for schemes for bridges over or tunnels under navigable waters, orders for diversion of navigable waters and supplementary orders).

9 Urban development corporations

Part XVI of the Local Government, Planning and Land Act 1980 introduced the concept of the urban development corporation. If the Secretary of State is of the opinion that it is expedient in the national interest to do so, he may by order designate any area of land as an urban development area (s 134 of the 1980 Act) and establish an urban development corporation with the specific objective of securing the regeneration of the area. As the orders are by statutory instrument requiring approval by resolution of each House of Parliament, there is no right to object and no 'prior proceeding'. To achieve its objective the corporation has wide powers to acquire, hold, manage, reclaim and dispose of land, to provide infrastructure and generally to do anything necessary or expedient for the objective or purposes incidental to it. Land may be acquired by agreement or compulsorily if it is in the urban development area, adjacent to it and required to discharge the corporation's functions, or elsewhere and required for the provision of services in connection with the discharge of functions (s 142). New rights can also be acquired compulsorily.

The development corporation may also have wide powers to take over various planning and other functions from the existing local authorities. There is special provision in s 141 for the Secretary of State to transfer to an urban development corporation land vested in a local authority, statutory undertaker or other public body.

In Circular No 23/88, 'Compulsory Purchase Orders by Urban Development Corporations', the Secretary of State drew attention to the special features and particular policies relevant to such orders. He pointed out that in reaching a decision on whether to confirm an order under s 142 of the 1980 Act, he would have in mind the statutory objectives of the UDC and will, inter alia, wish to consider:

(a) whether the UDC has demonstrated that the land is in need of regeneration;

(b) what alternative proposals (if any) have been put forward by the owners of the land or other persons for regeneration;

(c) whether regeneration is on balance more likely to be achieved if the land is acquired by the UDC;

(d) the recent history and state of the land;

(e) whether the land is in an area for which the UDC has a comprehensive regeneration scheme;

(f) the quality and timescale of both the UDC's regeneration proposals and any alternative proposals.

The Secretary of State goes on to recognise that it will not always be possible or desirable for a UDC to have detailed proposals for land use planning beyond their general framework for regeneration.

The circular points out that the ownership by a UDC of land in an area can stimulate confidence that regeneration will take place, and in this way help to secure investment. UDCs will often best be able to bring about regeneration by assembling land and providing infrastructure over a wide area in order to secure or encourage its development by others.

The Acquisition of Land Act 1981 applies to compulsory purchase orders made by urban development corporations, subject to some minor procedural changes to be found in Sched 28 to the Local Government Planning and Land Act 1980 (as amended).

Chapter 3

Procedure for Making a Compulsory Purchase Order

This chapter is concerned primarily with the mechanics of making a compulsory purchase order for the benefit of local authorities and others with powers of compulsory acquisition. It covers all the steps, some of which are amplified later.

It is appropriate at this stage to mention the statutes which are generally of most relevance in compulsory purchase procedures. First, the Acquisition of Land Act 1981 deals with the procedure for the making and confirmation of compulsory purchase orders. It re-enacts much of what was previously contained in the Acquisition of Land (Authorisation Procedure) Act 1946 and is used in a wide variety of cases—but as mentioned in Chapter 1 it does not apply at all in some cases and in others it applies subject to modifications.

The Compulsory Purchase Act 1965 deals with procedures following the confirmation of the compulsory purchase order, ie, the service of notice to treat, entry on the land, and compensation for disturbance, severance and injurious affection. It applies to those orders to which the 1981 Act applies, and also in other cases. It re-enacts equivalent provisions from the Lands Clauses Consolidation Act 1845 although, as mentioned earlier, some modern private legislation still incorporates the 1845 Act.

The Land Compensation Act 1961 sets out the basis of the compensation code, ie, the procedure for the assessment of compensation for which land has been compulsorily acquired. The code provides for the payment of open market value (unless there is no general demand or market, in which case compensation may be payable on the equivalent reinstatement basis).

The Land Compensation Act 1973 supplements the compensation provisions by providing for such matters as depreciation caused by public works, powers to mitigate injurious effect and for new types of payment such as the home loss payment.

Numerous other statutes may be relevant but in most cases of compulsory acquisition the statutes mentioned form the basic framework for the procedures.

Appendix 2 gives a useful checklist for the benefit of anyone concerned to follow through the detailed statutory procedure involved in making a compulsory purchase order. Those who have to make compulsory purchase orders should bear in mind the time-scale involved, and begin procedures well in advance of land actually being required. Even for an unopposed order at least six months should be allowed from enquiries as to ownerships, etc, until notice of entry. For an opposed order involving a public inquiry at least a year should be allowed (Appendix IV to the Memorandum annexed to Circular Roads No 1/81 states that for a road proposal involving an opposed order at least 35 weeks will be needed as a minimum but on current experience that period will be insufficient).

The critical periods are the preliminary period to prepare land plans, schedule the ownerships, obtain planning permission, investigate the requirements of statutory undertakers and make and submit the order; the period leading up to the inquiry and for the inquiry itself and the preparation and submission of the Inspector's report; the time needed for the Secretary of State to reach a decision—tending to lengthen where environmental issues are raised; and for departmental action to issue the confirmation documents, which will be affected by the volume of cases currently in the Department and complications such as confirmation in part only.

The acquiring authority have control over only a small part of this process, and must recognise that it is a lengthy one.

Detailed guidance is given in Circular No 6/85 'Compulsory Purchase Orders: Procedures' issued by the Department of the Environment (and Welsh Office Circular 11/87). It deals with orders to which the Acquisition of Land Act 1981 applies. Minor amendments to the advice appear in Circulars 1/90 and 2/90. For advice on housing orders see 77/75 and Circulars 13/81. The Department has issued separate advice to New Town Corporations on orders made under the New Towns Act 1981. Circular No 23/88 (Welsh Office 43/88) gives advice and guidance about compulsory purchase orders by urban development corporations (see p 13). The following paragraphs deal with some of the issues which arise regularly in practice.

1 Preliminaries

(a) Schedule of ownerships

One of the first steps in the making of any compulsory purchase order is to ascertain the owners, lessees and occupiers of the land to be acquired. This is normally done as soon as possible after the making of the order has been authorised by an appropriate resolution of the authority specifying the land involved and the statutory power utilised.

Various Acts contain powers under which information as to ownership can be required (see, for example, s 297 of the Highways Act 1980, s 284 of the Town and Country Planning Act 1971 and s 16 of the Local Government (Miscellaneous Provisions) Act 1976): it will be important to use these powers because of the risk that an order could be quashed after confirmation because of failure to serve notices on those entitled (see p 25). Also use of the powers may prove that 'reasonable inquiry' has been made if individual service is to be dispensed with. It is necessary to check the scope of such powers. For example, urban development corporations do not have power to require information under the 1976 Act—although the Department of the Environment has indicated an intention to extend the power to such corporations.

(b) Dispensing with individual service

The Acquisition of Land Act 1981, s 6, provides that if the authority is satisfied that reasonable inquiry has been made and that it is not practicable to ascertain the name or address of an owner, lessee or occupier on whom any document has to be served, the document may be served by addressing it to 'the owner', 'the lessee' or 'the occupier' as the case may be and adding the description of the premises, for example, 'The owner of the unoccupied site of demolished buildings formerly known as Nos 12 to 18 Ashworth Cottages, Barset'.

The document must be delivered to someone on the premises, or if no person is on the premises to whom it may be delivered, the document or a copy must be fixed to some conspicuous part of the premises.

The procedure in the former Acquisition of Land Act 1946 required a Ministerial dispensation from individual service, but this control was abolished by the Local Government, Planning and Land Act 1980. As the new procedure requires 'the authority' to be satisfied, a suitable minute of a committee is needed or a general delegation of powers in this respect to a subcommittee or officer of the acquiring authority.

It is understood to be the view of the Department of Environment that the 'unknown owner' procedure enables acquiring authorities to meet their obligations in those cases where objectors fragment the ownership of sites needed for public development (the intention apparently being to frustrate authorities by requiring them painstakingly to track down each individual owner). However the Department have indicated that amending legislation may be introduced to provide for a declaratory statement of the obligations of an authority in such circumstances.

(c) Maps

The order must describe by reference to a map the land to which it relates. The best scale is usually 1:500, with a location plan showing the position of the site in the locality at a scale of 1:1250, or in rural areas 1:2500, superimposed. If a particular scheme involves acquiring many small plots, the use of insets on a larger scale is helpful. The north point should be shown.

The map should have an appropriate title, eg, the name of the authority and the authorising Act. This title or heading on the map should agree with the description of the map in the order. There should be space for sealing and the authority's usual attestation clause.It should be marked 'Map referred to in the . . . Compulsory Purchase Order 199 '.

The land to be acquired should be coloured and numbered 1 (2, 3, etc, depending on the number of parcels to be acquired) and the area of each parcel should be ascertained and shown in the order schedule.

Maps in monochrome can be submitted, but special care must then be exercised to identify clearly the lands to be acquired.

The map should contain the names of roads and such other information as will enable it to be related to the description of the parcels in the schedule to the order.

A similar unit of measurement should be used throughout: one plot should not be described as 1.7 acres and another as 1,500 square yards (or hectares and square metres). The Government is encouraging the use of metric units of measurement.

The boundaries between plots should be clearly marked. If in any case it is impossible to show a boundary precisely, the land in question should be shown as one plot and all parties believed to be interested should be included in the schedule against the plot number.

The Local Government (Miscellaneous Provisions) Act 1976 and the Highways Act 1980 give power to acquire rights over land as distinct from the land itself, eg, the right to place footings in land. Any plots affected by the acquisition of rights only should be coloured differently (or shown by a method which distinguishes them) from those involving acquisition of title.

On maps, see generally Appendix F to Department of Environment Circular No 6/85 and section E of Roads Circular No 1/81.

(d) Planning consent

No confirmation of a compulsory purchase order can be expected unless the acquiring authority have obtained planning clearance for any development intended after purchase. It is not always necessary to obtain a formal consent, although this is the safest course. In Appendix C to Circular No 6/85 it is stated that the Secretary of State will expect an authority as far as possible to establish before making an order that if the order is confirmed the scheme will be able to proceed without planning difficulties; it will be in the authority's interests to obtain any planning permission needed for the scheme before submitting the order for confirmation. When the order is submitted the Circular indicates that one of the following should be stated:

(a) outline or detailed planning permission has been given for the proposed development, or has been deemed to have been given;

(b) a planning application has been referred to the Secretary of State;

(c) an application will be made later and could not have been made before; or

(d) no planning permission is needed.

Moreover for orders made under s 112 (1) (a) of the Town and Country Planning Act 1971 (as amended) both the local authority and the Secretary of State are required by s 112 (1A) to have regard to the development plan, any planning permission in force and any other material consideration, and the Circular requires the authority to indicate the extent to which they have had regard to those matters.

In the case of urban development corporations, para 7 of Circular No 23/88 recognises that it will not always be possible or desirable to have specific proposals beyond the general framework for the regeneration of the area, and so planning permission may not be essential even in those cases where land is required for a defined end use.

In the case of development by local planning authorities, the position as regards planning consent is governed by the Town and Country Planning General Regulations 1976.

Where the acquiring authority is also the local planning authority, the procedure for obtaining planning consent will be to obtain a deemed consent as outlined in reg 4. The authority must pass a resolution seeking planning permission for the development; notify any owners and agricultural tenants; advertise the proposals in those cases where publicity would have been obligatory if an application had been made, ie, 'bad neighbour' cases, or those affecting the character of a conservation area or the setting of a listed building; and enter the resolution and plans in the planning register. At the end of the specified period (which varies according to whether advertisement was necessary), the authority may pass a second resolution, and then planning permission is deemed to have been granted by the Secretary of State. The procedure is designed to identify objections and to give the Secretary of State an opportunity to call the matter in. The permission does not enure for the benefit of the land, but only for the authority.

However there is an alternative procedure (reg 5) unlikely to be appropriate in compulsory purchase cases, whereby if land is vested in the authority but the development is to be carried out by a third party, deemed permission can be obtained which will enure for the benefit of the land.

In cases where the authority is using compulsory powers to assemble a site to be developed by a third party, it may well be better for the third party to make an application for permission in the normal way. For difficulties arising in 'deemed permission' cases see *Sunbell Properties Ltd* v *Dorset County Council* (1979) 253 EG 1123 and *JJ Steeples* v *Derbyshire County Council* [1981] JPL 582.

The deemed planning procedure is not available if works to alter or extend a listed building are involved—the Secretary of State deals with the application. If the development is a departure from the development plan, the authority must follow the procedure laid down in the Town and Country Planning (Development Plans) (England) Direction 1981: and see Appendix D, Circular No 2/81 from the Department of the Environment. One example under this head is where the proposed route of a highway differs from that shown on the current development plan (or is not shown at all). In Greater London the procedure is set out in the parallel Greater London Direction 1986.

In some cases planning consent is granted by the Town and Country Planning General Development Order 1988, eg, highway improvements on land outside, but abutting onto, the present highway limits (see Pt 13 of Sched 2 to the Order).

Section 40 of the Town and Country Planning Act 1971 allows Government departments to direct that permission shall be deemed to be granted when authorising the local authority's proposals under an enactment. On the whole this is not of much value in compulsory acquisition cases.

(e) Listed building consent

If a compulsory purchase order involves the demolition of a building included in the statutory list maintained under s 54 of the Town and Country Planning Act 1971, it is most unlikely to be confirmed unless listed building consent has been obtained under the Act. Consent is also needed for works of alteration which would affect the character of the building. Where the acquiring authority are also a local planning authority, listed building consent must be obtained from the Secretary of State for the Environment.

When submitting an order concerning listed buildings, the authority must provide a certificate in the form set out in Appendix H to the Department of the Environment Circular No 6/85. The certificate is needed for buildings listed under s 54 of the Town and Country Planning Act 1971; those notified as qualified for listing but not yet formally listed; those subject to a building preservation notice; and those of list quality (as to which see Circular No 8/87 Appendix 1). The certificate should also state whether the order will involve the demolition of any unlisted buildings in conservation areas.

If a listed building is being acquired under s 114 of the 1971 Act, the notice to owners will contain additional paragraphs (see Compulsory Purchase of Land Regulations 1990, reg 4 and form 8). These are dealt with in Appendix J of Circular No 6/85. See also *Robbins v Secretary of State for the Environment* [1989] 1 WLR 201.

(f) Crown land

In accordance with general legal principles, compulsory purchase legislation does not bind the Crown except where expressly stated or by necessary implication. Therefore it is not possible to acquire compulsorily the interest of a government department in land. However s 266 of the Town and Country Planning Act 1971 provides that any power to acquire land compulsorily under Pt VI of the Act (which includes the commonly used s 112) may be exercised in relation to any interest in the land which is held otherwise than by or on behalf of the Crown—so long as the consent of the 'appropriate authority' (ie, the Crown Estate Commissioners, the government department, the Chancellor of the Duchy of Lancaster or the Duchy of Cornwall) is obtained.

Much of the Land Compensation Act 1973 applies to the Crown —see s 84 of that Act and p 245.

(g) Special lands

During the preliminary stages, the acquiring authority must consider whether any of the land is in the ownership of an owner with special protection against compulsory acquisition; or whether any of the land is of a special category, eg, a common, open space or fuel or field garden allotment land. Chapter 11 deals with these special cases.

(h) Acquisition of new rights

The requirements for showing rights on maps have already been mentioned under head (c). Further guidance is given in Appendix K to Circular No 6/85 as to the heading of the order; the wording of an order for the acquisition of both land and of new rights (whether or not for the same purpose); the wording of an order relating solely to new rights; and to the procedure where it is proposed to create a new right over one of the categories of special lands referred to under head (f) above. Powers to acquire new rights for highway purposes are also available under the Highways Act 1980 and guidance on these powers is given in Circular Roads No 1/81.

(i) Orders for planning purposes

Appendix M to Circular No 6/85 stresses the need to state clearly which provisions of s 112 of the Town and Country Planning Act 1971 are being relied upon. Section 112 (1) (a) is used frequently in town centre developments but where comprehensive development is not involved it may be more appropriate to use s 112 (1) (b).

(j) Draft order

Most Ministries are prepared, without prejudice to their later formal consideration, to look through a draft compulsory purchase order. It should be accompanied by the map and, if possible, by the proposed statement of reasons. Such a perusal can avoid difficulties later particularly where there are problems in drafting or legal points to be cleared, but it will be of a technical nature only and will not extend to the merits of the proposed order.

2 Making the order

The order is made in the appropriate form prescribed by the Compulsory Purchase of Land Regulations (usually Form 1).

The enabling powers must be correctly stated, as it seems that the confirming Minister cannot make alterations to the citation of the enabling powers.The purpose of acquisition should be described in the words of the section of the Act authorising purchase but should be wide and comprehensive enough to achieve the desired purposes. In the case of purchases under s 112 of the Town and Country Planning Act 1971, the Department require the authority to state precisely the subparagraph relied upon (head (*i*) above). See *Capital Investments v Wednesfield Urban District Council* [1965] Ch 774 for the sort of argument which can arise where the statutory provision is not followed.

The importance of correctly stating the purpose of acquisition in paragraph 1 of the prescribed forms has been emphasised more than once in departmental circulars, as have the difficulties which can occur through a description of purpose not clearly tied to the wording of the enabling Act.

Department of Environment Circular Roads No 1/81, para 41, contains useful guidance as to the drafting of the statement of purposes in highway acquisition and provision of parking place orders as follows:

(a) Where the construction of a new length of highway, as well as the improvement of the existing highway, is involved, both purposes should be clearly stated.

(b) Highways to be improved should be named or briefly described.

(c) New lengths of highways should be briefly described (eg, "a new highway to by-pass (name of village)", "a new highway from High Street to John Street in the said Borough", etc).

(d) Where the scheme for the construction of a new highway involves the construction of ancillary roads to connect the new highway with the existing highway system, or related improvements to existing roads, this should be made clear in the statement of purposes.

(e) Where the order is made in reliance on s 239 (6) of the 1980 Act, the statement of purposes should include a reference to land adjoining or adjacent to the highway, as well as to the frontages to the highway, if any significant area of land outside the proposed boundaries of the highway are to be acquired.

(f) Where part of the land in a parking place compulsory purchase order is required for the provision of a means of entry to and exit from the parking place this must be clear in the statement of purposes (see the wording of s 28 (1) of the Road Traffic Regulation Act 1967).

Section 27 of the Compulsory Purchase Act 1965 (which requires an authority to make good any deficiency in rates during works) should be excluded, ie, para 2 in the draft order should *not* be struck out.

Parts II and III of Sched 2 to the Acquisition of Land Act 1981 (broadly replacing ss 77 and 78–85 of the Railways Clauses

Consolidation Act 1845) should, conversely, be included in the order so that the authority need not purchase any minerals under the land except to the extent specified by it and also has powers to regulate subsequent working of minerals not acquired (see Chapter 12).

Each plot should be described in ordinary language, eg, 'pasture land', 'arable land', 'woodland', 'part of the front garden to dwelling-house No ', 'dwelling house and garden No '. If Ordnance Survey field numbers are quoted the sheet numbers and the date of the edition should be included in the description.

Property especially in urban areas should be described by name or number in relation to the road or locality, and where appropriate a part of a property should be described by reference to any separate postal address. Particular care needs to be taken if individual properties have been known by another name or number. The description should be amplified to avoid any possibility of mistaken identity.

Land which falls within the special categories to which Pt III of the 1981 Act applies should be shown twice in Sched 1 to the order, once in the main body of the schedule and again separately at the end (see note (*R*) to the prescribed form of the order).

Owners or reputed owners (column 3). If the name of an owner (or lessee etc) cannot be ascertained the word 'unknown' should be entered in the appropriate columns of the schedule. As regards dispensing with service, see p 16. If there is a dispute or any doubt, all claiming parties should be named in the column and served. Contractual purchasers or lessees should be included.

Lessees or reputed lessees (column 4). A dash should be inserted in this column if there are none.

Occupiers other than tenants for a month or less (column 5). If there is an owner-occupier, the owner's name will have appeared in column 3. In column 5, either his name can be reproduced or preferably the word 'owner' inserted—or 'lessee' in a case where the occupier is a tenant in occupation. A dash should be inserted if the occupier is a monthly, weekly or a statutory tenant. If there is any doubt as to the legal status of an occupier it is safer to include his name and serve him for it will not matter if he later turns out to be, say, merely a weekly tenant. If the property is unoccupied, the column should be marked 'unoccupied'.

It is important that special care is taken to identify and correctly describe all the interests in land proposed for compulsory purchase. The Secretary of State's power of modification is circumscribed by s 14 of the Acquisition of Land Act 1981. This requires that the order as confirmed shall not, unless all persons interested consent, authorise the compulsory purchase of any land which the order would not have authorised the authority to purchase if it had been confirmed without modification.

Although it is not obligatory in law to include the addresses of owners, lessees or occupiers in the schedule to a compulsory purchase order, it is helpful to do so, and Departments encourage the practice.

3 Statement of reasons

Although it does not form part of the statutory procedure, it is common practice today for a statement of reasons to be prepared and served with the statutory notices at the time of making the order instead of waiting for the Inquiries Procedure Rules to create an obligation. The 1990 Rules create an obligation to serve a statement of case soon after the expiry of the period for objections—see p 37.

The statement should be as comprehensive as possible so that those whose interests are affected are fully informed about the intentions of the authority. In addition to serving those entitled to notification of the order, short term tenants and also applicants for planning permission in respect of the land should be served (see para 15 of Circular No 6/85). Appendix B of that Circular indicates that the statement should contain a description of the land, an outline of the case for acquisition and of the proposed use and development, details of the planning position, information required by government policy statements, details of special considerations, eg, listed buildings, the views of any government department, proposals for rehousing or relocation and details of any related order. Paragraph 9 of Appendix B has been superseded by paragraph 15 of Circular 1/90 and so it is no longer necessary to indicate whether the statement is intended to discharge the statutory obligation under the Inquiry Procedure Rules or to provide a list of documents with the statement of reasons. Instead it will be necessary to serve the statutory statement earlier than under the previous rules.

4 Press advertisement and deposit

The form of press advertisement is prescribed in the 1990 Regulations as Form No 7. It must be published in a local newspaper in two successive weeks.

As the purpose of the press notice is to warn those people who do not receive individual notice, it is not necessary (though it is convenient) that the period for expiry of the objections invited under the press notice should run out on the same date as that fixed in the individual notices.

Sometimes a newspaper will forget to publish the second notice, ie, publishes only one. In this case it is necessary to advertise again so that there can be publication in two successive weeks. Inevitably, the overall objection period will be extended as a result because the full 21 days must be allowed after republication.

A copy of the order and map must be placed on deposit at some place in the locality. There is no objection to the deposit being made at more than one place, eg, public libraries or citizens' advice bureaux, and it is believed that the Department of the Environment are anxious to see wider publicity given to proposed compulsory acquisitions. Where the notified place of deposit is not the offices of the acquiring authority, it is important to send it to the place of deposit a day or two before the date of service on the owners to allow for the owner who presents himself at 9 am at the place of deposit on the morning he receives notice. This deposited copy order and map is in addition to the requirement (which arises from the terms of the prescribed form of compulsory purchase order) to have a sealed map deposited in the offices of the acquiring authority and confirming Minister. The correct description in the prescribed form in the case of the Department of the Environment is 'the offices of the Secretary of State for the Environment'—no address need to be mentioned. The same holds good for the Department of Transport mutatis mutandis. So far as the Ministry is concerned this sealed map is usually deposited when the order is sent forward for confirmation. This should be done as soon as both press advertisements are available and before the end of the objection period. See Appendix 2 for details of the submission to the Minister.

5 Service of notices

Notices on owners, etc, take two forms:
(*a*) Form No 8 in the case of a normal order;
(*b*) Form No 9 where a compulsory purchase order is made on behalf of a parish or community council.

Notice must be served on every owner, lessee and occupier (except an occupier who is 'a tenant for a month or any period less than a month'). Monthly or weekly tenants need not be served. A statutory tenant under the Rent Act 1977 or the Rent (Agriculture) Act 1976 is deemed to be a tenant for a period of less than a month, and so is not entitled to notice. The same applies to a licensee under an assured agricultural occupancy under Pt 1 of the Housing Act 1988 (1981 Act, s 12(2)).

However few difficulties can arise from serving too many people.

Occasionally, a mistake is made and some party fails to get served. It is then only necessary to serve the person concerned giving him the full period of 21 days for objection. As with a defective press advertisement, this will inevitably delay the time at which the Minister can consider the order as the overall objection period is extended but there is no other ill-effect.

The following are the rules for service in special cases:

(a) Where a firm or partnership is concerned all the partners should be served and their names shown in the schedule.

(b) Companies should be served at the registered or principal office and other incorporated bodies at their principal office. Service should be on the secretary.

(c) Individual executors or trustees should all be named and served.

(d) In the case of unincorporated bodies such as clubs, chapels, charities, etc, the names of individual trustees should be shown and each should be served.The secretary can be safely served only if specifically authorised by the trustees.

(e) Where land is ecclesiastical property (ie, Church of England property as defined in s 12 (3) of the Act of 1981) notice of the making of the order must be served on the Church Commissioners as well as on the owners. In the case of land the subject of a charitable trust it is advisable that the Charity Commissioners should be served at their headquarters, as well as the trustees.

Where any person has furnished an address for service, this will be the address for service (1981 Act, s 6 (3)). This is a useful provision and can save such work as discovering registered offices and so forth. Where service is made on solicitors, the authority should make sure that the person to be served has authorised service on his solicitors. The solicitor should be asked to confirm his authority to act, and to furnish the names and addresses of all those for whom he will accept service.

Service of notices can be made personally or by leaving at the person's proper address—a procedure usually adopted where the persons to be served are also occupiers of the premises to be acquired.

Most notices are served by post, using recorded delivery or registered post. It is important to preserve the registration or recorded delivery receipt slip. If a notice is served but is returned through the post marked 'gone away' this will not amount to service (*Hewitt* v *Leicester Corporation* [1969] 1 WLR 855). See also *Moody* v *Godstone Rural District Council* [1966] 1 WLR 1085.

Correct service of notices is important because of the risk that a challenge may be made at a very late stage, ie, after the confirmation of the order. Thus in *George* v *Secretary of State for the Environment* (1979) 38 P & CR 609, a wife jointly owned a property with her husband. Notice of the order was served on the husband but not on the wife. The Court of Appeal held that she had not been substantially prejudiced and so was not entitled to upset the order. However, in *Fagan* v *Knowsley Metropolitan Borough Council* (1985) 50 P & CR 363, the Court of Appeal held that service on the brother of the owner, who lived near the order property and who had been given full authority to act as his agent, was insufficient.

Service is deemed to have occurred unless the contrary is proved —Interpretation Act 1978, s 7. This means that normally the onus is on the addressee to prove that he did not receive a notice (*Chiswell* v *Griffon Land & Estates Ltd* [1975] 1 WLR 1181. However where a letter is returned undelivered, the sender must also be able to demonstrate, on sufficient admissible evidence, that the posting of a notice has actually occurred—see *Mustafa Hussein* v *Secretary of State for the Environment and Hackney L B C* [1984] JPL 431 where an order was quashed because of an alleged failure to serve notice of the public inquiry.

How service is effected where individual service has been dispensed with has already been mentioned on p 16.

6 Local land charges

In the absence of express statutory provision requiring registration (eg, vesting declarations under s 3 of the Compulsory Purchase (Vesting Declarations) Act 1981), an order is not registrable as a local land charge. Although it is the practice of some authorities to register in all cases so as to ensure that prospective purchasers learn of the order, the better procedure is for an order which is not registrable by statute to be disclosed in answer to the additional enquiries which usually accompany a local search. However, there can be difficulty in discovering the existence of a compulsory purchase order which is made by a body other than the local authority, since the relevant question on the Additional Enquiries Form deals only with orders or resolutions by that authority. Even if a specific enquiry is raised with the authority they may be unaware of orders made by other bodies or unwilling to reveal details of those of which they have been made aware.

7 Objections

The confirming authority has to consider objections and representations duly made and may—in most cases, must—order a public local inquiry or hearing.

This part of the procedure is considered in detail in Chapter 4.

8 Confirmation of order

Where a submitted order raises obvious legal difficulties, the Department of the Environment have set out the procedures which they will follow in paras 18 and 19 of Circular No 6/85. If the Secretary of State is satisfied that there is a serious risk of challenge in the High Court and that defects cannot be remedied, he will issue a reasoned decision letter formally refusing confirmation. The way is then opened for the authority to submit a fresh order, if necessary after a fresh resolution.

If the confirming authority confirms the order, with or without modifications, the local authority must, as soon as possible, publish in the local press a notice that the order has been confirmed. Form No 10 in the 1990 Regulations is the one to use.

Form No 10 is also the appropriate form to serve notice on the individual owners, lessees and occupiers who were required to be served with notice of the submission of the order under s 12 of the Act of 1981. A copy of the order as confirmed must also be served with the notice.

Orders are confirmed by endorsement, and any modifications may be made either by manuscript amendments to the order or by setting them out in the endorsement. No decision letter will, as a rule, precede the confirmation of the order. The confirming authority will indicate how many copies of the confirmed order it needs for official use.

When the confirming authority modifies the order, it may not include additional land in the order without the consent of the parties. The confirmation may cut down but not enlarge the terms of the order (Acquisition of Land Act 1981, s 14).

Cases used to occur on highway schemes where part of the proposal was not objected to, but part was contested. It was not possible in these circumstances for the Secretary of State to confirm the order in regard to the agreed part, and to defer consideration of the contested part. Section 55 of the Highways Act 1971 overcame the difficulty and has been re-enacted in s 259 of the Highways Act 1980. Where an order is confirmed in part, that part and the remaining part will be treated as becoming separate orders for procedural purposes. It is understood that the Secretary of State will not confirm part and defer consideration of the remainder unless satisfied that the interests of objectors to the deferred part will not be prejudiced by part confirmation (Circular Roads No 1/1981, para 96). Form 10 of the 1990 Regulations provides for such confirmation in part. There are other cases where there can be part confirmation of a compulsory purchase order with postponement of the remainder. See s 132 of the Town and Country Planning Act 1971 and the Local Government, Planning and Land Act 1980, Sched 28, para 2.

Confirmation of the order is the first opportunity to give the prescribed form of notice which is a prerequisite to the use of the general vesting declaration procedure in the Compulsory Purchase (Vesting Declarations) Act 1981 (see Chapter 16).

The order comes into operation on the day on which the first press advertisement appears (s 26 of the Act of 1981).

9 Validity

The validity of a confirmed order can be questioned in the High Court during a period of six weeks from the day on which it comes into operation on the ground that it is ultra vires, or that the procedure has been faulty, except in a case—probably very exceptional—where the order has been confirmed by an Act of Parliament under s 6 of the Statutory Orders (Special Procedure) Act 1945. Apart from this, a confirmed compulsory purchase order cannot be questioned in any legal proceedings whatever (Acquisition of Land Act 1981, s 25).

Challenge to the validity of orders is considered in Chapter 6, which also deals with the possibility of an application for judicial review in the case of non-confirmation (see *Islington London Borough Council* v *Secretary of State for the Environment* (1982) 43 P & CR 300; [1982] JPL 739).

10 Notice to treat and taking possession

Notice to treat under s 5 of the Compulsory Purchase Act 1965 may not be served until after the order comes into operation.

Notice to treat is dealt with in Chapter 7.

At any time after it has been served the authority may enter and take possession on giving 14 days' notice of their intention to do so, without waiting for completion of the purchase. (There is also a little used alternative procedure in s 11 (2) of and Sched 3 to the Compulsory Purchase Act 1965.) The acquiring authority have the right to withdraw notice to treat in the circumstances referred to in s 31 of the Land Compensation Act 1961 (see p 58). If the notice to treat is not served within the period referred to in s 4 of the Act of 1965, the compulsory powers lapse. This period is three years from the date on which the compulsory order becomes operative, ie, three years from the press notice of confirmation.

Notice of entry is dealt with in Chapter 8.

11 Acquisition of rights

The compulsory acquisition of rights over land, rather than the land itself, requires specific statutory authority. Section 28 of and Sched 3 to the Acquisition of Land Act 1981 apply to the creation of new rights under s 13 of the Local Government (Miscellaneous Provisions) Act 1976 and under the other statutory provisions listed in the section. The acquisition of rights is dealt with in Chapter 13.

Section 29 of the 1981 Act deals with compulsory rights orders under the Opencast Coal Act 1958. The 1981 Act is applied, subject to certain modifications, to enable British Coal to acquire temporary rights of occupation and use of land. Objections may be disregarded if they relate to the question of whether opencast planning permission should be granted.

Section 30 applies the provisions of the 1981 Act to the compulsory purchase of a right to store gas underground under s 12 of the Gas Act 1965.

Chapter 4

Objecting

(See also Chapter 14—Some practical points.)

1 Use of compulsory powers

Many purchases which could be made under compulsory powers are in fact concluded by agreement. However, there is always a balance of cases in which the authority having the compulsory powers feel obliged to use them.

Apart from straightforward cases of failure to reach agreement, formal compulsory proceedings are likely to be taken in three classes of acquisition:

(*a*) if there is a large number of properties to acquire for the scheme, because the inability to reach agreement in a single case may hold up the whole scheme;

(*b*) if compensation problems are likely to prove difficult, because the ability to serve notice to treat ensures that in the last resort there can be recourse to the Lands Tribunal to settle disputed questions;

(*c*) if the scheme must be carried out to a predetermined timetable, because the authority can serve notice of entry after notice to treat and so secure possession (or alternatively use the general vesting declaration procedure described in Chapter 16).

The use of compulsory powers is therefore not as a matter of last resort, to be undertaken only after lengthy efforts to reach agreement have failed. Circular No 6/85 (para 8) suggests that large urban sites in multiple ownership and urgently required sites are examples where it may be appropriate to seek compulsory powers at the same time as attempting to purchase by agreement.

2 Notice of order

In the case of compulsory purchase orders, unlike development plans and the like, an owner need not be afraid that an order will be made over his head. Nor is it necessary to read the *London Gazette* with homoeopathic minuteness.

The Acquisition of Land Act 1981, ss 11 and 12, provide that the acquiring authority must:

(*a*) advertise the making of the order for two successive weeks in a local paper; and

(*b*) serve notice upon every owner, lessee and occupier (except tenants for a month or any period less than a month) (see p 25).

The authority may dispense with individual service, eg, if there are multiple ownerships and reasonable enquiries have failed to produce a complete book of reference (see p 16). The special position in new towns has already been noted (see p 5).

3 Considering line of action

The prescribed form of notice indicates the time within which, and the way, to make representations against the order. Usually no more than the minimum period of 21 days is allowed, and it is sensible to put in a holding objection whilst considering the client's case. With the notice an owner should have received a copy of the authority's reasons for making the order. This is not at present a statutory requirement but rests on Ministerial advice to local authorities (see Circular No 6/85, para 15 and p 24).

In the case of compulsory purchase orders made under s 290 of the Housing Act 1985 (clearance areas), a local housing authority is under a statutory obligation (para 4 (2) of Sched 22) to serve on any objector who claims that his house is not unfit a notice stating the main grounds on which unfitness is alleged. The authority's statement in writing, therefore, will normally deal in general terms with the condition of the unfit houses in the clearance area in addition to setting out the authority's reason for the acquisition both of the houses in the clearance area and of any adjoining land included in the order.

A copy of any minutes of the authority dealing with the purchase can be requested, and a copy of the deposited plan will usually be provided on payment. With the aid of this information a line of action must be determined. (By virtue of the Local Government (Access to Information) Act 1985 local authorities are obliged to provide copies of documents in specified circumstances.)

Obviously each case raises its own peculiar features, and only the most general guidance can be given as to the best line to pursue. Some of the important questions which require answers are as follows:

(1) Has the principle of acquisition been settled by any preliminary proceeding? On this, see Chapter 2. Even if the principle of the proposal has been settled, there may be scope for securing modifications of detail which will be of value to the client, as outlined in para (5) below.

(2) Can the need for the acquisition be challenged? In the case of a responsible authority there should be little scope for suggesting that the road, school, fire station, or housing site is unnecessary. Sometimes, however, the degree of 'necessity' may be so low as to justify objection. At any rate the 'need' should never be taken for granted.

(3) Is there any alternative proposal which can be put forward? Even if the need for, say, a new school is accepted, it may be that an alternative site can be suggested (cases concerning alternative routes are dealt with in Chapter 6). In the case of an alternative route for a road the special provisions of s 258 of the Highways Act 1980 must be considered (see p 34). At one end of the scale the submission of an alternative may involve calling expert evidence at the inquiry: at the other, the alternative may be put forward as a matter of argument, and the authority's witnesses cross-examined as to whether they would or would not accept its practicability.

Expert witnesses are expensive, and obviously they will not be used unless there is a good case, and some chance that their evidence will impress the inspector at the inquiry. If a technical expert is to be called for an objector, it is always worth considering whether any agreement can be reached between the technical experts on both sides before the public inquiry. Agreement is likely to save expense and delay. In most cases there is an area within which the experts on each side can reach agreement (with a little give and take) and an area in which there is a dispute about facts or interpretation.

(4) Would the acquisition still be necessary if specified works were to be carried out? For example, where orders are made for the purchase of housing in poor condition, the authority might agree that if improvement works are carried out in a reasonable time the owner can retain the property. See p 46 for cases where undertakings were given by authorities not to acquire.

(5) Can modifications of detail be secured which will benefit the client? Very often common sense will indicate that there is a genuine need for the project covered by the compulsory

purchase. This does not mean that the whole of the authority's proposals must be swallowed; they cannot stand in the client's shoes, and may have failed to realise the damaging effect of their proposal on the client's property. It is likely, too, that their proposals may have been designed to optimum standards, which may be capable of reduction without material detriment to the scheme as a whole.

Examples of modifications which might be sought are:

(*a*) a reduction in the radius curve of a road to keep it further away from a client's house;

(*b*) amendment to the boundary of school playing fields involving the acceptance of one or more substandard playing pitches;

(*c*) reduction in the overall width of a carriageway, involving a reduced pavement, to save a screen of trees;

(*d*) variation in the alignment of an approach road to a new roundabout, so as to minimise the effect on a front garden;

(*e*) altered disposition of buildings on site to reduce visual impact on neighbouring property;

(*f*) landscaping of site by acquiring authority to protect amenities;

(*g*) mounding of earth or provision of a wall or planting of trees on land adjoining a proposed new road to reduce effects of noise or traffic, etc;

(*h*) road to be built in a cutting instead of at ground level to reduce noise and visual impact;

(*i*) building of acquiring authority to be heated by alternative means to avoid boiler house and tall chimney flue;

(*j*) underpass or bridge to be provided to minimise effects of severance.

In any case it is desirable to ask for an exploratory meeting with the acquiring authority's advisers. Just as an acquiring authority may fail to realise an owner's position so, too, may the owner fail to appreciate the difficulties of the authority. A 'without prejudice' discussion can sometimes resolve an objection and will usually narrow the field of disagreement.

4 Alternative route—road scheme

Difficulties have been caused in the case of road schemes by the absence of any requirement that objectors must furnish particulars of alternative routes which they may wish to put forward at the public inquiry. Section 258 of the Highways Act 1980 provides that an objector to a compulsory purchase order who wishes to propose an alternative route at a public inquiry into objections can be directed to furnish the Secretary of State with sufficient particulars of the alternative route to enable it to be identified. This does not mean that a plan must be provided if the alternative can be accurately described without one. Objectors must be given at least 14 days in which to prepare their particulars. They are required to submit them not less than 14 days before the date of the inquiry.

Objectors to the order will normally receive notice of any direction under s 258 in the notice of the public inquiry which goes out at least six weeks ahead of the inquiry date.

Where an objector fails to submit details of his alternative, the Secretary of State and the inspector at the inquiry have a discretion (which they may or may not exercise) to disregard the objection in so far as it consists of a submission about an alternative route.

5 Disregard of objection

If an owner, after being asked for his reasons, objects on grounds exclusively related to compensation, he may find his objections disregarded (Acquisition of Land Act 1981, s 13 (4)).

If in the case of disputed compensation there is no prospect of agreement, it may be desirable to refer the issue of compensation straight to the Lands Tribunal by consent, as though the compulsory purchase order had been confirmed.

Where the only issue between the parties is as to the amount of compensation, the owner may be willing to enter into a contract providing for compensation to be settled by the Lands Tribunal in default of agreement. Appendix 5 contains a draft form of agreement which may be suitable where there is agreement about the principle of selling, but not as to price. See *Marchment and others* (*Executors*) v *Hampshire County Council* (1979) 43 P & CR 436.

6 Neighbouring owners

One purpose of the press advertisement is to alert owners whose lands will not be taken for the scheme, but who may be affected by it. They cannot force a public inquiry in the way that persons served with notice can, but their objections or representations will be considered by the confirming authority who may decide to afford them an opportunity to be heard even if there are no statutory objectors (see p 39).

Chapter 5

Inquiry into Objections

1 Inquiry or hearing

Where an objection to a compulsory purchase order is made by an owner, lessee or occupier and is not withdrawn, then, unless satisfied that the objection is exclusively related to compensation, the confirming authority must arrange for either a public local inquiry or a hearing before an inspector appointed by the Minister (Acquisition of Land Act 1981, s 13).

It the ordinary way, it makes little practical difference which procedure, ie, hearing or public inquiry, is adopted. But at a hearing, the inspector cannot compel the attendance of witnesses or take evidence on oath, and the Minister cannot award costs to either side (1981 Act, s 5 and the Local Government Act 1972, s 250). If any of these matters is important, an objector will clearly wish to represent that there should be a public inquiry and not just a hearing. It is understood that the Department of the Environment have decided to hear all future objections to compulsory purchase orders for which they are responsible at a public local inquiry.

2 The Inquiries Procedure Rules

Where the compulsory purchase order is made by a local authority under the 1981 Act, the procedure before, at and after the hearing or inquiry will be governed by the Compulsory Purchase by Non–Ministerial Acquiring Authorities (Inquiries Procedure) Rules 1990 (SI 1990 No 512), set out in Appendix 4.

The Rules came into force on 31 March 1990, although by virtue of transitional provisions (r 3) the previous 1976 Rules will apply to orders submitted before that date and where no inquiry had opened or decision been issued. The new Rules are based on the same principles as those applying to inquiries arising from planning appeals and they contain similar provisions. The scope of the previous Rules has been extended so that the new ones apply to clearance orders made under s 290 of the Housing Act 1985 and to compulsory rights orders under s 4 of the Opencast Coal Act 1958. They do not apply to orders under the New Towns Act 1981.

Guidance on the new Rules is set out in Department of the Environment Circular 1/90 (Welsh Office Circular 1/90). This also amends certain of the advice given in DoE Circular 6/85 on compulsory purchase order procedures.

Local enquiries into highway schemes will take place in accordance with the Highways (Inquiries Procedure) Rules 1976 (SI 1976 No 721), which are modelled on the rules for planning and compulsory purchase order inquiries. The main difference is in the definition of 'statutory objector'. The table in the Rules lists (in effect) as statutory objectors:

(*a*) those statutory bodies and persons who have a right to be served under the Highways Act 1980;

(*b*) those owners, lessees and occupiers of land likely to be required for the execution of highways works;

(*c*) those persons likely to be able to claim compensation under Pt 1 of the Land Compensation Act 1973 as a result of traffic noise, fumes, etc, depreciating their property.

The Rules equate the procedure for public inquiries with those of hearings, except that, for a hearing, public notices and advertisements are dispensed with (r 2).

In many road schemes, the acquiring authority will be the Secretary of State for Transport. In the case of purchases for highway or other purposes by Ministers, the procedure is that laid down in the Compulsory Purchase by Ministers (Inquiries Procedure) Rules 1967 (SI 1967 No 720). These are likely to be revised soon so that they are similar to those applying to local authorities.

3 Procedure before inquiry

Not later than 14 days after the end of the objection period or after the submission of the order to the Secretary of State, he must give notice that an inquiry will be held. The date of the notice is the 'relevant date' which triggers other procedures. Perhaps the most significant change in the new Rules is that at least 28 days before the inquiry and not later than six weeks after the relevant date, the acquiring authority must serve its statement of case on the Secretary of State and each statutory objector (ie, any owner, tenant or occupier entitled to notice of the order who has objected). The statement must contain full particulars of the case to be put forward at the inquiry, copies of any documents to which reference is made (or relevant extracts) and a list of documents to be put in evidence.

Even if a statement of reasons for making the order was circulated when it was made, the requirements relating to the service of the statement of case must be observed. The statement must include any views in support of the order expressed in writing by a government department. Any person (ie, statutory objectors and third parties) must be given an opportunity to inspect and, where practicable, take copies of the authority's statement and documents.

There is a discretionary power for the Secretary of State to require statutory objectors and others wishing to appear at the inquiry to provide a statement but this power will be used very sparingly and normally only for complex inquiries (Circular 1/90).

An inspector may hold a pre-inquiry meeting if he thinks it desirable: 14 days notice must be given. There is a further power for the Secretary of State to cause pre-inquiry meetings to be held (r 6) and there are procedures for publicity, outline statements and notification and conduct of such meetings.

The inquiry must take place not later than 22 weeks after the relevant date unless this is impracticable (r 11). At least 42 days written notice must be given to those entitled to appear and the public will also learn of the inquiry from site and newspaper notices published at least 14 days before the inquiry.

4 Appearances at inquiry

Those entitled to appear are the acquiring authority, any statutory objector and any other person who has served a statement of case. The inspector may permit any other person—eg, a neighbouring owner—to appear.

Where a government department is supporting the authority a representative must attend if requested by the authority or objector. The representative will give evidence and be cross-examined like any other witness, but cannot be required to answer questions directed to the merits of government policy.

5 Statements of evidence

The Secretary of State has a discretionary power, which will be used in more complex cases, to require those appearing to serve a copy of their proof of evidence on the inspector not later than three weeks before the inquiry or their scheduled appearance at it. The inspector may require a written summary. If the acquiring authority send proofs or a summary to the inspector they must at the same time send copies to statutory objectors and others entitled to appear. Similarly any other person who provides a proof to the inspector must send it to the authority. Where summaries have been provided the witness will normally read only that summary at the inquiry (r 14).

6 Procedure at inquiry

Unless otherwise determined by the inspector, the acquiring authority has a right to begin the inquiry, when they will, by opening statement, evidence and cross - examination, make their case for confirmation of the order. They also have the right of final reply. Other parties appear in the order determined by the inspector.

A statutory objector may call evidence and cross - examine, and any person entitled to appear may call evidence and, at the discretion of the inspector, cross - examine. In practice permission is always given.

The rules of evidence do not apply at a public local inquiry and the inspector may, with some provisos, admit any evidence in his discretion. He may refuse to hear evidence or to permit cross - examination which is irrelevant or repetitious, and he may require any person behaving in a disruptive manner to leave the inquiry. As to the refusal of an inspector to allow an objector to cross - examine local authority witnesses, leading to substantial prejudice, see *Nicholson* v *Secretary of State for Energy* (1977) 245 EG 139.

The inspector may take into account (subject to disclosure) written representations received before the inquiry from any person who does not attend.

If the acquiring authority (or anyone who served a pre - inquiry statement of case) wishes to amend it or add to the list of documents, they may be permitted to do so providing other persons entitled to appear are given adequate opportunity of considering any fresh matter or documents. This may result in an adjournment which may have implications for an award of costs.

7 Site inspection

The inspector may make a site inspection either during or after the close of the inquiry and representatives of the authority and statutory objectors are entitled to accompany him. There may also have been an unaccompanied visit before or during the inquiry. The inspector generally tries to make arrangements convenient to all parties, but is not obliged to secure their attendance on the appointed day. The acquiring authority or a statutory objector may before or during the inquiry require that a site inspection be made (r 16). As to the dangers of obtaining the views of persons on site in the absence of objectors, see *Hibernian Property Co Ltd* v *Secretary of State for the Environment* (1973) 27 P & CR 197.

8 Procedure after inquiry

Rule 17 requires the inspector to include in his report to the Secretary of State his conclusions and recommendations, and deals with the report of any assessor. If the Secretary of State differs from the inspector on a matter of fact which is material to a conclusion, or takes into consideration new evidence or facts, and is disposed to disagree with the inspector's recommendation as a result of this new evidence, then he must notify the persons entitled to appear at the inquiry who appeared and to give them an opportunity of making representations within 21 days; if he has received new evidence he must, on request, re-open the inquiry.

9 Decision letter

The Secretary of State must notify his decision to the acquiring authority, every statutory objector, any person entitled to appear who did so, and any other person who appeared at the inquiry and asked to be notified. The decision must contain reasons. Where a copy of the report of the inspector is not sent with the decision letter it must contain the conclusions of the inspector and his recommendations. Anyone entitled to the decision letter can request a copy of the inspector's report within four weeks. Provided application is made within six weeks of the publication of notice of confirmation of the order, the recipient of the report can inspect any documents, photographs or plans appended.

10 Costs

Department of Environment Circular No 2/87 (Welsh Office 5/87) deals with the award of costs to the successful objectors to compulsory purchase orders. If a statutory objector to a compulsory purchase order is successful an award of costs will be made unless there are exceptional reasons for not doing so. For an award to be made, the objector must have made a formal objection to the order, the order must have been the subject of a public inquiry which the objector must have attended (or been represented at) and at which the objector must have been heard as a statutory objector (in the case of orders under s 290 of the Housing Act 1985 (clearance areas) certain expenses may be awarded where there has been no inquiry or where the objector did not attend). If the Secretary of State refuses to confirm the order, or excludes from the order the whole or part of the objector's property, then an award will be made against the authority. The making of an award does not in itself imply unreasonable behaviour, which is the normal criterion for an award of costs in planning proceedings. It is possible that an award of costs may be made to an unsuccessful objector in compulsory purchase proceedings, or to the authority which made the order, because of unreasonable behaviour by the other party. This is likely to relate to procedural matters such as unreasonably causing an adjournment of the public inquiry.

It is not necessary for costs to be applied for at the public inquiry (as already noted, costs are not payable in the case of hearings). The Secretary of State will raise the question in his decision letter refusing to confirm the compulsory purchase order. Normally, the parties will be given an opportunity to agree on the amount; if legally represented, any dispute will lead to costs being taxed in the High Court.

A partially successful objection will lead to an award of a proportion of the costs incurred. For example, the Secretary of State when confirming an order may exclude part of the objector's land.

Chapter 6

Operation and Validity of Order

A compulsory purchase order comes into operation normally on the day on which the press advertisement of confirmation first appears (see p 29).

(see p 29).

The validity of the order can be questioned in the High Court during a period of six weeks from the day on which it comes into operation on the ground either that it is ultra vires, or that the procedure has been faulty, including failure to comply with the requirements of the Tribunals and Inquiries Act 1971 or of any rules made under that Act and for the Government departments' orders in 1967 (Compulsory Purchase by Ministers (Inquiries Procedure) Rules 1967) in respect of acquisitions under the Act of 1946—to be read as referring to the Acquisition of Land Act 1981, see Sched 5 thereto.)

The application is made under RSC Ord 94, and the court may, by interim order, suspend the operation of the order until final determination of the proceedings (Act of 1981, s 24 (1)). Provided that the application is made in time, the grounds of appeal may be amended out of time, with leave of the court (*Hanily* v *Ministry of Local Government and Planning* [1951] 2 KB 917).

If an applicant takes a procedural point, he will have to satisfy the court that his interests have been subtantially prejudiced by the non-observance of the statutory requirements (Acquisition of Land Act 1981, s 24 (2)).

The onus appears to be on the person seeking to oppose the order to show on the balance of probabilities that he is entitled to relief (per Roskill LJ in *George* v *Secretary of State* (1979) 38 P & CR 609). In *Parker* v *Secretary of State for the Environment and another* (1980) 257 EG 718 CA, Lord Denning said that a decision letter and an inspector's report should not be gone through like a statute. As long as it is broadly correct and no injustice done the order should not be upset by the courts.

Once the period for challenge has passed, the order cannot be challenged in any legal proceedings whatsoever—even if bad faith is alleged (*Smith* v *East Elloe Rural District Council* [1956] AC 736; *Uttoxeter Urban District Council* v *Clarke* (1952) 3 P & CR 70; *Cartwright* v *Ministry of Housing and Local Government* (1967) 18 P & CR 499). And see s 25, Acquisition of Land Act 1981.

In *Smith* v *East Elloe Rural District Council* the court allowed the action against the clerk of the council to proceed. 'The bad faith or fraud upon which an aggrieved person relies is that of individuals, and . . . even if the validity of the order cannot be questioned and he cannot recover the land that has been taken from him, yet he may have a remedy in damages against those individuals', per Viscount Simonds at p 752.

Smith v *Elloe* was approved by *R* v *Secretary of State for the Environment ex parte Ostler* (1976) 32 P & CR 166. Denning MR said of the remedy to challenge the order in the courts:

But he must come promptly. He must come within six weeks. If he does so, the court can and will entertain his complaint. But if the six weeks expire without any complaint being made the court cannot entertain it afterwards. The reason is that, as soon as that time has elapsed, the authority will take steps to acquire property, demolish it and so forth. The public interest demands that they should be safe in doing so.

It should be noted that the restriction on court proceedings in s 25 of the 1981 Act does not prevent the courts from acting in the case of a challenge to a resolution to make an order (See *R* v *Camden L B C, ex parte Comyn Ching and Co (London) Limited* (1983) 47 P & CR 417) or where judicial review is sought during a public inquiry because of the exclusion of evidence (see *R* v *Secretary of State for the Environment, ex parte Royal Borough of Kensington and Chelsea* [1987] JPL 567).

It should also be noted that in spite of the restriction in s 25, where circumstances change between the confirmation of an order and its planned execution, the court could intervene (see *Simpsons Motor Sales (London) Limited* v *Hendon Corporation* [1963] Ch 57).

If an order is not confirmed, the action of the Minister with powers of confirmation can be challenged by means of an application for judicial review under s 31 of the Supreme Court Act 1981 (*Islington London Borough Council* v *Secretary of State for the Environment* (1982) 43 P & CR 300, but decided in 1980). See also *R* v *Secretary of State for the Environment, ex parte Wellingborough Borough*

Council (1983) 45 P & CR 98. Failure to comply with the statutory rules or other legal obligation, taking into account irrelevant considerations or a breach of natural justice, might all be sufficient to found an application for judicial review. Such an application can only be made with leave of the court, and must be made promptly and, normally, within three months of the date when the grounds for the application arose. Before granting leave the court will have to be satisfied that the applicant has a 'sufficient interest' in the proceedings (*Inland Revenue Commissioners* v *National Federation for the Self Employed and Small Businesses* [1981] 2 WLR 722).

1 The tests to be applied

It is stated in para 7 of Circular No 6/85 that 'proposals for compulsory purchase may often cause uncertainty and anxiety for owners and occupiers and should not be made unless there is a compelling case in the public interest'. That may be the policy but the courts have rejected the concept of a 'compelling case' and have indicated that whilst a compulsory purchase order must be justified on its merits before it can be confirmed, there are no special rules or tests to be applied. This view has emerged as a result of several cases in each of which alternative sites or routes have been proposed, and so the cases are of interest both from the point of view of the general duty of the Secretary of State when considering an order and also in cases where an alternative is proposed.

In *Brown and another* v *Secretary of State for the Environment* (1978) P & CR 285, a compulsory purchase order was made to provide a site for gipsies. The Secretary of State failed to consider the merits of alternative sites, including one owned by the acquiring authority. The order was quashed because it was a material consideration that there were other sites available but that the Secretary of State had regarded that consideration as immaterial. Per curiam, the court suggested that if the acquiring authority is itself in possession of other wholly suitable land, no reasonably Secretary of State could come to the conclusion that it was necessary for it to acquire land compulsorily for precisely the same purpose. Necessity for the exercise of compulsory purchase powers is what must be shown in a case of this character.

In *Prest and Straker* v *Secretary of State for Wales* (1982) 81 LGR 193, a water authority made a compulsory purchase order for the provision of a new sewage works on land owned by the applicants. At the inquiry the applicants offered two possible alternative sites at existing use (agricultural) value. In confirming the order the Secretary of State failed to take into account the cost of acquiring the order land as against the alternative sites offered. By the time the case reached the Court of Appeal fresh evidence was available showing that it was highly probable that planning permission would be granted for the development of the order land for industrial purposes, which would increase its value considerably. The order was quashed. Lord Denning stated that 'no citizen is to be deprived of his land by any public authority against his will, unless it is expressly authorised by Parliament and the public interest decisively so demands: and then only on condition that proper compensation is paid'.

These two cases were reviewed by the Court of Appeal in *R* v *Secretary of State for Transport, ex parte de Rothschild* [1989] 1 All ER 933. The highway authority made an order to acquire land owned by the appellants for the construction of a by-pass. The appellants objected and put forward four alternative routes on other land which they owned and were prepared to sell. The Secretary of State confirmed the order, stating that he did not believe that any of the suggested alternatives had sufficient advantages to justify their adoption over the order scheme.

The appellants argued that there were special rules applicable when the court was considering a challenge to a compulsory purchase order. These went beyond the decisions on unreasonableness in *Associated Provincial Picture Houses Limited* v *Wednesbury Corporation* [1947] 2 All ER 680 and in *Ashbridge Investments Limited v Minister of Housing and Local Government* [1965] 3 All ER 371. These special rules placed the onus on the authority to justify the order; required that there should be a 'compelling case in the public interest' before an order could be confirmed; required that any doubt be resolved in favour of the owner; precluded compulsory powers if equally suitable alternative land was available; and required the authority to demonstrate that compulsory acquisition was necessary rather than the landowner to demonstrate the converse.

The court rejected the submission, holding that there were no special rules. The '*Brown*' and '*Prest*' cases were merely examples based on the conventional *Wednesbury/Ashbridge* grounds. However the draconian nature of a compulsory purchase order will itself render it more vulnerable to a successful challenge on *Wednesbury/ Ashbridge* grounds; no reasonable Secretary of State would be likely to confirm an order in the absence of what he perceived to be a sufficient justification for his decision on its merits or to impose such an order on an unwilling landowner, if the owner was willing to sell other land which would serve the same purpose equally well taking all relevant considerations, including delay and cost, into account.

The court also indicated that it could not be right to analyse each sentence of the Secretary of State's letter as if it were a sub-section in a taxing statute. Moreover, the form of the public inquiry and the decision taken by the Secretary of State was not appropriate for the discharge of a burden of proof. The Minister had to perform a balancing exercise involving numerous factors, ultimately making a value judgement on whether or not the order was justified in the public interest.

2 Undertakings by the acquiring authority

There have been several cases where the courts have considered whether undertakings given by the authority are valid. In *Sovmots Investments* v *Secretary of State* [1976] 3 All ER 720 an undertaking not to acquire the freehold interest was held not to be incompatible with the statutory purpose of the order (see p 58). In *Varsani* v *Secretary of State for the Environment and Islington LBC* (1980) 40 P & CR 354, the Council made a compulsory purchase order on properties in a Housing Action Area. They gave undertakings to owners not to acquire any house which was satisfactorily repaired. Confirmation was challenged on the grounds that the lawful purpose of the order was to enable acquisition and that the Council disabled themselves by their undertakings from exercising that power. The court upheld the order and indicated that it would be unfortunate if authorities were debarred from giving and recording such undertakings.

In *Mullins* v *Secretary of State and another* [1982] JPL 576 a similar undertaking was given and the confirmed order was challenged on the ground that the Secretary of State had been misled by the undertaking. The court found that the Secretary of State had not relied on the undertaking, which was merely part of the background to the decision.

In these two cases the undertakings could limit the discretion of the authority but were not incompatible with the basic purpose of the order. However, in *R* v *Secretary of State for the Environment, ex parte Leicester City Council* [1987] JPL 787, the decision of the Secretary of State not to confirm an order was upheld by the court where an undertaking had been given that the order would not be enforced if owners made an appropriate contribution towards the construction of roads and sewers. The order had been made under s 112 of the Town and Country Planning Act 1971 for redevelopment, but if owners made the contributions they could retain their land. The purpose of the order was therefore to encourage owners to make financial contributions towards a cost which would otherwise have to be borne by the ratepayers.

3 Cases on the validity of orders

The following are some cases dealing with the validity of compulsory purchase orders:

Darlassis v *Minister of Education* (1954) 4 P & CR 281. Communication between Ministries after inquiry: natural justice.

Steele v *Minister of Housing and Local Government and West Ham County Borough Council* (1956) 6 P & CR 386. Inspector's report: no substantial prejudice by technical mistake: natural justice.

Richardson v *Minister of Housing and Local Government* (1956) 8 P & CR 29. Failure to comply with requirement for special Parliamentary procedure leads to order being quashed.

Grice v *Dudley Corporation* [1958] Ch 329. Order made in 1937: notice to treat served in 1939: compulsory purchase sought to be completed in 1954: original plans for development changed. Declarations made that the authority had no powers to acquire under the compulsory purchase order.

Goddard v *Minister of Housing and Local Government* [1958] 1 WLR 1151. Consideration of matters precedent to making of order: council acting through committee under Housing Acts.

London and Westcliff Properties Ltd v *Minister of Housing and Local Government* [1961] 1 WLR 519. Purchase for improper and ultra vires purpose makes order ultra vires.

Simpsons Motor Sales (London) Ltd v *Hendon Corporation* [1963] Ch 57. In the absence of any challenge to the bona fides of the acquiring authority, a change in the type of housing scheme did not invalidate the notice to treat: nor did delay which had originally been at the owner's request. See also *R* v *Carmarthen DC, ex parte Blewin Trust Ltd* [1990] 8 EG 101 —attempt to restrain execution of general vesting declaration.

Hanks and others v *Minister of Housing and Local Government and another* (1963) 15 P & CR 246. Relevant considerations before making compulsory purchase order under Housing Acts.

Webb and others v *Ministry of Housing and Local Government and another* [1964] 1 WLR 1295. Compulsory purchase under Coast Protection Act 1949—bad faith.

Capital Investments Ltd v *Wednesfield Urban District Council* [1965] Ch 774. Notice to treat held to be valid, although school site substituted for housing following confirmation of compulsory purchase orders under Housing Act powers.

Ashbridge Investments Ltd v *Minister of Housing and Local Government* [1965] 3 All ER 371. Courts may only intervene if Minister acts on no evidence; or comes to a conclusion to which on the evidence he could not reasonably have come; or has wrongly interpreted the statutory provision; or taken into account matters which he should not have. The court refused to hear fresh evidence as to whether premises were 'a house'.

Crabtree (A) & Co Ltd v *Minister of Housing and Local Government* (1965) 17 P & CR 232. Alternative accommodation in comprehensive development area for displaced traders a matter for Minister not courts.

Cartwright v *Minister of Housing and Local Government* (1967) 8 P & CR 499. Court without power to consider validity of planning permission and compulsory purchase order.

Bass Charrington (North) Ltd v *Minister of Housing and Local Government* (1971) 22 P & CR 31. Inspector's report must be considered as a whole in deciding whether adjoining land properly included in a compulsory purchase order for a clearance area under Housing Act 1957.

Coleen Properties Ltd v *Minister of Housing and Local Government* [1971] 1 WLR 433. There must be some evidence to support an assertion that an acquisition 'was reasonably necessary for the satisfactory development or use of the cleared area'. The ipse dixit of the acquiring authority was insufficient.

Gordondale Investments Ltd v *Secretary of State for the Environment* (1972) 23 P & CR 334. Court considered what must be included in an official representation as to unfitness by medical officer of health: housing authority held to be under no duty to rehouse tenants to facilitate private scheme to remedy unfitness.

Hibernian Property Co Ltd v *Secretary of State for the Environment* (1973) 24 P & CR 197. Inspector heard views of residents in clearance area in absence of objectors: confirmation of compulsory purchase order a breach of rules of natural justice as there was a risk of prejudice which constituted a breach of the requirements of para 3 (3), Sched 3 to the Housing Act 1957. Approved in *Performance Cars Ltd* v *Secretary of State for the Environment* (1977) 34 P & CR 92. See also *Lake District*

Special Planning Board v *Secretary of State for the Environment* [1975] JPL 220 where in a planning appeal the appellants had written to the Minister after the close of the inquiry, but the court held that no unfairness had resulted from these representations not being circulated to all parties.

WH Gibbs Ltd v *Secretary of State for the Environment* (1973) 229 EG 103. Inspector's report inadequate to inform Minister of the appellant's case.

Fairmount Investments Ltd v *Secretary of State for the Environment* [1976] 1 WLR 1255. Order under Housing Act 1957 quashed because the Secretary of State had been in breach of the rules of natural justice in basing his decision on the opinion of his inspector as to the inadequacy of the foundations, when this had formed no part of the council's case and the objectors had no opportunity of refuting it.

Brinklow v *Secretary of State for the Environment* (1976) 241 EG 461. Order quashed as Minister had not considered as relevant the absence of alternative sites for relocating uses carried on in properties to be acquired under the order.

Eckersley v *Secretary of State for the Environment and another* (1977) 34 P & CR 124. Sufficiency of financial resources for carrying into effect a clearance area and redevelopment scheme were purely a matter for consideration by the acquiring authority not the Secretary of State. However, order quashed as Secretary of State had failed to take into account the relative costs of clearance and redevelopment as compared with the cost of retention and rehabilitation.

Sovmots Investments Ltd v *Secretary of State for the Environment* [1979] AC 144. No power to local authority to acquire ancillary rights under Housing Act 1957 unless rights in existence at the time of making the order. (But see now Chapter 13.)

Meravale Builders Ltd v *Secretary of State for the Environment and another* (1978) 36 P & CR 87. Housing compulsory purchase order included land to be used as a principal traffic route. Court held that the road was not reasonably incidental to the provision of housing accommodation, and whole order quashed.

London Welsh Association Ltd and another v *Secretary of State for the Environment and another* [1980] JPL 745. Where the Secretary of State in confirming a compulsory purchase order stated that he accepted the findings of fact, conclusions and recommendations of an inspector relating to the order and had not differed on any relevant matter, he was not wrong in including in his decision letter some of the material considerations and omitting the others.

Ackerman and another v *Secretary of State for the Environment* (1980) 257 EG 1037. No denial of natural justice when objector failed to appear at inquiry in mistaken belief that order was to be withdrawn in respect of objector's property.

Robbins v *Secretary of State for the Environment* [1989] 1 WLR 201. Local authority served repairs notice under s 115 of the 1971 Act on the owner of a listed windmill specifying works some of which were necessary for preservation and others for restoration. After failure to comply with the repairs notice the authority made a compulsory purchase order under s 114 of the 1971 Act. The confirmation of the order was challenged on the grounds that the repairs notice was invalid. The House of Lords held that preservation had to be given its ordinary meaning in contrast to restoration so there was an objective limitation on the works that could be specified; the relevant date for determining whether works were repair or restoration was the date of listing, not of the repairs notice; and that if the notice contained items of restoration rather than preservation it remained valid so long as the items of preservation justified the notice—the invalid items could be disregarded.

Chapter 7

Notice to Treat

After a compulsory purchase order has been confirmed, the acquiring authority will be able to proceed either by way of the notice to treat/notice of entry procedure, or alternatively by making a general vesting declaration (as described in Chapter 16). The choice of procedures will be influenced by whether there is a need to secure title or whether possession is sufficient. By using the notice to treat, early possession can be obtained and often this is sufficient for the authority, the title being sorted out later. The general vesting declaration takes longer and is more complex, but the authority will gain ownership of the land and this may be important if commercial development is involved. Notice to treat is served on all owners, mortgagees and lessees. Usually the notice incorporates or attaches a form of claim, which must be returned within 21 days.

Curiously enough, the phrase 'notice to treat' had no statutory origin for upwards of 100 years. The procedure commonly known as serving notice to treat rested upon s 18 of the Lands Clauses Consolidation Act 1845, which required the promoters by notice to demand from all the parties interested in the lands 'the particulars of their estate and interest in such lands, and of the claims made by them in respect thereof'. Now, s 5 of the Compulsory Purchase Act 1965 uses the phrase 'notice to treat' to describe the notice to be given by the acquiring authority to all the persons interested in, or having power to sell and convey or release the land.

Section 4 of the 1965 Act provides that the powers of the acquiring authority shall not be exercised after three years from the date on which the order becomes operative. This means that notice to treat must be served within three years of publication of notice of confirmation. As long as the notice is served within the three years, entry may be taken outside that period.

The section requires the notice to give particulars of the land to which it relates; to demand particulars of the recipient's interest in the land and of his claim; and to state that the acquiring authority are willing to treat for the purchase and as to the compensation to be made for damage sustained by execution of the works.

Failure to deliver an adequate notice of claim may result in the Lands Tribunal depriving a claimant of his costs. This is provided for in s 4 (2) of the Land Compensation Act 1961, under which a claimant must state the exact nature of the interest in respect of which compensation is claimed and give details of the compensation claimed, distinguishing the amounts under separate heads and showing how the amount claimed under each head is calculated. As to what the notice of claim must contain in a case where equivalent reinstatement is claimed (p 184), see *Trustees for Methodist Church Purposes* v *North Tyneside Metropolitan Borough Council* (1979) 250 EG 647.

In *Hull and Humber Investment Co* v *Hull Corporation* [1965] 2 QB 145, a letter from the district valuer opening negotiations was accepted as a valid notice to treat, but the Lands Tribunal in *Parker* (*Trustees of the Ware Park Estate*) v *Hertford Borough Council* (1967) 18 P & CR 315, held the opposite: the authors prefer this view.

See also *Bostock Chater & Sons Ltd* v *Chelmsford Corporation* (1973) 26 P & CR 321, for an unsuccessful attempt to set up a letter confirming a compulsory purchase order from the appropriate Minister as amounting to notice to treat.

In *Cohen v Haringey London Borough Council* (1981) 42 P & CR 6, it was held that a notice to treat could be served after entry into possession, even if that possession was unlawful. The fact that the notice had been back-dated, in an attempt to regularise the position, did not make the notice invalid.

1 Main effects

There are three main effects of service of a notice to treat:
(1) Service of the notice creates a relationship analogous to that between vendor and purchaser (*Adams* v *London & Blackwall Railway Co* (1850) 19 LJCh 557). The owner may deal with the property, but may not increase the burden to the acquiring authority (*Cardiff Corporation* v *Cook* [1923] 2 Ch 115). It binds the authority to purchase and the owner to sell at a price to be ascertained (*Mercer* v *Liverpool St Helen's and South Lancashire Railway Co* [1903] 1 KB 652, 664 CA).
(2) Where there is an unconditional agreement fixing the price

—whether in writing or by word of mouth—it is the equivalent of a binding contract between the parties (*Harding* v *Metropolitan Railway Co* (1872) 7 Ch App 154) quoted by Lord Denning MR in *Munton* v *Greater London Council* (1976) 32 P & CR 269. Lord Hatherley LC said in *Harding's* case 'when the price is ascertained... you have then all the elements of a complete agreement and in truth it becomes a bargain made under legislative enactment between the railway company and those over whom they were authorised to exercise their power'.

(3) The authority can get entry on the lands without the owner's consent. See Chapter 8.

2 Date for assessing compensation

For many years it had been regarded as settled law that the date of notice to treat determined the date as at which compensation would be assessed. See, for example, *Square Grip Reinforcement Co (London)* v *Rowton Houses* [1967] 2 WLR 160. The House of Lords in 1969 decided that the date of notice to treat is not the correct date as at which to assess compensation (*Birmingham Corporation* v *West Midlands Baptist (Trust) Association (Incorporated)* [1970] AC 874 HL). The House of Lords decided that the correct date is either the date of taking possession, or the date of assessment of compensation (by agreement or by the Lands Tribunal as the case may be), whichever date is the earlier. There have been a number of decisions as to the correct date for valuation, following the decision in the *Birmingham* case:

Bradford Property Trust v *Hertfordshire County Council* (1973) 27 P & CR 228—freehold interest no longer encumbered by tenancies at date of entry to be valued as unencumbered interest: the true rule being that interests as well as values must be taken as at the date of valuation or entry unless the owner has done something which so altered the interests as to increase the burden of compensation to the acquiring authority. Only interests subsisting at the date of notice to treat can qualify.

This case is one of a number in which it has been held that the interest to be valued and the surrounding circumstances are both to be considered as they are at the date of entry (or valuation) and valued as at that date. The alternative view is that the interest to be valued and the surrounding circumstances should be considered as they were at the date of notice to treat, but should be valued on the basis of the values which applied at the date of entry. Whilst the second alternative has been followed on some occasions, it would seem that the first alternative has generally been applied.

Burson v *Wantage Rural District Council* (1974) 27 P & CR 556—actual date of possession taken as the relevant date, although notice of entry would have permitted earlier possession.

W & S (Long Eaton) Ltd v *Derbyshire County Council* (1974) 29 P & CR 552—the Lands Tribunal concluded that there were three events which might determine date of assessment: entry by acquiring authority; the making of an enforceable contract; and date of hearing before the tribunal. The tribunal held that an accepted purchase notice, creating a deemed notice to treat (which could not be withdrawn), was not a contract for sale in the absence of agreement on price, so that the third alternative applied. The Court of Appeal affirmed the tribunal's view of the law and elaborated the third alternative. The date of valuation was to be the date of the award, 'which as a practical matter means the last date of the hearing before the Lands Tribunal'. See the same case at (1976) 31 P & CR 99. (*Corporation of Hull Trinity House* v *County Council of Humberside* (1975) 30 P & CR 243, had, prior to the appeal, considered the third alternative in the *Long Eaton* case, and preferred the date of reference. This opinion was dissented from by the Court of Appeal in the *Long Eaton* case.)

It had also been thought that, after notice to treat, the property was at the risk of the acquiring authority who should therefore insure. The House of Lords overruled *Phoenix Assurance Co* v *Spooner* [1905] 2 KB 753, on which this view was based.

There are two main side-effects from the decision in the *Birmingham* case:

(1) It is not possible for local authorities to stabilise values by serving notice to treat. They can only do this by taking possession either by agreement or after serving notice of entry.

(2) As property is not at the risk of the authority merely because they serve notice to treat, the owner must safeguard his property against physical deterioration or damage. He cannot therefore leave the property after notice to treat without taking some risk that deterioration may reduce its value by the time compensation falls to be assessed. The exclusion of changes in value due to the scheme (see p 186 below) may be some safeguard to the owner, but he should preferably not vacate until the authority have agreed to take possession. Circular No 35/70 from the Ministry of Housing and Local Government

suggests that owners should be made aware of their continuing liability after service of notice to treat: see also p 101 below.

Where there has been agreement about the principle of selling, with the price to be on the compulsory purchase basis, the date for assessing that price will be the date of possession and not the date of contract—see *Marchment* v *Hampshire County Council* (1979) 43 P & CR 436. (See Appendix 5 for a draft form of agreement.)

If a local authority rehouse a residential tenant before they have served notice of entry or reached agreement on compensation, they may create vacant possession value by so doing. In order to prevent this, and in view of the doubts created by the House of Lords decision in *Rugby Joint Water Board* v *Foottit and others* [1972] 1 All ER 1057, s 50 (2) of the Land Compensation Act 1973 provides that compensation for the landlord's interest shall not be enhanced by the fact that the landlord has obtained possession (or has prospects of obtaining possession) after the date of the notice to treat by the authority rehousing the tenant in fulfilment of their duty under s 39 of the 1973 Act (as to which see p 155 below). If the landlord obtains possession before the notice to treat or otherwise than by virtue of s 39, there is nothing in s 50 to prevent vacant possession value being created.

In *Paul* v *Newham LBC* (Lands Tribunal 16 November 1989) tenants of a house divided into two flats were rehoused after notice to treat but before notice of entry. The owner claimed vacant possession value because one tenant was rehoused voluntarily by the acquiring authority due to the condition of the property and the other was rehoused by another authority; therefore in neither case was the rehousing in consequence of the order. It was held that the tenants were compelled to leave in consequence of the acquisition so compensation was payable on a sitting tenant basis.

If the authority rehouse a residential owner, s 50 also provides that the compensation is not to be reduced because of the provision of accommodation.

3 Effect on existing agreements, etc

Anyone who has acted in a compulsory purchase will know that quite a long time can elapse between the announcement of the authority's intentions and the confirmation of the order.

During this period the owner may well find it difficult to do anything with his land. It may be possible to serve a blight notice if the owner wishes to sell (see Chapter 18) and the following propositions apply:

(1) If the owner creates a new interest, the holder may be debarred from claiming compensation (*Mercer* v *Liverpool, St Helens and South Lancs Railway Co* [1904] AC 461). The determination of an interest may have the same result: see *Banham* v *London Borough of Hackney* (1970) 22 P & CR 922.

(2) If the owner sells or assigns his interest, the purchaser or assignee will merely stand in the vendor's shoes (*Cardiff Corporation* v *Cook* [1923] 2 Ch 115).

(3) If there is a contract for sale between the owner and a third party, it will not be frustrated by service of notice to treat. The owner must convey the land to the third party but subject to the notice to treat (*Hillingdon Estates Co* v *Stonefield Estates Ltd* [1952] Ch 627).

(4) If the owner erects any building, does any work or carries out any alteration or improvement on the land or other land with which the owner is directly or indirectly concerned, the Lands Tribunal shall not take into account any interest or enhancement in value, if satisfied that the works etc, were not reasonably necessary and were undertaken with a view of obtaining compensation or increased compensation (Acquisition of Land Act 1981, s 4).

4 Binding contract

A notice to treat has been described as a neutral act. When, then, is there a contract for sale which will bind the owner? The answer is when there is agreement between the parties on price, or when the price has been assessed following reference to the Lands Tribunal. Specific performance will then be granted. (This is subject to the provisions of s 31 (5) of the Land Compensation Act 1961, which allows an authority to withdraw when a claimant has failed to deliver a claim.) (*Harding* v *Metropolitan Railway Co* (1892) LR 7 Ch 154.)

For there to be a binding agreement following notice to treat it is not necessary that there should be a written contract for sale which satisfies the requirements of s 2 of the Law of Property (Miscellaneous Provisions) Act 1989 (the successor of s 40 of the Law of Property Act 1925 and, before that, the Statute of Frauds 1677). In *Pollard* v *Middlesex County Council* (1906) 95 LT 870, Parker J said 'It is quite true that statutory agreements arising out of notices to treat are not within the statute of frauds and that oral evidence of them may therefore be admitted'. See also *Harding* v *Metropolitan Railway Co* (1872) 7 Ch App 154 at p 158.

In *Duttons Brewery Ltd* v *Leeds City Council* (1980) 42 P & CR 152 agreement on a purchase price was reached in 1968 'subject to a contract to be prepared by me [the Town Clerk]'. The council did not enter on the property until 1976, although at the time of agreement on price entry had been expected about 1971. The court at first instance held that there was no firm agreement between the parties if entry was not made within the period contemplated in 1968. Compensation fell to be assessed at the date of entry. This decision was affirmed by the Court of Appeal but on the grounds that 'subject to contract' meant that compensation had not been unconditionally agreed, following the decision in *Munton* v *Greater London Council* (*sub nom*) *Munton* v *Newham London Borough Council* (1976) 32 P & CR 269CA. Here agreement on price was reached but the words 'subject to contract' were used by the solicitors and surveyor for the house-owner. It was held that there was no binding agreement as to price 'It is important that no doubt should be thrown on the effect of the words' said Lord Denning.

Both *Dutton's* and *Munton's* cases contain useful reviews of the law relating to notice to treat and the consequential effects of serving such notice.

A notice to treat is not registrable as an estate contract in the land charges register: it is often registered as a local land charge, but whether it needs to be so registered is doubtful (*Capital Investments Ltd* v *Wednesfield Urban District Council* [1965] Ch 774).

5 Who is entitled to notice?

In practice the authority will serve all parties whom they know to have a legal or equitable interest in the land, other than the owners of short tenancies who can be dealt with under s 20 of the Compulsory Purchase Act 1965 (formerly s 121 of the Lands Clauses Consolidation Act 1845) (see p 68).

A—The following *are* entitled to notice:
  (i) any person who is a necessary party to the conveyance of an interest which the authority wish to acquire;
 (ii) mortgagees, whether legal or equitable (see p 107 below);
(iii) persons with equitable rights, eg, arising under a building agreement (*Birmingham & District Land Co* v *London & North Western Railway* (1888) 40 ChD 268)—unless presumably these would be overreached on conveyance of the

legal estate;
(iv) lessees, other than tenants having no greater interest than for a year, or from year to year. Weekly, monthly, quarterly or yearly tenants, therefore, need no notice to treat.

B—The following *are not* entitled to notice
 (i) holders of short tenancies (see (iv) above);
 (ii) licensees (eg, directors having a right to use a room: *Municipal Freehold Land Co v Metropolitan and District Railways Joint Committee* (1883) 1 C & E 184);
(iii) persons having the benefit of easements over, or restrictive covenants against, the land to be acquired (see pp 92 and 94 below).

Whilst the authority normally serves notice to treat on all interests, it does not have to do so. Provided that notice to treat is served on all owners of any particular interest, it is not essential that every interest is acquired. Thus an authority can choose to serve notice on the owner of a leasehold interest but not on the freehold. In *Sovmots Investments v Secretary of State for the Environment* [1976] 3 All ER 720 Camden LBC as acquiring authority undertook not to serve notice to treat in respect of the freehold interest of the Greater London Council and the GLC undertook not to oppose the confirmation of the order. The court held that the undertaking did not render the order invalid since it was not incompatible with the statutory purpose behind the order.

6 Withdrawal of notice

A property owner will usually greet with some enthusiasm news that an acquiring authority intend to go into reverse over a proposed compulsory purchase. The question of supervening loss is, however, an important one, and it is on this aspect of the matter that professional advisers are most likely to be consulted.

Power to withdraw a notice to treat appears in s 31 of the Land Compensation Act 1961. This permits the authority to withdraw within six weeks of the delivery of a valid statement of claim under s 4 of the 1961 Act. The authority then become liable to the owner 'for any loss or expense occasioned to him by the giving and withdrawal of the notice'. The compensation under these heads will in default of agreement be settled by the Lands Tribunal. The compensation will include a sum for any loss flowing directly from the receipt of the notice, eg, inability to develop or let the land (*London County Council v Montague Burton Ltd* [1934] 1 KB 360 at p 364). For cases before the Lands Tribunal involving the payment of fees of professional advisers where an acquisition was not proceeded with, see *Duke of Grafton v Secretary of State for Air* (1955) 5 P & CR 290; reversed on appeal (1956) 6 P & CR 374; and *Atkins and Atkins v Lymington Corporation* (1962) 14 P & CR 148.

The statutory power in s 31 is not available when entry has been made on the land under the powers in s 11 of the Compulsory Purchase Act 1965, because there is then an obligation to pay compensation. See p 61.

Section 31 also deals with the less usual case of an invalid claim being received. This point was considered in *Trustees for Methodist Church Purposes and another v North Tyneside Metropolitan Borough Council* (1979) 38 P & CR 665, where the notice of claim was merely that compensation would be claimed on the basis of equivalent re-instatement of the chapel. The claim was held not to comply with s 4 of the Land Compensation Act 1961, and the authority was accordingly entitled to withdraw the notice to treat and not to proceed with the purchase.

If no statutory power exists, a notice can always be withdrawn by consent (*Tawney v Lynn and Ely Railway Co* (1847) 16 LJCh 282). The owner can then lay down his terms for agreement.

The following special rules relating to withdrawal should be noted:

(1) A notice to treat cannot be withdrawn by the acquiring authority where notice is deemed to be served in purchase notice cases under Pt IX of the Town and Country Planning Act 1971 (see s 208 and p 120).

(2) A notice to treat can be withdrawn if the owner requires the authority to take all or nothing under s 8 of the Compulsory Purchase Act 1965 (see Chapter 10).

(3) In the case of compulsory purchases by an acquiring authority who have made a general vesting declaration under the Compulsory Purchase (Vesting Declarations) Act 1981, the following special rules as to withdrawal apply:

(a) The constructive notice to treat which the acquiring authority are deemed to have served cannot be withdrawn after the interest has vested, ie, normally the authority can withdraw only in the period (usually 28 days) between the making and coming into effect of a vesting declaration (s 7 of the Act of 1981).

(b) The constructive notice can be withdrawn within three months of the owner's objection in cases where an owner has objected to the acquisition on the grounds of severance, ie, says to the acquiring authority 'take the whole or nothing' (para 4 (1) (*a*) of Sched 1 to the Act of 1981).

7 Abandonment

In *Simpson's Motor Sales (London) Ltd* v *Hendon Corporation* [1963] Ch 57 and [1963] 2 WLR 1187, the court put forward four principles of general application:

(1) Where notice to treat has been served, it is the duty of the acquiring authority to proceed to acquire the land within a reasonable time. If they fail to do so, they may lose their rights. Only considerable delay will normally invalidate the notice, and it is therefore important that an authority who have served notice to treat are not allowed to go to sleep on the matter thereafter. In the *Hendon* case, although there had been a delay of some two and a half years, it had been acquiesced in by the owners. The acquiring authority never communicated any intention to abandon to the owners, and in the absence of misconduct or any action which could be regarded as ultra vires, the order was held to be valid.

(2) The authority may evince an intention to abandon the notice to treat. Delay is usually an element in abandonment. For example, in *Grice* v *Dudley Corporation* [1958] Ch 329, an authority served notice to treat in 1939 but did not proceed under it until 1954, by which time the scheme had materially changed. The notice was held to be invalid. If either party 'sleep upon their rights' they may lose their right to proceed under the notice to treat (*Tiverton and North Devon Railway Co* v *Loosemore* (1884) 9 App Cas 480) and the authority may be estopped by conduct from acting on the notice (*Hedges* v *Metropolitan Railway* (1860) 3 LT 643).

(3) The authority may act ultra vires. Cases of abandonment are to be contrasted with those where the authority show a continuing intention to acquire the land, but for a purpose not authorised by the compulsory purchase order (see *Capital Investments Ltd* v *Wednesfield Urban District Council* [1965] Ch 774 and *Meravale Builders Ltd* v *Secretary of State for the Environment* (1978) 36 P & CR 87).

(4) Either party may lose the right to enforce the notice to treat against the other by misconduct.

Chapter 8

Powers of Entry

It will already have been noted that one of the main advantages of proceeding by compulsory purchase is the ability of the acquiring authority to get entry on the land in advance of the settlement of the price, and in the absence of agreement.

Sometimes entry by consent is sought by the authority after the compulsory purchase order has been confirmed. It should be noted that consent to the entry, once given, cannot be revoked (*Knapp* v *London, Chatham and Dover Railway Co* (1863) 11 WR 890). A mortgagee's consent should be obtained as well as the mortgagor's (*Ranken* v *East & West India Docks and Birmingham Junction Railway Co* (1849) 12 Beav 298). Interest is payable in accordance with normal conveyancing practice where entry by consent is obtained.

1 Under the Act of 1845

The procedure under the Lands Clauses Consolidation Act 1845 was elaborate. It is now contained in Sched 3 to the Compulsory Purchase Act 1965, where it is entitled 'alternative procedure for obtaining rights of entry'. The promoters must lodge in court as security either the amount claimed by any party not consenting to entry or an amount determined by a surveyor as the value of the lands, and also give a bond for payment of the sum due together with interest.

2 Under the Act of 1965

The old Lands Clauses procedure will be little used today, because of the much simpler procedure available in s 11 of the Compulsory Purchase Act 1965. Following notice to treat, the authority can take possession after 14 days' notice has been served upon every owner, lessee and occupier. For a case where a lessee was estopped from asserting his claim to receive notice, see *Milford Haven Urban District Council* v *Foster* (1961) 13 P & CR 289. Unless a mortgagee is in possession, he will not get notice of entry. Once the power of entry has been exercised it will not be open to the authority to withdraw the notice to treat except by agreement. This is specifically provided for in cases going before the Lands Tribunal (see Land Compensation Act 1961, s 31 (2)), and appears to be implied by s 11 (4) of the Compulsory Purchase Act 1965.

There is not infrequently a longish period between the service of notice and actual entry. The expiry of the period of notice does not amount to entry. As to what amounts to entry see *Courage Ltd* v *Kingswood District Council* (1978) 247 EG 307.

The continuing liabilities of owners pending actual entry are discussed in Chapter 14, and the relationships between landlords and tenants in Chapter 9.

Although the procedures in the 1965 Act apply generally to orders made under the Housing Act 1985, there are restrictions on the recovery of possession—see ss 582–3.

If the authority or their contractors fail to observe the procedure in s 11 of the 1965 Act, they become liable to penalties (unchanged since 1845) for unauthorised entry—see s 12. The penalties will only apply if the entry is 'wilful', ie, there is an absence of an honest belief that the procedure has been followed. Other remedies are not excluded by the statutory provision, so damages or an injunction may be available to an owner.

3 Under vesting declaration

Where an acquiring authority have executed a general vesting declaration upon the compulsory purchase of land by them under the Compulsory Purchase (Vesting Declarations) Act 1981, the powers of entry just described and contained in s 11 of the Compulsory Purchase Act 1965 are excluded by s 8 (3). This is because the coming into effect of the vesting declaration confers the right to enter and take possession as against all but minor tenants or those with a long tenancy about to expire. The latter can only be dispossessed after notice to treat and a 14-day notice of entry (s 9 of the Act of 1981; and see pp 71 and 114).

4 Omitted interests

It may happen that the acquiring authority enter on the land and then discover that they have failed to purchase or pay compensation for an interest. Section 22 of the Compulsory Purchase Act 1965 safeguards their position so long as the entry was through mistake or inadvertence and they purchase or pay compensation for the interest within six months of having notice of the interest or the establishment of the claim. In *Advance Ground Rents* v *Middlesbrough Borough Council* (1986) 280 EG 1015, it was held that the s 22 could not be used where the authority did not purchase or pay compensation to a mortgagee within six months after title was proved.

5 Unknown owners

Difficulties may arise if s 22 cannot be utilised, eg, if prior to entry the authority discover that there is a strip of land with no apparent owner. If this had been discovered at the 'referencing' stage, then the various notices could have been served on 'the owner' under the procedure outlined in on p 16. However, it may be that, at the 'referencing stage', ownership was claimed which subsequently could not be substantiated. For example, occasionally ownership is claimed of a courtyard or passageway and so no further enquiries are made; later it may be established that the 'owner' can prove title to, eg, rooms above the passageway but not to the passageway itself. Alternatively, it may happen that an owner claiming to hold the freehold has in fact only a long lease. What action should the authority take? Is there any difference between situations where the interest is known but the owner is unknown, and where the interest itself has not been disclosed?

It is submitted that if reasonable enquiries suggested that an interest was owned by someone who later proves to have no title, then s 22 can be utilised, although not until possession has actually been taken. If ownership is established prior to entry, then it would probably be desirable to serve notice to treat. In any event, if compensation has not been agreed by the end of the six-month period allowed by s 22, then the matter should be referred to the Lands Tribunal. If the owner remains unknown, then the compensation, when agreed, should be paid into court.

It would seem from *Cooke* v *London County Council* [1911] 1 Ch 604 that s 22 would not be available in cases where the authority know that there is a mortgagee but do not insist on the name of the mortgagee being disclosed. There is no 'mistake or inadvertence'. Nevertheless the authority was held to be not precluded from giving notice to treat to the mortgagee and retaining possession.

If an interest is not disclosed at all (eg, because a freeholder does not reveal a lease) then—again assuming that reasonable enquiries were made—it seems that the s 22 procedure would be appropriate.

6 Survey

There are special provisions in the 1965 Act where the authority wish to enter to survey only (see s 11 (3)). A survey may be made after giving to the owners and occupiers not less than three nor more than 14 days' notice. The authority will have to pay compensation for any damage occasioned during the survey. The power is exercisable only after the compulsory purchase order has been confirmed, unlike the wider power conferred by s 15 of the Local Government (Miscellaneous Provisions) Act 1976.

7 Interest

Where entry is made under the above powers, interest is payable on the purchase money from the date of entry. The rate is prescribed by regulations made under s 32 of the Land Compensation Act 1961 —see the Acquisition of Land (Rate of Interest after Entry) Regulations, which are regularly made adjusting interest rates. The interest is paid subject to deduction of tax at the basic rate (s 54 (1) (a) Income and Corporation Taxes Act 1970)(see Chapter 33).

In *Chilton* v *Telford Development Corporation* [1987] 3 All ER 992 the acquiring authority served notice of entry on 67 acres of agricultural land. Soon after they took possession of five acres but thereafter took possession of the remainder of the land piecemeal on seven separate dates over 28 months. It was held that for the purposes of calculating compensation for disturbance, possession of the whole of the 67 acres had been taken when the authority first entered onto the land and took possession of the first parcel.

See also *Simmonds* v *Kent County Council* on p 263.

8 Failure to give up possession

In any case where the owner or occupier refuses to give possession, the authority may issue their warrant to the sheriff to deliver possession (Compulsory Purchase Act 1965, s 13). An authority can enter without warrant if they can do so peaceably (*Loosemore* v *Tiverton and North Devon Railway Co* (1882) 47 LT 151). The sheriff can be put in to give possession even if the occupier would otherwise enjoy the protection of landlord and tenant legislation.

Chapter 9

Leasehold Interests

This chapter brings together a number of points which only or mainly affect tenants of the land to be acquired.

1 Service of order

A lessee is entitled to notice of the making of the compulsory purchase order and its confirmation, unless he is 'a tenant for a month or any period less than a month'. Monthly, weekly or statutory tenants need not therefore be served, although on grounds of caution an acquiring authority may serve everyone known to be interested—for there is no penalty for serving too many parties.

2 Notice to treat

Notice to treat must be served on all lessees, including those holding under agreements which in equity are equivalent to a lease (*Walsh* v *Lonsdale* (1882) 21 ChD 9); but not on tenants having no greater interest than as tenant for a year or from year to year (s 20 of the Compulsory Purchase Act 1965).

The owners of these short tenancies are dealt with by means of what used to be called 'a s 121 notice', this section being the fore-runner in the Lands Clauses Acts of s 20 of the Act of 1965 (see head 3 below).

If the acquiring authority serve notice to treat and then discover that the interest is a 'short tenancy', the compensation will fall to be assessed under s 20 of the Act of 1965, ie, when possession is required. If this is after the end of the tenancy, then the tenant has not had to give up possession and so is not entitled to compensation. He cannot require that he be compensated under the notice to treat (*London Borough of Newham* v *Benjamin* [1968] 1 All ER 1195).

Following notice to treat, the leasehold interest can be acquired, as in the case of freeholds. Failure to register as an estate contract an agreement for a lease will not deprive the tenant of his right to compensation, in spite of s 13 (2) of the Land Charges Act 1925 (*Blamires* v *Bradford Corporation* (1965) 16 P & CR 162).

If nothing is done under a notice to treat served on a lessee, and meanwhile the lease runs out, no compensation for the compulsory acquisition will be payable (*Holloway* v *Dover Corporation* [1960] 1 WLR 604). The Lands Tribunal followed this decision in *Cleaners (JV)* v *County Borough of Luton* (1968) 20 P & CR 465. The reasoning in this type of case is that there is nothing for the acquiring authority to acquire. There is no expropriation, and no subject matter for which the authority are liable to pay compensation. Removal expenses, temporary losses and expenses in connection with acquiring other premises were allowed in *Soper and Soper* v *Doncaster Corporation* (1964) 16 P & CR 53, although Sir Michael Rowe in the *Luton* case just mentioned doubts if *Soper's* case was rightly decided in strict point of law. Compensation for extinguishment of goodwill was allowed by the tribunal in *Koch* v *Greater London Council* (1968) 20 P & CR 472, in a case where a tenant of a fried fish shop stayed in business after expiry of his lease, notice of entry having being served a year before the expiry, and the tenant having finally determined the lease under s 27 (2) of the Landlord and Tenant Act 1954.

Cases have arisen when a lease contains an option to determine sometimes exercisable by the landlord and sometimes by the tenant. What is the position if this option is exercisable after notice to treat? In the light of *Birmingham Corporation* v *West Midlands Baptist (Trust) Association (Incorporated)* [1970] AC 874 HL, it would seem that the position must be assessed as at the date when possession is taken by the acquiring authority or when compensation is assessed. Cases such as *Square Grip Reinforcement Co (London) Ltd* v *Rowton Houses* [1967] Ch 877 must be regarded as overruled by the *Birmingham* case noted previously. As compensation is no longer assessed as at the date of notice to treat, it would seem that options which if exercised by a tenant would give rise to a longer lease may have to be taken into account even if they are exercisable after the date of notice to treat. See also *R* v *Kennedy* [1893] 1 QB 533.

The Lands Tribunal assumed that a new lease would be granted by the landlord in *Trocette Property Co Ltd* v *Greater London Council and the London Borough of Southwark* (1974) 27 P & CR 256, in order that the tenant could benefit from a planning consent for redevelopment which the tribunal assumed would be granted (decision subsequently confirmed by the Court of Appeal (1974) 28 P & CR 408). This case can be contrasted with *Davy Ltd* v *London Borough of Hammersmith* (1975) 30 P & CR 469, where on different facts the tribunal held that landlords would wait for an existing lease to fall in.

Suppose on the other hand the landlord has the power to determine which he does not exercise on the due date, assuming this to be after notice to treat. Here it would seem that the acquiring authority would have to pay for their own inactivity in not serving notice of entry on the tenant or alternatively acquiring the landlord's interest and exercising the option to determine. The tenant would in this case have done nothing himself to increase the liability, and would be entitled to have his interest valued as it existed at the time of entry or agreement on compensation.

Where the tenant vacates the premises because he is rehoused by the local authority in pursuance of the rehousing obligation provided by s 39 of the 1973 Act, the landlord will not get vacant possession value (s 50 of the Land Compensation Act 1973, and see also p 55 above).

An acquiring authority will not always serve notice to treat upon lessees. If they can acquire the freehold interest, they stand in the shoes of the former owner. They may therefore terminate a tenancy in accordance with the terms of the tenancy agreement and subject to any statutory protection, eg, the Landlord and Tenant Act 1954; and compensation will not be payable under the legislation relating to compulsory purchase (*Syers* v *Metropolitan Board of Works* (1877) 36 LT 227). A tenant who has received notice to quit from the acquiring authority after they have acquired the reversion may be entitled to compensation under landlord and tenant legislation, eg, for tenant's improvements under s 1 of the Landlord and Tenant Act 1927. He may also claim a disturbance payment under s 37 of the Land Compensation Act 1973, if this is more favourable than compensation based upon rateable value under s 39 of the Landlord and Tenant Act 1954. He cannot get both payments (s 37 (4) of the Act of 1973).

Where an acquiring authority become owners of the freehold reversion of agricultural land, the service of notice to quit by them on the agricultural tenant will bring into play the provisions of s 59 of the Land Compensation Act 1973. The tenant can elect to have compensation assessed as if the notice to quit were a notice under s 20 of the Act of 1973. Section 59 does not apply only to cases where notice to quit has been served by the landlord from whom the authority are purchasing the freehold of the farm (*Dawson* v *Norwich City Council* (1979) 37 P & CR 516).

An authority who intend to act as landlord must give themselves time to follow through the procedures in the Landlord and Tenant Act 1954, so that in due course the former tenant is left without any compensatable interest but only his claim to a disturbance payment or one based upon rateable value.

3 Section 20 procedure (formerly s 121)

A tenant who has no interest greater than as a tenant for a year, or from year to year, is not entitled to a notice to treat, but is entitled to compensation if he is required to give up possession before his term has expired (s 20 of the Compulsory Purchase Act 1965). It has been held that, in the case of a lease for more than a year with an unexpired residue of the term less than a year at the time possession is taken, the tenant's interest is no greater than that of the tenant for a year or from year to year (*R* v *Great Northern Railway Co* (1876) 2 QBD 151). Where tenants of business premises held over under the provisions of s 24 of the Landlord and Tenant Act 1954 after expiry of their lease, the Lands Tribunal held that their interest could properly be determined under s 121 of the Lands Clauses Act 1845, the forerunner of s 20, under which most cases have been decided (*Selborne (Gowns) Ltd* v *Ilford Corporation* (1962) 13 P & CR 350). See *Runcorn Association Football Club Ltd* v *Warrington and Runcorn Development Corporation* (1983) 45 P & CR 183 for a case involving equivalent reinstatement and the application of s 20 to leasehold club premises.

Where required to give up possession before his interest has expired, such a tenant is entitled to 'compensation for the value of his unexpired term or interest, and for any just allowance which ought to be made to him by an incoming tenant, and for any loss or injury he may sustain'. In *Ministry of Transport* v *Pettit* (1968) 67 LGR 449, it was held that 'loss or injury' was not confined to financial loss or injury but was wide enough to cover the inconvenience and upset suffered by the claimant. In practice, this means that a holder of a short tenancy will receive compensation in exactly the same way and under the same heads as if he had received notice to treat, and in default of agreement can have it assessed by the Lands Tribunal. See *DHN Food Distributors Ltd* v *London Borough for Tower Hamlets* (1975) 30 P & CR 251, for a claim under s 20 where several tenancies and subsidiary companies were involved.

The s 20 procedure is not needed if the tenant's interest is due to expire by effluxion of time or if it can be terminated by the acquiring authority giving notice to quit in their capacity as landlord.

Where a tenant moved after notice to treat, but before notice of entry, he was held not to be entitled to compensation under the former s 121 (*Roberts and Midland Bank* v *Bristol Corporation* (1960) 11 P & CR 205) because he had not been 'required to give up possession' within s 121.

In the case of business premises, s 39 of the Landlord and Tenant Act 1954 provides a compensation payment based on a multiplier of the rateable value. It excluded, so far as assessing compensation is concerned, the right of a tenant to apply for a new tenancy, but this was repealed by s 47 of the Land Compensation Act 1973. The right to a new tenancy can be expected to enhance the value of the tenant's interest if he has carried out improvements, because this could leave him with a profit rental value. The right to renewal could also enhance the value of the business goodwill, which could be an item of compensation for 'any loss or injury' sustained if the business is extinguished or interrupted.

See p 222, as to a tenant's claim for disturbance.

A tenant entitled to compensation under s 20 would require to be served with notice of entry (see Chapter 8) before possession is taken, unless compensation has been paid or tendered by the authority in accordance with s 20.

4 Landlord and tenant relationship

The mere service of a notice to treat or even notice of entry will not alter the position under the lease as between landlord and tenant. In the absence of agreement to the contrary, the tenant is responsible for payment of the rent and for performing the tenant's covenants in the lease.

It used to be considered that the doctrine of frustration did not apply to leases. However, in *National Carriers* v *Panalpina (Northern)* [1981] 2 WLR 45, the House of Lords held that the doctrine of frustration was in principle applicable to leases though the cases in which it could properly be applied were likely to be rare. Once the acquiring authority has entered into possession, so that the subject matter of the lease has been expropriated, it would seem that there may be 'an eviction by title paramount' thus distinguishing compulsory purchase from wartime requisition in such cases as

Whitehall Court Ltd v *Ettlinger* [1920] 1 KB 680, where the requisition was held to be a notice showing that the government required no more than the occupation of the premises for an undefined period.

Once the authority has taken possession it seems therefore (although surprisingly there is no authority on the point) that there is an eviction by law, and whether on that account or the principle of frustration as enunciated in the *National Carriers* case, the lease must be regarded as terminated. It is worth nothing in this connection that the time of disposal for capital gains tax purposes is the date when the authority enters the land if earlier than the date of settlement of the compensation. In cases where a demolition order or closing order has been made under the Housing Act 1985, it is interesting that there is special provision made in s 317 for a county court judge to make an order determining the lease—but no parallel provision is made for compulsory purchase orders in any enactment.

The landlord's compensation will carry interest from the date of entry into possession and this interest can be regarded as equivalent to the rent. The tenant for his part will have to pay rent for alternative accommodation and so gains nothing by being relieved of his obligation to pay rent under the agreement.

Until the obligations under the lease can be regarded as terminated, the tenant remains liable under his repairing covenants. This means that the tenant should not do anything which might damage the value of the reversion, for example, leaving the premises unoccupied and liable to vandalism. It is usual, however, for the repairing covenant not to be enforced, but to deal with the matter by adjustment of the compensation as between landlord and tenant. The reversion will be valued on the basis that there is a claim for dilapidations. The valuation of the tenant's interest will take into account the liabilities of the tenant under the lease. If a large claim for dilapidations is in issue, it is desirable for the parties to discuss the matter with the valuer for the acquiring authority. If, as is often the case, the acquired property will later be demolished, it is obviously wasteful for actual repairs to be carried out, and discussions between the parties will usually produce a fair and sensible solution.

In *Leek* v *Birmingham City Council* (1982) 44 P & CR 125, a freehold was acquired by the city council under a general vesting declaration which vested in the council the right to sue in respect of breaches of the repairing covenants in a lease of the property. The Lands Tribunal held that a claimant was entitled to be compensated for the loss of the right to enforce the repairing covenants. The amount awarded turned upon the value of the tenant's covenants having regard to the fact that the tenant was a subsidiary of an international company of repute.

5 Procedure under vesting declarations

When an acquiring authority vest land in themselves by executing a vesting declaration (see Chapter 16) they will not serve notice of execution on a holder of an 'minor tenancy', or on a holder of a 'long tenancy which is about to expire' (Compulsory Purchase (Vesting Declarations) Act 1981, s 6). Apart from this every occupier has to be served.

'Minor tenancy' means a tenancy for a year or from year to year, or any lesser interest: this would include a controlled or regulated tenant or a short business tenant (Act of 1981, s 2 (1)). These tenants, who are not entitled to notice to treat under the general law, are accordingly put in a similar position in regard to notice of the vesting declaration.

If the acquiring authority wish to get possession in such a case, they must serve a notice to treat followed by a 14-day notice of entry. The vesting will be subject to the tenancy until the expiry of the notice of entry, or the tenancy comes to an end in the normal way. When the notice of entry expires, the tenant's rights become rights to compensation under s 10 of the 1981 Act.

The same scheme of things applies to a 'long tenancy about to expire'; the acquiring authority can specify in the general vesting declaration those tenancies which they wish to except from the vesting. The aim is to leave undisturbed people the acquiring authority do not need to move, but to require notice to treat and notice of entry if for any reason possession is required.

A 'long tenancy about to expire' must—

(*a*) originally have been granted for more than one year, and
(*b*) have more than one year to run but, on the vesting date, not longer than the specified period.

In deciding the unexpired term, it shall be assumed that tenants will exercise any option to renew, and conversely, landlords will exercise any option to terminate (see s 2 (2) of the Act of 1981).

General vesting declarations are dealt with in detail in Chapter 16.

Chapter 10

Taking the Whole or Nothing

It often happens, particularly in the case of acquisitions for highway purposes, that the authority do not want to acquire the whole of a property. Sometimes the acquisition of part presents no difficulty: but sometimes the owner will feel that no amount of compensation for injurious affection can compensate for the damage to be caused by the authority's scheme to the part he will retain. A consideration of this sort may lead to an objection being lodged to the scheme itself.

Apart from this, however, the owner may be able to say to the authority: 'Take the whole or nothing'. By virtue of s 8 of the Compulsory Purchase Act 1965 (derived from s 92 of the Lands Clauses Act 1845), no person can be required to sell a part only of a house, building, or manufactory, or a part only of a park or garden belonging to a house, if he is willing and able to sell the whole. In the case of a dispute as to the applicability of the provision, the Lands Tribunal will determine the issue by asking one of two questions: Can part be taken without material detriment to the house, building or manufactory? Alternatively, in the case of a park or garden, can part be taken without seriously affecting the amenity or convenience of the house?

In the past opinions differed as to whether, in considering if part can be taken without material detriment to the remainder, regard can be had:

(a) only to the effect of severance of the part;

(b) to the severance of the part and also to the works proposed to be carried out on, and the use proposed to be made of, the part proposed to be taken; or

(c) to the effect of severance of the part and also to the totality of the works comprised in the scheme for which the part is proposed to be taken, whether on the land taken or not.

Section 58 of the Land Compensation Act 1973 removed any doubt on this point by providing that in determining whether part can be taken without material detriment to the remainder the Lands Tribunal shall take into account not only the effect of the severance but also the use to be made of the part proposed to be acquired, and in a case where the part is proposed to be acquired for works or other purposes extending to other land, the effect of the whole of the works and the use to be made of the other land.

Accordingly it is open to the tribunal to take into account the effect of the whole of the works, whether adverse or beneficial, and in particular, where an access is interfered with, to take into account any proposal by the acquiring authority to provide an alternative access on other land. The same question is required to be considered by the Lands Tribunal under s 202 (2) of the Town and Country Planning Act 1971 in relation to blight notices, and under Sched 1 to the Compulsory Purchase (Vesting Declarations) Act 1981 in relation to vesting declarations executed by an acquiring authority in respect of part of the claimant's land.

Section 58 (2) provides that the matters required to be taken into consideration under sub-s (1) shall also be taken into account in determining under s 8 (1) of the Compulsory Purchase Act 1965 when rights can be compulsorily acquired over land without material detriment to the remainder of the land. Section 58 (1) is applied, subject to necessary modifications, by various provisions which correspond to or are substituted for s 8 (1)—for example, para 8 of Sched 3 to the Gas Act 1986.

The provisions of the Act of 1965 take the place of s 92 of the Lands Clauses Consolidation Act 1845, and it may be found helpful to refer to the annotations to the earlier Act in a standard text-book if, for example, any difficult question arises as to the meaning of 'house', 'park' or 'garden' or as to the respective rights of owners or lessees. 'House' has, for example, been widely interpreted so as to include a shop or inn (*Richards* v *Swansea Improvement Co* (1878) 9 ChD 425), a vacant piece of land (*Marson* v *London Chatham & Dover Rly* (1868) LR 6 Eq 101), and a warehouse and a stable yard used with a shop (*Siegenburg* v *Metropolitan District Rly* (1883) 49 LT 554). In *London Transport Executive* v *Congregational Union of England and Wales (Incorporated)* (1979) 37 P & CR 155, it was held that a substantial place of worship was within the expression 'any house or other building'. This case, which arose on an application for a declaration, was decided on the wording of s 92 of the Lands Clauses Consolidation Act 1845.

In *Ravenseft Properties Ltd* v *London Borough of Hillingdon*

(1968) 20 P & CR 483, the Lands Tribunal considered what amounts to material detriment—'less useful or less valuable in some significant degree' after part has been taken. It was held that a building used for business purposes could still be a house within the section.

In practice s 8 should not cause difficulty, and an authority should not refuse to meet an owner's request to purchase the whole of his interest. It is true that the authority will have to finance a larger purchase than they originally contemplated. But when the scheme has been completed they will have surplus land which they can sell in the open market. Whether they buy part only and pay compensation for injurious affection to the remainder, or buy the whole and later sell off the part not required at a price which will reflect the depreciation caused by the scheme, the financial results should be broadly the same to them.

1 Procedure

The old cases under s 92 of the 1845 Act show that a requirement to take the whole was usually notified to the authority by means of a counter-notice to the notice to treat. Under modern practice, a letter to the authority—albeit a reasonably formal and precise one—is all that is required.

There is everything to be gained by sending this letter at the earliest possible opportunity, because so often, when an owner says 'I am prepared to sell the whole, but not part', he adds a mental reservation: 'Provided the price for the whole is right'. The best course will often be to lodge a holding objection to the order itself, whilst exploring, on a 'without prejudice' basis, the possibility of a sale of the whole property at a price agreeable to the owner.

Once there is an enforceable contract for the sale of part (which can arise by agreement on the amount of the compensation following notice to treat), it will be too late to exercise the right of requiring the authority to take the whole under s 8 of the 1965 Act.

In an exceptional case, an acquiring authority may be satisfied that the owner is entitled to have the whole acquired but may be unwilling to proceed on that basis. They are in this event entitled to abandon the purchase (*Schwinge* v *London etc Railway* (1855) 24 LJCh 405) and are similarly entitled to abandon the purchase if they have referred the question of detriment to the Lands Tribunal and get a decision which requires them to take the whole or nothing (*Ashton Vale Iron Co Ltd* v *Bristol Corporation* [1901] 1 Ch 591).

2 Intersected lands

The provisions about small portions of intersected lands originally in ss 93 and 94 of the 1845 Act are somewhat similar in intention, but arise less frequently in practice. They are now to be found in s 8 (2) and (3) of the Compulsory Purchase Act 1965. Section 8 (2) gives an owner of rural land the right to require the purchase of any small piece of severed land less than half an acre. The provisions of s 8 (3) only come into play if the authorising Act gives the owner a right to call for the provision of a bridge or tunnel to avoid the severance of his land by the authority's scheme. The acquiring authority can avoid providing an expensive accommodation work if the part severed is less than half an acre or if the part severed is of less value than the cost of the connecting bridge or tunnel, provided that in either case the intersected piece is an isolated one so that the owner has no other land adjoining it. Instead of providing the accommodation work, the authority are empowered to buy the piece of land severed by the scheme.

3 Objection to severance (vesting declaration)

Schedule 1, para 2 (3) to the Compulsory Purchase (Vesting Declarations) Act 1981 makes s 8 of the Compulsory Purchase Act 1965 inapplicable to land included in a general vesting declaration. The cases in which the owner can say 'take the whole' are the same as in s 8, but the Schedule provides instead a detailed procedure for cases where an owner objects to severance.

The procedure, which is not specified in s 8, is fully detailed in the case of a vesting declaration and occupies no less than two and a half pages of the Schedule. The salient points are as follows:

(1) The owner must serve a 'notice of objection to severance' within 28 days after receipt of the notice of making of the vesting declaration. An objection may be allowed out of time where there has been some failure in the service of the vesting declaration notices, provided that the owner acts within 28 days after he learns of the making of the vesting declaration. If the notice of objection is made so late that the vesting declaration has become operative, the acquiring authority cannot withdraw—they must either buy the whole or refer the case to the Lands Tribunal.

(2) A notice of objection stops the vesting declaration taking effect.

(3) Within three months the acquiring authority must decide on one of three courses of action:
  (a) withdraw from the proposed purchase;
  (b) proceed, but purchase the whole; or
  (c) refer the notice to the Lands Tribunal.
  If they fail to act, they are deemed to have withdrawn from the purchase.
(4) The Lands Tribunal may decide that there is no case to require the taking of the whole, applying the same tests as in s 8 of the Compulsory Purchase Act 1965, ie, 'material detriment' or 'seriously affecting' amenity or convenience. Alternatively, it may determine the area that shall be taken.

4 Special provisions for agricultural holdings

(a) Notice to treat for part of farm

Section 53 of the Land Compensation Act 1973 confers in respect of agricultural land a comparable right to that given by s 8 of the Compulsory Purchase Act 1965 to the owners of houses, buildings, etc. It does not in any way diminish earlier law relating to intersected lands, etc (see above).

Where an acquiring authority serve notice to treat for part of an interest in an agricultural unit, the owner may within two months serve a counter-notice requiring the purchase of the residue of his interest. To do so he must claim in his notice that the residue of the unit is not capable of being farmed as a separate agricultural unit either by itself or in conjunction with any agricultural land outside the unit which he may occupy as owner or lessee.

The right may be exercised by persons who have a greater interest than as tenants for a year or from year to year. It therefore covers owner occupiers; landlords who have parted with the land to lessees or tenants; and lessees who hold under a lease for a term of years of which at least two remain unexpired. Both the landlord and such a lessee will be entitled to serve a counter-notice. The authority must decide within two months whether or not to accept the counter-notice as valid. Disputes will be dealt with by the Lands Tribunal.

In considering land outside the existing unit, the test is whether the land is effectively at the disposal of the claimant. Land he owns but has let will not be taken into account. Nor will land which he occupies as a tenant for a year or from year to year. Any land already subject to compulsory purchase will also be disregarded.

In order that the other parties may know the position, a copy of the counter-notice must be served on any person with an interest in the other land, ie, the residue.

Certain deemed notices to treat (s 53 (5)) have the same effect as actual notice to treat.

There are two safeguards for the claimant built into s 54. The first is to prevent an acquiring authority from withdrawing the deemed notice to treat for the land covered by the counter-notice. The second and more important is that if the claimant is unable to reach agreement with the acquiring authority on compensation, he can withdraw his counter-notice either before reference to the Lands Tribunal or within six weeks of the tribunal's determination, ie, if he does not like the award he can withdraw. Compensation will not include anything for development value: it will be based on existing use as agricultural land (s 54 (5)).

A problem may arise in the case of leasehold land where the lessee has served a valid counter-notice but the landlord has not done so. The solution in s 54 is to require the authority to offer to surrender the lease to the landlord on such terms as the authority consider reasonable. If within three months the parties have not agreed upon terms, the authority must (unless the lessor has already done so) refer the matter to the Lands Tribunal. Within one month of the tribunal's award (or on a date to be specified by the tribunal) the lessor is deemed to have accepted the surrender. The section imports the provisions of s 9 of the Compulsory Purchase Act 1965 to deal with a recalcitrant lessor.

(b) Yearly tenants

Section 55 of the Land Compensation Act 1973 makes similar provision for tenants of agricultural holdings. When served with notice of entry, the tenant for a year or from year to year can by notice elect to treat the notice as one relating to the entire holding. A copy of the counter-notice must be served on the landlord. The general requirements are similar to those in s 59 for enlarging notices to treat.

A special problem arises in the case of yearly tenants which does not apply in the case of notice to treat for owners and lessees. The notice of entry which is served upon an ordinary yearly agricultural tenant can provide for the taking of possession at a very short notice, ie, 14 days. The notice can therefore take effect before the validity of any counter-notice has been determined. The tenant can as a result find himself in possession of the residue well after he has given up possession of the land which was the subject of notice of entry. Section 56 (2) makes a special provision for this situation. Provided that the tenant gives up possession of every part of the holding to the acquiring authority within 12 months, the authority are deemed to have taken possession of the residue on the day before the expiry of the current year of the tenancy.

This device preserves the tenant's full entitlement to compensation. He should receive as a minimum under s 48 the value of an unexpired term of interest for at least one year, based on loss of the profit rental value and loss of profits.

The landlord (who has been served with a copy of the tenant's counter-notice) will of course have received a notice to treat and can get rid of his residue by counter-notice under s 53. A problem may arise when the landlord chooses not to serve or fails to serve a valid counter-notice under s 53. The landlord must then take over the residue of the holding from the authority as soon as the tenant gives up possession. Any increase in value of the residue because it is taken back with vacant possession will be deducted from the landlord's compensation for the acquisition of the original part of his holding. Other provisions protect the authority and the claimant from possible action by the landlord and transfer to the authority rights and liabilities of the tenant against the landlord on such matters as dilapidations, rent arrears and tenant right. Compensation to the tenant will have taken account of these.

Most notices of entry on agricultural tenants will be by virtue of s 11 (1) of the Compulsory Purchase Act 1965. There are, however, other provisions which enable authorities to take possession of agricultural land. Section 57 applies the provisions just outlined in these cases with the necessary modifications.

See Chapter 30 (p 254) for the position where the acquiring authority serve notice to quit instead of notice of entry, and there is a residue of land difficult to farm.

5 Other cases

The provisions of s 8 of the Compulsory Purchase Act 1965 are applied to compulsory acquisitions in new towns (New Towns Act 1981, s 4) in urban development areas (Local Government Planning and Land Act 1980, Sched 28) and in clearance areas under the Housing Act 1985 (see s 579 (2) (*a*))). A power to compel the acquisition of the whole of his interest is given by s 252 of the Highways Act 1980 to an owner from whom a highway authority seek to acquire a right over land (as opposed to acquiring the land itself).

Chapter 11

Special Kinds of Land

In Chapter 2 we drew attention to certain cases where an owner might find his rights of objection curtailed. In this chapter we deal with certain exceptional classes of land where safeguards have been introduced into the procedure of compulsory acquisition.

Part III of the Acquisition of Land Act 1981 deals with these special kinds of lands which are as follows:

(*a*) land of *statutory undertakers*;

(*b*) land the property of a *local authority*;

(*c*) inalienable land of the *National Trust*;

(*d*) *commons, open spaces*, fuel or field garden allotment;

(*e*) certain *ancient monuments*.

The safeguards introduced by Pt III are of two sorts:

(1) a certification procedure for statutory undertakers' land under which the acquisition can only proceed if accompanied by a certificate from an appropriate Minister (s 16); or

(2) making the order subject to special Parliamentary procedure in the case of objection (s 17). This special protection was excluded by the Community Land Act 1975 and, after the repeal of that Act, by s 20 of the Local Government, Planning and Land Act 1980. It was restored by the Acquisition of Land Act 1981. However, it is only a limited restoration because if the acquiring authority is one of those specified in s 17 of the Act of 1981, special Parliamentary procedure will not apply.

1 Statutory undertakers—certification procedure

Statutory undertakers are defined in s 8 of the Act of 1981 to include electricity supply and transport undertakings; dock and harbour undertakings; the Civil Aviation Authority and the Post Office; the list has been reduced with the change to private status of the former gas, telephone, airport and water undertakers.

The certification procedure for operational land of statutory undertakers allows the undertakers to prevent acquisition if they can convince the appropriate Minister that acquisition would cause serious detriment to the carrying on of their undertaking. It is more likely to be used than for reliance to be placed on the need for special Parliamentary procedure (as to which see the next head).

The protection of a certificate is given to land of statutory undertakers only if the land was acquired for the purposes of their undertaking (not, for example, as an investment), and is used for such purposes or held for such purposes.

The protection only comes into play if the undertakers make representations to the appropriate Minister (normally the Minister responsible for the statutory function but the Treasury can decide in case of doubt) before the expiry of the period for objecting to the compulsory purchase order and satisfy the Minister that the land in question falls into the protected class. The order may then only be confirmed if the Minister certifies that the nature and situation of the land are such that:

> (a) the land can be purchased and not replaced without serious detriment to the carrying on of the undertaking; or
>
> (b) the land can be replaced by other land owned or available for acquisition without serious detriment to the carrying on of the undertaking.

If a certificate is given, the acquiring authority must publish notice of it in at least one local newspaper (see Form No 11 in the Compulsory Purchase of Land Regulations 1990).

In certain cases an order can be confirmed on operational land of statutory undertakers even though no certificate is given under s 16.

Section 31 of the 1981 Act applies to acquisitions of the operational land of statutory undertakers under the Town and Country Planning Act 1971, by the Land Authority for Wales, or by an urban development corporation. In these special cases there must either be a certificate given by the appropriate Minister, as described above, or alternatively the order must be confirmed or made by the appropriate Minister jointly with the Minister who has the power to confirm or make the order. The advice given at para 6 of Appendix G to Circular No 6/85—that joint confirmation is necessary in the absence of a certificate only if representations have been made—would appear to be incorrect.

2 Local authorities and statutory undertakers—special Parliamentary procedure

Land which is the property of a local authority or statutory undertaker may not be acquired compulsorily, without resort to special Parliamentary procedure, if the local authority or undertaker have lodged an objection which has not been withdrawn. This cumbersome procedure is little used and in any event, if the acquiring authority is one of those specified in s 17 of the Act of 1981, the special protection is lost, ie, the provisions for special Parliamentary procedure will no longer apply. The owning authority (or undertaker) will have either to rely on making its case for objection to the confirming Minister in the normal way, or in the case of a statutory undertaker who can prove serious detriment, use the certification procedure described earlier. Those acquiring authorities who are specified in s 17 and therefore can acquire the land of other authorities and undertakers without fear of possible resort to special Parliamentary procedure are:

(a) local authorities, ie, county councils, district councils, London Borough Councils, the Common Council of the City of London and the Council of the Isles of Scilly;

(b) the Land Authority for Wales;

(c) the Peak Park Joint or Lake District Special Planning Board;

(d) the British Coal Corporation or any other undertaker specified by order of the Minister;

(e) any Minister.

An urban development corporation is therefore not specified in s 17.

By virtue of s 254 of the Highways Act 1980, special Parliamentary procedure does not apply to the compulsory acquisition of rights over land of a local authority or a statutory undertaker needed for the purposes of constructing a bridge or of road drainage. See also s 247 of the same Act as to special Parliamentary procedure in the case of acquisitions by bridge owners.

There are special provisions relating to the assessment of compensation on the acquisition of 'operational ' land of statutory undertakers (Land Compensation Act 1961, s 11; Town and Country Planning Act 1971, ss 238 and 239). Undertakers whose land is compulsorily acquired without the appropriate Minister's certificate (as previously described) may choose between 'market value' under s 5 of the 1961 Act, or 'replacement value' under s 238 of the Act of

1971. See *National Carriers Ltd* v *Secretary of State for Transport* (1978) 35 P & CR 248 for a consideration of the scope of this provision.

3 National Trust

In the case of land held inalienably by the National Trust special Parliamentary procedure will still apply if an objection to the compulsory purchase order is made by the Trust and not withdrawn (s 18, Act of 1981).

Special Parliamentary procedure (which is described at the end of this chapter) also applies to the acquisition of certain other special types of land.

4 Commons, etc

A compulsory purchase order authorising the acquisition of land forming part of a common, open space, fuel or field garden allotment (this means an allotment set out under an inclosure award and not the modern allotment) is subject to a special Parliamentary procedure apart from any objection, unless the Secretary of State for the Environment certifies either:

(1) that equivalent land has been or will be given in exchange, or

(2) that the land does not exceed 250 square yards in extent or is required for the widening or drainage of an existing highway or partly for the widening and partly for the drainage of such a highway, and the giving of other land in exchange is not necessary (Acquisition of Land Act 1981, s 19). The Secretary of State will not in respect of any one common or open space give a certificate under *both* heads of para 2.

Although s 19 requires the Secretary of State to give public notice of his intention to give a certificate—no method is prescribed. It would seem that a clear notice inserted in two local newspapers is sufficient, provided the land is correctly described—see *Wilson* v *Secretary of State for the Environment* [1973] 1 WLR 1083.

It may be necessary to apply for consent from the Secretary of State under s 22 of the Commons Act 1899. Without this consent the grant or inclosure of common land purporting to be made under the general authority of an Act incorporating the Lands Clauses Consolidation Act 1845 or Pt I of the Compulsory Purchase Act 1965 will not be valid. However, if planning permission has been obtained for the development, s 22 will be overridden by s 129 of the Town and

Country Planning Act 1971. This applies to land being a common, open space, or fuel or field garden allotment which has been acquired by a Minister, a local authority or statutory undertakers under the Town and Country Planning Act 1971, or appropriated by a local authority for planning purposes, or acquired compulsorily under any other enactment by a Minister, local authority or statutory undertaker. It allows the land to be used by a Minister for the purposes of the acquisition and in any other case, in any manner in accordance with planning permission, 'notwithstanding anything in any enactment relating to land of that kind or in any enactment by which the land is specially regulated'.

The giving of a certificate by an Minister will not prevent a claim for equality of exchange (*McKay* v *City of London Corporation* (1966) 17 P & CR 264). On the other hand if the certificate is given, the owner of common land cannot prefer to take monetary compensation in lieu of the exchange (*Freeman* v *Middlesex County Council* (1965) 16 P & CR 253). In *Wilcock* v *Secretary of State for the Environment* (1974) 232 EG 1385, a certificate was quashed by consent where it related to land which was proposed to be given in exchange but which was not yet laid out and used as public open space.

The compulsory purchase of commons gives rise to the additional requirements set out in s 21 of and Sched 4 to the 1965 Act, dealing in particular with the distribution of compensation.The compensation on the acquisition of a common may be payable in respect of the soil to the lord of the manor and in respect of commonable rights to the commoners. See, for example, *College Royal of the Blessed Mary of Eton* (*Provost of*) v *Eton UDC* (1959) 11 P & CR 66; *Vardon* v *Ministry of Agriculture, Fisheries and Food* (1960) 11 P & CR 153; *Hancock and Roborough Parish Council* v *Ministry of Agriculture* (1960) 11 P & CR 362.

5 Ancient monuments

There are special safeguards (1981 Act, s 20) in relation to the acquisition of an ancient monument. Here again, special Parliamentary procedure applies unless the Secretary of State is the acquiring authority or gives a certificate that suitable conditions will be observed as to the use of the land. The conditions must be embodied in an undertaking to be given by the acquiring authority.

The ancient monuments which obtain protection are:

    (*a*) those with respect to which an interim preservation notice is in force under s 10 (1) of the Historic Buildings and Ancient Monuments Act 1953, or

(b) those within the definition of ancient monument in the Ancient Monuments Acts 1913 and 1931 (now s 61 of the Ancient Monuments and Archaeological Areas Act 1979, which came into effect on 9 October 1981 by SI 1981 No 1300 but without substituting new definitions).

There are special provisions where an ancient monument is a listed building. A listed building, or any land or object comprised within the curtilage of such a building, will not obtain the protection of s 20 of the Act of 1981 as an ancient monument unless specified in the Schedule to the Ancient Monuments Protection Act 1882 or specified in a list published under s 12 of the Ancient Monuments Consolidation and Amendment Act 1913. A certificate is therefore needed only for listed buildings so specified and not in other cases. An acquiring authority will of course need a listed building consent under s 55 of the Town and Country Planning Act 1971 if their scheme involves demolition or material alteration.

As to compensation for injurious affection by a preservation order on ancient monuments, see p 280.

6 Consecrated ground

Where a compulsory purchase order includes a burial ground, difficulties can arise. The expression covers any ground which has been set aside for interment, whether in use or disused. Burial grounds provided by local authorities are not as such consecrated, nor are those provided by denominations other than the Church of England.

If land is consecrated, it is usual to apply to the Diocesan Chancellor for a faculty to use the land for secular purposes. If it is granted, purchase can proceed by agreement. Note that the transference of human remains will require a licence from the Home Secretary under s 25 of the Burial Act 1857 unless they are removed under the authority of a bishop's faculty.

A faculty cannot authorise the erection of buildings and there may be other difficulties which will necessitate the use instead of the powers in s 128 of the Town and Country Planning Act 1971. This section and the regulations made under it (Town and Country Planning (Churches, Places of Religious Worship and Burial Grounds) Regulations 1950) provide a code to permit consecrated land and burial grounds to be used in accordance with planning permission. The section applies to land acquired by a Minister, a local authority or statutory undertakers, or appropriated by a local authority for planning purposes. It also applies to a compulsory acquisition by these bodies under any other enactment. The prescribed code takes the place of s 25 of the Burial Act 1857 in regard to removal of human remains. The section enables the difficulties created by ecclesiastical law to be overcome, and its wide application makes it usable in the case of any compulsory acquisition.

7 Ecclesiastical property

Where a compulsory order contains ecclesiastical property, notice of the making of the order must be served on the Church Commissioners as well as on the owner or owners of the property (s 12(3) of the Act of 1981).

8 Special Parliamentary procedure

Where an order is subject to special Parliamentary procedure, the Statutory Order (Special Procedure) Acts 1945 and 1965 apply. The order is laid before Parliament by the confirming Minister, who has to give notice of this at least three days previously in the *London Gazette*. Twenty-one days are allowed for petitions, which are heard by a Joint Committee of both Houses in much the same way as petitions against a private Bill. The Lord Chairman of Committees and the Chairman of Ways and Means report to the House of Lords and House of Commons respectively as to whether there are petitions, and whether they are either petitions of general objection or petitions for amendment. Within 21 days of the Chairman's report, either House may pass a resolution for the annulment of the order. If no petition is lodged and no annulment resolution is passed, the order becomes operative at the end of the second period of 21 days, unless in the case of orders reported with amendments, some later date is specified in the order.

For the purposes of the procedure three additional order maps are required, one of which must be specially prepared for deposit in the House of Lords. The specially prepared map should be drawn in ink and/or printed by a lithographed or 'true to scale' process on stout cartridge paper and then backed with fine linen, and the paste used should be a polyvinyl acetate. A signed certificate, in the following form, should be endorsed on the treated copy of the plan: 'I/We certify that this plan has been prepared by being (drawn in ink) (and) (printed by a lithographed process) (printed by a "true to scale" process) on stout cartridge paper and backed with fine linen, and that the paste used was a polyvinyl acetate.' (Circular No 6/85, Appendix G). The Joint Committee which hears the petitions has powers to award costs (s 7, 1945 Act). Petitioners are entitled to recover costs from the promoters if the committee find that petitioners have been unreasonably or vexatiously subjected to expense; promoters may recover costs from petitioners whose opposition is unfounded.

Chapter 12

Minerals

In the prescribed form of compulsory purchase order will be found a third paragraph which reads as follows: 'Parts II and III of Sched 2 to the Acquisition of Land Act 1981 are hereby incorporated with this order, subject to the modifications that ....' Then follow suitable drafting modifications. What does all this mean?

If Pt II of Sched 2 to the Acquisition of Land Act 1981 is incorporated, mines and minerals (except minerals necessarily extracted or used for the purposes of the acquisition) will not be included in the purchase except to the extent to which express provision is made for their inclusion. Therefore by incorporating Pt II the authority is enabled to purchase surface land without being obliged to buy the minerals. The adviser to the authority must therefore decide whether the minerals need to be acquired, and will bear in mind that the value of the minerals will usually be reflected in the compensation, that value turning in most cases upon the prospect of obtaining planning permission to work them. In most cases the minerals need not be purchased with the land. Even if the minerals are not acquired initially, the authority may compulsorily purchase them after it has acquired the surface land (see *Errington* v *Metropolitan District Railway* (1882) 19 Ch D 559).

If they are not acquired, the incorporation of Pt III will regulate the relations between the surface owner and the mineral owner (including British Coal, for coal cannot be acquired in any event). Part III reproduces the effects of ss 78–85 of the Railways Clauses Act 1845, often referred to as the 'mining code'. This code imposes, broadly, a requirement to give notice of intent before minerals within a specified distance are worked. The surface owner can then decide whether to prevent the working of the mineral and compensate for the mineral owner. It thus allows the question of payment for the minerals to be deferred until the minerals are actually worked.

The Department of the Environment has indicated that the mining code should not be incorporated automatically or indiscriminately since it may well result in the sterilisation of minerals (including coal reserves). The Department suggests that existing statutory rights to compensation or repair of damage might provide an adequate remedy in the event of damage to land or buildings caused by mining subsidence. In areas of coal working, authorities are asked to notify British Coal if they make an order which incorporates the mining code (see Appendix E, Department of Environment Circular No 6/85). However with regard to orders made under s 290 of the Housing Act 1985 (clearance areas) it is specified in s 580 that the mining code shall be incorporated.

'Minerals' must be interpreted according to normal commercial usage. It has been held that minerals do not include sandstone or sand and gravel (*Waring* v *Foden; Waring* v *Booth Crushed Gravel Co Ltd* [1932] 1 Ch 276) but include limestone (*Midland Rlwy and Kettering Thrapston etc Rlwy* v *Robinson* (1889) 15 App Cas 19). The definition of minerals in s 290 of the Town and Country Planning Act 1971 is not relevant to interpretation under Pts II and III..

Chapter 13

Rights, Easements and Restrictive Covenants

1 Acquisition of easement

Until the passing of the Local Government (Miscellaneous Provisions) Act 1976, there was no general power which enabled an acquiring authority to compel an owner of lands to grant or create an easement.

The authority could obtain the benefit of existing easements appurtenant to the land to be acquired—and this without any need for the easement to be specified or mentioned in the schedule to the order. But the authority could not purchase compulsorily new rights which were not in existence when the order specifying them was made.

By virtue of s 13 of the Act of 1976 rights over land can be compulsorily acquired. The rights must be specified in the order and where necessary the land over which the rights are to be exercisable must also be specified.

The statutory provision in 1976 was largely made necessary by the litigation culminating in the decision of the House of Lords in *Sovmots Investments Ltd* v *Secretary of State for the Environment* [1979] AC 144. This concerned the compulsory purchase by Camden London Borough Council of the maisonettes forming part of the Centre Point complex of buildings. The maisonettes were unusable without the use of the fire escapes, lifts and various other facilities. Because the building had never been occupied the right to use the facilities had never been brought into existence, so that there were no existing rights, whether as easements or quasi-easements, appurtenant to the maisonettes. The House of Lords held that no new rights could be created by the compulsory purchase order whether or not they were specified in the order.

The power in s 13 supplements some other powers, eg, under the Highways Act 1980 (see head 2 below) or the Pipe-lines Act 1962.

The procedure and machinery for assessing compensation for acquiring rights are usually obtained by treating easements as if they were 'land' within the meaning of the statutory compensation code.

As to the drafting of an order to enable the acquisition of rights under the 1976 Act, see Appendix K of Circular No 6/85 which gives detailed guidance.

Section 28 of and Sched 3 to the Acquisition of Land Act 1981 apply the procedures of the 1981 Act not only to the compulsory acquisition of rights under s 13 of the 1976 Act but also to a number of other statutes which authorise the acquisition of rights—for example by urban development corporations under s 142 (4) of the Local Government Planning and Land Act 1980.

Schedule 3 sets out the modifications which apply where rights are acquired over the various special kinds of land which were dealt with in Chapter 11—for example land of statutory undertakers. With regard to the assessment of compensation, Pt II of Sched 1 to the 1976 Act sets out the adaptations of s 7 of the Compulsory Purchase Act 1965 where rights are acquired by local authorities under s 13. Similarly, where rights are acquired by urban development corporations under s 142 (4) of the 1980 Act the 1965 Act applies as modified by Pt IV of Sched 28 to the 1980 Act. In cases where the acquisition of rights is required it will be necessary to check the authorising statute for modifications to the compensation procedures.

2 Highway easements

The inadequacy of the general law as to the acquisition of an easement was remedied insofar as highways are concerned by the Highways Act 1971: the provisions now appear in the Highways Act 1980. There are frequently cases where there is no call to deprive an owner of the land itself provided some facility can be obtained. For example, the authority may wish to place piers on land to carry a superstructure; to execute drainage works to carry water from the highway; to regrade the levels of land outside the highway limits or to erect snow fences or barriers. Section 250 et seq of the Highways Act 1980 make provision for the creation of rights over land by compulsory purchase orders.

Clearly these powers are inappropriate if the creation of the easement will in reality deprive the owner of the use and enjoyment of his land. The sections do not allow the compulsory acquisition of rights for a limited period only, but these can nevertheless be acquired by agreement. See hereon generally Circular Roads No 1/81, paras

78–81.

The procedure for acquiring rights is much the same as for acquiring full title. For example, in the case of special lands like open spaces, the certification procedure described in Chapter 11(p 82), is applicable.

Sections 254 and 255 of the Highways Act 1980 also contain powers to acquire rights over land belonging to a local authority or statutory undertakers, for the construction, maintenance, improvement or alteration of a bridge, or for any system of road drainage.

3 Temporary easement

An acquiring authority may sometimes require a temporary easement to enable it to carry out the works forming part of the scheme. It may, for example, wish to enter upon land or a building to allow it more easily and cheaply to demolish adjoining buildings or in the case of the construction of a new highway, working areas may be required during the construction period. There would appear to be no power to acquire temporary easements compulsorily. The advice in Department of Transport Circular Roads No 1/81 is that the statutory powers do not provide for the compulsory creation of rights for limited periods. Land or premises needed for a temporary easement may therefore be included in a compulsory purchase order and then the powers of acquisition not exercised, once agreement has been reached as to the temporary rights required.

Clearly there is nothing wrong in an acquiring authority proceeding in this way, provided that both parties reach a formal agreement before being irreversibly committed to the compulsory purchase. An authority might, for example, serve notice to treat in a case where the owner had agreed that he would grant the desired temporary rights. If the owner responds with a statement of claim, the authority will be unable to avoid purchasing the premises unless it acts within the six weeks after delivery of the statement of claim allowed for withdrawal by s 31 Land Compensation Act 1961 (see p 58 above). Similarly an owner who has merely had an informal indication that his property will not be acquired cannot stop the compulsory acquisition if he allows the compulsory purchase to proceed apace without any unequivocal letter of undertaking from the authority to say that the order is only intended to secure a limited period easement.

The grant and exercise of temporary easements are best dealt with by formal agreements between the parties. These agreements may be written against the background of compulsory purchase proceedings, or preferably may be entered into at an earlier stage, making use of compulsory powers unnecessary.

4 Acquisition of land subject to easement

Cases sometimes arise where the land being acquired is subject to an easement, which the acquiring authority propose to interfere with.

Examples

(a) The authority may propose to erect a building which will interfere with and obstruct a right to light.

(b) They may propose to close a private right of way in carrying out authorised works.

(c) Their operations may remove or diminish a right of support.

In all these cases, the person entitled to the easement cannot call on the authority to purchase the easement before they proceed to interfere with it. His remedy is compensation for injurious affection to the dominant tenement under s 10 of the Compulsory Purchase Act 1965. Some Acts give special powers to interfere with easements, eg, the New Towns Act 1981, s 19 and s 127 of the Town and Country Planning Act 1971: there can be then no question whether a particular interference is justified by the Act authorising purchase or not. For an example of an unsuccessful claim for injurious affection following interference with alleged easements, see *Roberts* v *Holyhead Urban District Council* (1962) 14 P & CR 358.

As we have already seen persons entitled to easements are not entitled to notice to treat (*Thicknesse* v *Lancaster Canal Co* (1838) 4 M & W 472). Interference with an easement is also not an entry on lands and so the dominant owner is not entitled to notice of entry (*Clark* v *London School Board* (1874) 9 Ch App 120).

In the absence of express statutory provision an easement is not extinguished until compensation has been paid, but will bind the land in the hands of persons other than the acquiring authority (*Manchester, Sheffield & Lincolnshire Rly* v *Anderson* [1898] 2 Ch 394).

Because of this, it is important that careful thought be given to cases where the acquired land is to be sold or leased to a third party and its subsequent use or development might be hindered by the existence of an easement enforceable against the third party, though not against the acquiring authority itself. Section 127 of the Town and Country Planning Act 1971 can be particularly valuable in cases of this sort. For example, a local authority may be acquiring land with a view to the carrying out of a commercial development, probably by way of a building agreement and a grant of a long lease. The developer may worry that an owner of adjoining land could seek to prevent the development because it would infringe, eg, a right of light or a right of way.

Section 127 provides that the erection of a building on land acquired or appropriated by a local authority for planning purposes, whether done by the authority or by a person deriving title under them, is authorised if it is done in accordance with planning permission, notwithstanding that it involves interference with an easement, right or other interest to which the section applies. Compensation is payable and it should be noted that if a person deriving title under a local authority fails to discharge a liability for compensation, then it is enforceable against the authority. The section also applies to restrictive covenants (see p 95).

It should also be noted that the definition of a person deriving title under a local authority is extended by s 290 (7) of the 1971 Act to include any successor in title of that person.

The forerunner of s 127 was considered in *Dowty Boulton Paul Ltd v Wolverhampton Corporation (No 2)* [1972] 2 All ER 1073. The plaintiffs had a right to use a municipal airfield provided by the Corporation. When the Corporation no longer needed the airfield they decided to build houses on it and appropriated the land for planning purposes. The plaintiffs sought confirmation that their right to use the airfield continued, but it was held that the airfield had been validly appropriated for planning purposes and that, subject to planning permission and the payment of compensation, the Corporation were entitled to proceed with their housing scheme notwithstanding its effect on the plaintiffs' right over the airfield.

In connection with appropriation for planning purposes under s 127, authorities should consider whether any consent of the Secretary of State is required. The requirement for consent formerly contained in s 23 (2) of the Town and Country Planning Act 1959 was relaxed when the section was amended by virtue of the Local Government, Planning and Land Act 1980 (Sched 23, para 3). However consent is still necessary in respect of certain common land (Town and Country Planning Act 1971, s 122 (2)) and in relation to garden allotments (s 23 (3)). Also, a proposed appropriation of open space must be advertised and objections considered (s 23 (2), 1971 Act, s 122 (2B) and Local Government Act 1972, s 122 (2)).

Whilst s 127 of the 1971 Act does give a wide power to override easements and other rights, it does not enable a local authority or a corporate body deriving title under them to act in a way which would be ultra vires—see s 133 (2).

A claim for compensation for interference with a right of way may be defeated if it can be shown that an alternative access has been provided so that there has been no loss in value of the land—see *Ward* v *Wychavon District Council* (1986) 279 EG 77.

Similar powers to override easements etc are available to new town development corporations (s 19, New Towns Act 1981) and to urban development corporations (para 6 of Sched 28 to the Local Government Planning and Land Act 1980).

5 Restrictive covenants

Also of frequent occurrence is the case where an authority wish to use the property in a way which would normally be prevented by a restrictive covenant. For example, they may wish to use as a children's home a house which is restricted by the covenant to use as a private dwelling-house only.

A person entitled to the benefit of the restrictive covenant may not bring an action for breach of covenant by the promoters in exercise of their statutory powers. His remedy is also compensation under s 10 of the Compulsory Purchase Act 1965 (*Long Eaton Recreation Grounds Co* v *Midland Railway Co* [1902] 2 KB 574).

Cases under the Lands Clauses Act suggest that compensation is payable where the execution of the works rather than the user gives rise to a breach of a restrictive covenant. However, it seems likely that today a wide interpretation would be given to the concept of 'execution'.

In the case of purchases by agreement after 1 April 1974, s 120 (3) of the Local Government Act 1972 allows an acquiring authority to contravene restrictive covenants subject to payment of compensation. Purchases by agreement before 1 April 1974 could be put in much the same position by Ministerial order following a resolution under s 14 of the Local Government (Miscellaneous Provisions) Act 1976.

Some authorities have local Act powers based on a well precedented clause, entitled 'Application of Lands Clauses Acts to purchases by agreement', and can override covenants in any purchase, whether compulsory or not. There is also a growing tendency for modern Acts to make specific provision with the same objects in view. Section 260 of the Highways Act 1980 allows a highway authority to include, in a compulsory purchase order, land in which the authority have already acquired an interest by agreement but which is burdened by restrictive covenants. Lessees of, or contractors operating, a service, picnic or lorry area may under the same section use the land for these purposes as if they were the highway authority, notwithstanding the existence of restrictive covenants.

It will be seen from the foregoing that where the use to be made of the property in breach of a restrictive covenant is use by the acquiring authority for its statutory purposes, no problem is likely to arise. However, at some later date the authority may wish to dispose of the property and, if compensation has not been paid for discharge of the covenant, the purchaser may wish to know whether it could be enforced against him.

In such a case the prudent course is for the local authority to appropriate the land for planning purposes under s 127 of the Town and Country Planning Act 1971 and ensure that there is a planning permission to cover the purchaser's use of the land. The purchaser will then obtain the protection of the section which covers interference with any 'easement, liberty, privilege, right or advantage annexed to land and adversely affecting other land, including any natural right to support'. In *Edmunds* v *Stockport MBC* (1990) 1 PLR 1 it was held that s 127 applied to restrictive covenants.

If no statutory protection (such as that under s 127 or given to lessees and contractors in s 260 of the Highways Act 1980 referred to above) is obtained, it would seem clear that the covenants become enforceable once the land ceases to be used for the statutory purposes for which it was acquired and passes into the hands of some third party.

In *Marten* v *Flight Refuelling Ltd* [1961] 2 All ER 696 the Air Ministry in 1942 requisitioned part of the Crichel Estate for use as an airfield. The farm was later sold subject to a covenant restricting it to agricultural use. In 1947 the Air Ministry allowed an industrial concern to occupy the land (mainly for purposes in connection with the Air Ministry and the defence of the realm). In 1958 the Air Ministry bought the farm compulsorily, subject to the restrictive covenant. The former owner sought to enforce the restriction. It was held that the compulsory acquisition had not freed the land from the restrictive covenant which was still binding. The plaintiffs were nevertheless not entitled to enforce it so as to restrict use by or on behalf of the Air Ministry for the statutory purposes for which it had been acquired. However, they were entitled to an injunction to restrain other uses by the industrial company, ie, non-defence of the realm uses.

It is clear from the *Marten* case that so long as work is done in accordance with and for the statutory purposes for which it was acquired, it makes no difference if it is carried out by the acquiring authority or by an independent contractor, or if a lease or licence is granted. Wilberforce J said at p 717: 'It cannot in my view make any difference that instead of doing this type of work himself he commits it to an individual or a company nor that having chosen his instrument he uses the latter as an independent contractor rather than as an agent'. A lessee from a local authority should therefore be protected from attack—although compensation may still be payable—provided that he is using the land for the statutory purposes for which it was acquired.

6 Extinguishment of rights over land compulsorily acquired

Section 118 of the Town and Country Planning Act 1971 provides that on the completion by the acquiring authority (ie, government department, local authority or other body by whom the interest is acquired) of the compulsory acquisition under Pt VI of the Act —which includes s 112—all private rights of way and rights of laying down, erecting, continuing or maintaining any apparatus on, under or over the land are extinguished and any such apparatus is vested in the authority. The provision does not apply to statutory undertakers or telecommunications operators; provision is made for these in s 230. Any person who suffers loss because of the extinguishment of a right or the vesting of any apparatus under the section is entitled to compensation.

Similar provisions appear in other legislation—for example, s 16 of the New Towns Act 1981 and Sched 10 to the Housing Act 1988.

Chapter 14

Some Practical Points

In this chapter an attempt is made to bring together some of the matters which should be present in the mind of a professional adviser who is consulted by a client threatened by a compulsory acquisition of his property. If the client wishes to object to the acquisition, well and good. The procedure for objecting is laid down, and Chapter 4 gives some practical advice as to how to make the case against acquisition. Many owners, however, seek advice in a more neutral frame of mind. They may accept the reason for the acquisition, for example, to construct a road to relieve a town centre of congestion. Even if doubtful about the real public benefit to be secured by the scheme of which the acquisition forms part, they may feel that the authority are bound to win in the end. Some may welcome the prospect of acquisition, because they have been contemplating a move. Some may simply want more information about their position, if the acquisition goes ahead.

1 The delay factor

One of the first points to be made is that compulsory purchases are often drawn out and protracted affairs. Matters for one reason or another tend to move slowly. There is the period for objecting. If objections are made and not withdrawn there will be a public inquiry. The confirming Ministry have to consider the inspector's report and reach a decision. Assuming confirmation and no challenge to confirmation in the courts, the acquiring authority have to serve notices to treat, unless they use the special procedure of executing a vesting declaration. Even if owners submit claims in response to the notice to treat, or notice of the vesting declaration, it may be many months before the authority actually want to enter upon the land. There may have been financial or political changes which make the implementation of the scheme less attractive than when the order was made. Of course there are schemes which proceed quickly, particularly road schemes where a grant may only be available if work begins within a specific financial year.

However, not infrequently the timetable will correspond to such cases as *Duttons Brewery Ltd* v *Leeds City Council* (1980) 42 P & CR 152. Here there was agreement on price in 1968 with entry expected in 1971, but this was in fact delayed till 1976, during which time inflation had invalidated the 1968 settlement.

2 Opting to move

It follows from the length of compulsory purchase procedures that one of their immediate and obvious effects is to create a period of uncertainty for owners of properties affected. The owner may be prepared to go, but the authority may be unwilling to buy him out at least until the scheme as a whole has received approval by confirmation of the compulsory purchase order. If the scheme as a whole is turned back because of objections, the authority will not want to find itself holding a few properties which were bought at an earlier stage in expectation of confirmation. Reductions in public expenditure have tended to make it more difficult for public authorities to buy early in order to reduce uncertainty to an owner.

The owner who is prepared to go will probably have to wait until the order has been confirmed, although there is no reason why an approach should not be made earlier. However, some caution needs to be displayed in indicating a willingness to move. If the move is seen as voluntary rather than forced, the authority's valuer may wish to reduce or reject the claim for compensation for disturbance. Disturbance is intended to cover the consequences of a forced sale and is not payable if an owner was going to move in any case. However, it is possible that a disturbance claim may be accepted where an owner wishes to move early. In *Prasad* v *Wolverhampton Borough Council* [1983] 2 All ER 140 the Court of Appeal indicated that the test was the 'inevitability' of dispossession. It may be that claims for costs incurred prior to notice to treat will be eligible where the causation for the move is the action proposed by the acquiring authority, whereas if the owner wants to move for reasons other than compulsory purchase (for example, to change employment) they would not be paid.

Also, there is an additional risk if expenditure is incurred early. It is always possible that the order will not be confirmed or that, even if it is, the authority will not proceed with the acquisition. In those circumstances reimbursement would not be possible.

3 Home owners

In regard to delay the residential owner-occupier probably has fewer problems than any other person whose interest is to be acquired. Before the decision in *Birmingham Corporation* v *West Midland Baptist (Trust) Association (Inc)* [1970] AC 874 HL, such an owner was liable to be caught in the inflation trap of having compensation assessed at the level of prices at the time of notice to treat but having to replace his home at the higher price levels operating at the time of dispossession. Since the *West Midland* case this trap should not catch any owner-occupier. When the authority are ready to take possession the owner can seek alternative accommodation knowing that the prevailing price level should govern both sale and subsequent purchase. Even an unreasonable authority will be likely to help the owner-occupier in order to keep down the disturbance element in the compensation claim.

The home loss payment for residential owner-occupiers who have been in occupation for the last five years prior to displacement is a useful tax-free 'plus payment'. The owner-occupier of residential premises has the special protection that he can require the purchase of his interest under s 70 of the Land Compensation Act 1973 at any time after an order has been submitted for confirmation (or prepared in draft by a Minister). Once a notice takes effect, the authority are in the position that they cannot withdraw. On the other hand, serving a blight notice (see Chapter 18) is not an irrevocable step for the owner. He can withdraw the notice up to six weeks after he has seen what compensation will be payable. There are two snags which must be noticed; they are often sufficient to deter the service of a blight notice in cases where compulsory purchase proceedings are dragging on interminably:

(1) no home loss payment is payable, because to qualify the claimant must be dispossessed (a consultation paper in March 1989 proposed to change this);

(2) any claim for disturbance may well be the subject of argument because the owner is seeking to move voluntarily. Valuers' fees in preparing the claim for compensation will be payable and the solicitors' costs of the sale (*Lee* v *Minister of Transport* [1966] 1 QB 111). But a claim for removal expenses or the costs in connection with the alternative

premises may be disputed unless the owner can show that he was moving because he was threatened with inevitable dispossession within the principle of the *Prasad* case above.

The owner-occupier of a small business has the same power to speed up compulsory proceedings by serving a blight notice. However, the loss of a disturbance claim would normally be a more serious matter than for a householder. This would be particularly the case for a trader aged 60 or more who could otherwise benefit from the total extinguishment provisions in s 46 of the Land Compensation Act 1973.

Because of the limitations on compensation which follow the service of a blight notice, this means of speeding up of acquisition will probably only be resorted to by those who must go and in practice cannot wait for the authority. Sometimes it will be possible because the blight notice procedure exists to persuade an authority to buy a single property in advance of the remainder on terms as to compensation satisfactory to both sides. There is obviously nothing lost by trying.

4 Commercial premises

Commercial and industrial premises tend to present the most complex problems for advisers. Many legal interests can be involved —head leases, underleases, flying freeholds, licences to occupy. All complicate the picture.

Sometimes a commercial property is omitted from a compulsory purchase order though properties around it are included. The first reaction of the owners may be to welcome this omission. However, more thought needs to be given to the position which may obtain if the compulsory purchase—and possibly an associated redevelopment scheme—goes much more slowly than first envisaged. If the commercial property depends for its customers or trade upon the adjoining properties, it may find itself existing for years in a desert of derelict or demolished properties with its trade in decline. The owner can object to the compulsory purchase order on the grounds that his premises should be included. However, he will not be a statutory objector, but merely a third party making representations, and so cannot force a public inquiry.

Commercial properties are often held by companies. One company may own the freehold, another carry out the trading operations and a third operate the transport and warehousing. In order to avoid legal issues or technical points being raised on the lines pursued in *DHN*

Food Distributors (*in liquidation*) v *Tower Hamlets London Borough* (1976) 32 P & CR 240, the adviser will want to consider how the corporate structure can be rearranged to forestall any possible complication over compensation.

A business threatened with compulsory acquisition of its premises will often be mainly concerned about alternative accommodation. Sometimes the acquiring authority will be able to offer an alternative site or premises acceptable to the owner and no problem then arises. More often the firm concerned will have to make its own search for premises in which to relocate itself. It is a settled principle that an owner should take what steps he can to mitigate his loss. On the whole it is desirable that no appreciable expenditure is incurred until notice to treat has been served, a claim made in response and the period for withdrawal by the authority allowed to elapse. However, in the light of *Prasad's* case, above, it seems that expenditure reasonably incurred in advance of notice to treat, where a move must be regarded as inevitable, is justifiable.

In seeking alternative premises, a business must bear in mind the rule which prevents compensation being paid for expenditure where the owner has received 'value for money expended'. If the alternative accommodation is larger or better equipped, the owner will not necessarily obtain any additional costs of operating in the new premises. The approach must be that of a prudent and reasonable man who wants to be in the same position as before, neither worse nor better. The pitfalls are discussed in Chapter 28 (p 217).

5 Entry into possession

Problems sometimes arise over the dates of entry and taking possession by the acquiring authority. Because notice to treat is served, it does not mean that the property is at the risk of the acquiring authority. As Lord Reid said in the *Birmingham Corporation* case, above, at p 1064, 'It does not at all follow from the fact that the owner cannot so act as to increase the burden of the promoters, that the burden on the promoters may not be diminished by events later than the notice to treat'. Even the service of a notice of entry will not shift the burden onto the promoters. The notice to treat must be followed either by unconditional agreement on compensation (which is relatively unusual) or actual entry, for the burden to pass to the acquiring authority. There are sometimes disputes as to what amounts to entry (see, for example, *Courage Ltd* v *Kingswood District Council* (1978) 247 EG 307) but usually keys are handed over and a receipt obtained or some act of 'ownership' by the promoters takes place such as demolition or partial site clearance. The owner must do his best to safeguard the property while he is still legally in possession. If he leaves it unoccupied to suit his own convenience, for example if the licensee of a public house is moved to suit the requirements of a brewery owner, he may not be able to claim compensation based on the physical condition at the date of vacation. To be sure, the market value must disregard any diminution in value which is the result of 'the scheme'. But if diminution results from a careless approach by an owner, the authority may seek to value the property in its physical condition as at the date of entry. See *Arrow* v *Bexley London Borough Council* (1977) 35 P & CR 237. The safest course is for the owner to see that the property is occupied or boarded up until the authority are ready to take physical possession. Provided he has acted with reasonable diligence and care, he should not lose as a result of vandalism or other damage.

In the case of slum clearance it is possible that vandalism will be regarded as flowing from 'the scheme' underlying the acquisition and the property will be valued in its unvandalised state. See the cases referred to in *Arrow* v *Bexley London Borough Council*, above. However, it may be successfully argued that damage from vandalism is just vandalism and that the resulting loss falls on the vendor, so that prudence is needed in all cases; see, for example, *Lewars* v *Greater London Council* (1982) 43 P & CR 129. Once entry has been made, it becomes in theory unnecessary to insure because there is an obligation on the acquiring authority to pay compensation based on the value as at the date of entry. However, before insurance is discontinued it is prudent to check that the acquiring authority accept responsibility for the risk.

Even after entry has occurred it may take a long time to settle the amount of compensation. The right to have an advance, up to 90 per cent of compensation, should be borne in mind (see s 52 of the Land Compensation Act 1973 and p 108).

Questions sometimes arise as to the effect of entry as between landlord and tenant. These are answered in Chapter 9 (p 69).

6 Delay after notice of entry

Problems sometimes arise as to whether a notice of entry can be withdrawn before entry has actually taken place. In some cases the answer will be that, irrespective of the notice of entry position, the notice to treat cannot be withdrawn except by consent because it has been followed by a valid notice of claim and the expiry of the six weeks' period for withdrawal afforded to the acquiring authority under s 31 of the Land Compensation Act 1961 (see p 58). However, not all notices to treat are responded to by valid notices of claim. There may have been a notice to treat; no claim in response; a notice of entry and then a period of occupation by the owner or tenant, with the authority taking no further steps on the notice of entry. Either party may then want to review its position.

Sometimes an owner wants the authority to proceed in the circumstances just envisaged. He may have taken steps on the assumption that he would sooner or later be expropriated. His remedy will be to seek to have the compensation settled if necessary by reference to the Lands Tribunal. If the authority can withdraw the notice to treat under s 31 of the Act of 1961 because there has been no valid notice of claim, it is difficult to avoid the conclusion that the authority cannot be forced to proceed. (See *Trustees for Methodist Church Purposes and another* v *North Tyneside Metropolitan Borough Council* (1979) 250 EG 647.) However, they would be liable to pay compensation 'for the expenses and loss incurred by reason of the service of the notice to treat', per Lord Evershed MR in *Holloway* v *Dover Corporation* [1960] 2 All ER 193 CA, paraphrasing the provision to that effect in s 31.

If on the other hand, the authority after sleeping on their rights come to life and seek to enter under the notice of entry, the owner can only stop them if it can be argued that the compulsory purchase or notice to treat has been abandoned. 'The courts have long ago come to the aid of unwilling vendors of property compulsorily acquired by purchasers who delay completion to the prejudice of those helpless vendors and have held that a notice to treat can be abandoned by lapse of time,' said Stephenson LJ in *Dutton's* case, above. But he went on to quote Lord Evershed MR in *Simpson's Motor Sales (London) Ltd* v *Hendon Corporation* [1963] Ch 57 at p 82, 'As regards delay the court will and should be somewhat less strict in the case of a local authority exercising the powers and duties relating to housing and like matters than it was in the past in cases of railway corporations which were regarded as private undertakers seeking to make profits for themselves.' See generally p 60.

7 Acquisition of part: injurious affection

It may sometimes happen that a scheme can be accomplished with or without the land of a particular owner. Before an owner seeks to have every part of his land excluded, he should be reminded that the compensation provisions when no land is taken are much more circumscribed than compensation for injurious affection where lands are taken. If the choice is between being excluded and having some small part included, it will normally be wise to seek inclusion within the terms of the order. See p 235.

An owner may conversely find that he is left with nothing conveniently usable after the compulsory acquisition has taken place. The owner's adviser should bear in mind the right to require the purchase of the whole interest provided that the case can be brought within the rules described in Chapter 10.

Most acquiring authorities are prepared to do accommodation works to reduce the damage to retained land of the vendor. The scope for such works should be carefully considered as often they will be more valuable in the long term than monetary compensation.

8 Professional advice

Fees for professional advice form part of the claim for disturbance (see p 223). The advice may be as to the claim itself or as to consequential matters flowing from the acquisition. If the claimant acts reasonably in seeking advice, he should have no difficulty in obtaining reimbursement. However, if he is extravagant because he believes that someone else will pay in due course, he may find his claim reduced. With this proviso, valuers' and accountants' fees on a claim for business disturbance and architects' fees on examining proposals for alternative accommodation are commonly allowed. Legal advice may be needed, provided that there is no duplication of the advice being obtained from valuation experts. The legal costs of the conveyance are always allowable and do not technically form part of the disturbance claim (see Chapter 15).

9 Disposal of surplus land

Since the *Crichel Down* case in 1954 it has been government policy to give former owners or successors in title a right of first refusal in respect of surplus government land which was originally acquired by or under threat of compulsion. Guidelines for the disposal of surplus land in new towns were issued by the Department of the Environment in August 1983. Rules and procedures for the disposal of surplus Crown land (the *Crichel Down* rules) are set out in Pt III of Circular

No 18/84. The circular indicates that the general principles underlying the rules are commended, where appropriate, for application to local authority land disposals. Therefore when a government department, a new town development corporation or a local authority wish to dispose of land to which the rules apply, former owners will as a general rule be given a first opportunity to repurchase the land previously in their ownership provided that it has not been materially changed in character since acquisition. 'Material change' means change such as the development of agricultural land with houses, afforestation of mainly open land, the redevelopment of an urban site with offices or substantial works to existing buildings which effectively alter their character.

In *Tomkins* v *Commission for the New Towns* (1988) 28 RVR 219, the Court of Appeal considered whether these guidelines applied where the former owner of agricultural land (who had remained a tenant of it) wished to repurchase it when it became surplus. Negotiations proceeded but the Commission then decided that the land should be sold on the open market by tender. The former owner claimed that the guidelines should apply but the Court held that only a general obligation was imposed whereas the Commission had an obligation to obtain the best consideration and this could only be achieved through a sale by tender as land values were rapidly rising. The former owner was entitled to submit a tender but not to have the first opportunity to repurchase in accordance with the guidelines.

Chapter 15

Completion and Costs

When an acquiring authority have obtained a confirmed compulsory purchase order, it is possible that they may delay the service of notice to treat in the hope of securing early agreement on price. When this happens, it will usually be found that a normal contract of sale is prepared, which will govern the rights of the parties in accordance with ordinary conveyancing rules. The purchase in such a case is technically a purchase by agreement under s 3 of the Compulsory Purchase Act 1965 (formerly s 6 of the Lands Clauses Act 1845). (See also s 119 of the Town and Country Planning Act 1971; sale by agreement in circumstances corresponding to a compulsory acquisition). For a Scottish case of an agreement referring the question of price to arbitration entered into after notice to treat, see *J & A Massie Ltd* v *Aberdeen Corporation* (1974) 28 P & CR 189.

1 Unwilling vendor

Even if notice to treat is served, it is common practice to have a contract of sale once the price has been agreed. Section 9 of the Compulsory Purchase Act 1965 deals with the position where an owner refuses to accept the purchase money; fails to make out a title to the land; or refuses to convey the land to the authority. Once in a while an owner, even after an arbitration on price, will remain intransigent. In such a case the authority are entitled to pay the purchase money into court 'to the credit of the parties interested in the land and the acquiring authority shall so far as they can give their descriptions'. The promoters can then execute a deed poll vesting the lands in themselves and are entitled to immediate possession. There are some limitations on this power, eg, it is not available if there are rival claimants (see s 6 and Sched 1, Administration of Justice Act 1965). For a relatively recent case dealing with the application of moneys paid into court, see *Re County of London* (*Devons Road, Poplar*) *Housing Confirmation Order* 1945 (1956) 6 P & CR 133.

Where an acquiring authority have taken the necessary steps to make a general vesting declaration (see Chapter 16) it will usually be simpler to use the vesting procedure than to operate the s 9 procedure in the Compulsory Purchase Act 1965.

2 Untraced owner

Another not uncommon case arises when the owner of the land cannot be traced. Here the price must be settled under s 5 of and Sched 2 to the Compulsory Purchase Act 1965 by a member of the Lands Tribunal appointed under s 1 (6) of the Lands Tribunal Act 1949. The authority can then execute a deed poll after the awarded compensation has been paid into court. Note that the procedure only applies where an owner cannot, after diligent inquiry, be traced, not in cases of doubt as to ownership. Also, it cannot be used if a general vesting declaration has been made (Compulsory Purchase (Vesting Declarations) Act 1981, s 10 (2)).

Where money has remained unclaimed in court for 12 years, the authority may seek payment out under s 29 of the Local Government (Miscellaneous Provisions) Act 1976.

3 Mortgages

Both mortgagor and mortgagee should be served with notice to treat (*Cooke* v *London County Council* [1911] 1 Ch 604). Where this has been done, the acquiring authority will usually deal with both parties as in a normal conveyance. They will pay off the mortgage, obtain a discharge from the mortgagee, and then take a conveyance of the unencumbered fee simple from the mortgagor.

An alternative procedure (more cumbersome and therefore rarely adopted) is to be found in s 14 of the Compulsory Purchase Act 1965, under which the acquiring authority may redeem the mortgage and then treat with the mortgagor for the equity of redemption. Before operating s 14, the mortgagee must be served with notice to treat. The authority must either give six months' notice of their intention to redeem or alternatively pay six months' interest in lieu, as well as the outstanding principal, interest and charges. The mortgagee must then convey or release his interest. If he fails to do so, the authority may deposit the principal and interest in the bank and execute a deed poll vesting in themselves the mortgagee's interest in the land.

Of more practical use are the provisions of s 15 of the Act of 1965 dealing with the position where the purchase money is insufficient to pay off the mortgage. Here, the agreement between mortgagee, mortgagor and the authority may prove difficult to reach. In the absence of agreement the compensation payable in respect of the mortgagee's interest and in respect of the equity redemption will be determined by the Lands Tribunal. See, for example, *Wilson* v *London County Council* (1954) 5 P & CR 122. Once again there are provisions under which the authority may execute a deed poll vesting the mortgagee's interest in themselves should he fail to convey or make a good title.

4 Rentcharges

Section 18 of the Compulsory Purchase Act 1965 introduces similar provisions as regards rentcharges to those just described in relation to mortgages.

5 Advance payment of compensation

Section 52 of the Land Compensation Act 1973 makes it obligatory upon acquiring authorities to make an advance payment of compensation on or after entry, upon request by the person entitled.

The section imposes no obligation to make an advance where the claimant needs the money to pay a deposit, etc, upon alternative accommodation and is still in occupation of his old premises. Authorities, however, were urged to make advances where the money is needed to allow the claimant to reinstate himself (para 14 of the Department of Environment Circular No 103/72 of 17 October 1972, now obsolete). Under s 583 of the Housing Act 1985 a local authority authorised to acquire a house compulsorily may, instead of taking possession after notice of entry, allow the occupier to continue in occupation. Where a written notice authorising such occupation has been served, the advance payment obligation will arise (s 52 (11) of the Act of 1973).

The request for an advance must be in writing and give particulars of the claimant's interest and such other information as the authority reasonably require.

Compensation will not usually have been assessed in advance payment cases. The advance cannot exceed 90 per cent of the assessed amount, or, as is more likely, the authority's estimate of the amount due. The money must be paid within three months of the request being made. If the claimant makes his request well before (ie, at least three months before) he is due to give up possession, he can get the advance on the day he gives up possession.

Where land is subject to mortgage there is no obligation to make an advance if the amount of the mortgage exceeds 90 per cent of the agreed or estimated compensation. Where the mortgage is for less than this 90 per cent figure, the authority will scale down the advance to the owner so as to secure that the balance ultimately payable after the advance will pay off the mortgagee.

An advance payment is registerable as a Local Land Charge and will be set off against any payment to a subsequent owner of an interest.

The section applies to the compulsory acquisition of rights over land as well as of land itself. It contains the usual provisions to deal with overpayment.

6 Costs

Most practitioners are aware that their costs will be paid by the acquiring authority, but few appreciate that the statutory provision is limited to the conveyancing costs.

The Compulsory Purchase Act 1965, s 23, provides that the costs of all conveyances and assurances of any lands and outstanding terms or interests compulsorily purchased, including deducing, evidencing and verifying title and furnishing abstracts, fall to be borne by the acquiring authority.

Where work has been done prior to agreement on price, the professional fees involved are not claimable under s 23, but may nevertheless be claimed as part of the compensation (*London County Council* v *Tobin* [1959] 1 WLR 354). The limitations of *Tobin's* case must, however, be kept in mind. In the light of that case it is reasonable for a claimant who has been served with notice to treat to see his solicitor both when the notice has been served and when the surveyors have completed their negotiations. But it is not reasonable for the solicitor to duplicate the work of the surveyor, and in general no claim can be made for work done *prior* to notice to treat. The Lands Tribunal refused to allow costs incurred prior to notice to treat in *Webb* v *Stockport Corporation* (1962) 13 P & CR 339, and *Watkin* v *Widnes Corporation* (1962) 13 P & CR 363. However in view of the decision in *Prasad* v *Wolverhampton Corporation* [1983] (see p 98) such costs may be recoverable if incurred for a reasonable and proper purpose. Costs incurred prior to, and in connection with, a reference to the Lands Tribunal are normally allowable (see *Radnor Trust Ltd* v *Central Electricity Generating Board* (1960) 12 P & CR 111). The costs of a successful appeal by the claimants to the Minister of Housing and Local Government against a certificate of alternative development were not allowed by the Court of Appeal in *Hull and Humber Investment Co Ltd* v *Kingston-upon-Hull Corporation* [1965] 2 WLR 161.

If interest is payable on compensation under s 32 of the Land Compensation Act 1961 because entry on the land has been made before payment of compensation, it would seem that it is payable on the surveyor's fees, as they form part of the compensation (*Lee* v *Minister of Transport* [1965] 3 WLR 533 CA). However, interest would not, it seems, be payable on the solicitor's 'costs of the conveyance' under s 23.

Sometimes a professional adviser may be approached by a client who has received a letter from an acquiring authority seeking to know whether he will sell land to them by agreement. The adviser will be well advised in such a case to stipulate in his first letter that his reasonable fees shall be paid by the authority whether or not the negotiations lead to an agreement and sale. If negotiations are later broken off, or if a purchase is abandoned after agreement on price, the purchaser is, in the absence of agreement, under no legal obligation to meet the vendor's costs.

Powers are given for taxation of costs in s 23 (3) of the Compulsory Purchase Act 1965.

For many years there was an extra-statutory scale of vendor's solicitor's costs on sales of land with unregistered titles, agreed between the Law Society and the Associations of Local Authorities. This was abandoned in 1977 (see the Society's *Gazette*, 26 October 1977, p 910). The basis under the Solicitors Remuneration Order 1972 now applies, as it does to costs payable by local authorities on sales of land with registered title.

7 Stamp duty

A Press Notice issued by the Inland Revenue on 22 April 1953 sets out the basis of stamp duty where compensation includes compensation for damage by severance or other injury to other lands of the vendor held therewith and not taken. Stamp duty is payable on the total payment where (as normally happens) the compensation for severance or other injury represents part of the price or compensation payable for the land.

As disturbance forms part of any compensation, stamp duty will be payable on the whole of the price paid for acquisition of an owner's interest, and the disturbance element cannot be deducted for stamp duty purposes. (See *Inland Revenue Commissioners* v *Glasgow and SW Railway Co* (1887) 12 App Cas 315.)

A deed poll executed under the Compulsory Purchase Act 1965 must be stamped as though it were a conveyance (s 28 (2)).

Stamp duty on general vesting declarations turns upon whether the compensation has been assessed in whole or in part when the declaration is executed. Where the compensation has been wholly determined, conveyance on sale duty is charged in respect of the total compensation to each owner. The declaration is regarded as a separate transaction between each owner and the authority for the purposes of the Finance Act 1958, s 34 (4). Where compensation has been partly determined, duty is charged in respect of the ascertainable compensation payable to each owner, and in addition 50 pence fixed duty is payable for each owner in respect of the remaining consideration. No certificate of value is admissible. Where the compensation is wholly undetermined —as is often the case—50 pence fixed conveyance duty is payable in respect of each acquisition, ie, a separate duty in respect of each owner. Adjudication is not necessary. As vesting declarations effect conveyances on sale, they require to be produced under the Finance Act 1931, s 28, even where the compensation is wholly undetermined.

8 Tax

As to liability for tax, see Chapter 33.

Chapter 16

General Vesting Declaration

There have been various means introduced to speed up compulsory acquisitions. The most recent is the general vesting declaration procedure contained in the Compulsory Purchase (Vesting Declarations) Act 1981, re-enacting provisions formerly contained largely in the Town and Country Planning Act 1968. The power in the Act is applied to any Minister, local or public authority authorised to acquire land by means of a compulsory purchase order.

Where the vesting declaration procedure is used the acquiring authority do not have to follow out normal conveyancing practice. They do not have to investigate title but obtain a good title without the need for a conveyance. They are entitled to vest in themselves the interest in the land by executing a general vesting declaration. Under this declaration, all the interests in land are converted into rights of compensation. The acquiring authority become entitled to possession of the land by virtue of the vesting declaration, but, in the case of yearly and shorter tenancies and some longer tenancies about to expire, must serve notice of entry before exercising the right of entry (see p 71).

Where a person retains a document of title relating to land which has vested, he is deemed to have given to the acquiring authority an acknowledgement for production and delivery of copies and (unless a trustee) for safe custody (Act of 1981, s 14).

1 Prescribed notice essential

The key to the vesting declaration procedure is to realise that a special notice must be published giving prescribed information about the procedure and inviting those entitled to compensation to give information about their interests.

This advertisement can be issued at either of two points of time in the procedure for making a compulsory purchase order:

(a) as part of the notice of confirmation of order; or

(b) as a separate notice issued after confirmation but before any notice to treat has been served.

The prescribed form of notice must be advertised and served in just the same way as if it were a notice of confirmation of the order. Prescribed forms will be found in the Compulsory Purchase of Land Regulations 1990 (Vesting Declarations). The notice must be registered as a local land charge (Act of 1981, s 3 (4)).

It follows from this that if any difficulties are likely about unwilling vendors, untraceable owners, etc, the prescribed notice should preferably be given with (Form 2) the notice of confirmation. It does not oblige the authority to use the procedure, as it is still open to them to serve individual notices to treat and to proceed normally in cases where they prefer— the declaration is 'in respect of *any* of the land', not all of it and the notice states they *may*, not must, acquire. It is, however, not possible to employ the procedure of vesting declaration after the service of notices to treat has revealed difficulties, for it will then be too late.

Where a general vesting declaration comprises part only of any house, building or factory, or a park or garden belonging to a house, there are provisions in Sched 1 to the Act of 1981 similar to those described in Chapter 10, under which the owner may require the whole interest to be acquired.

2 Timetable

The procedure for making a vesting declaration after notice in the prescribed form has been given can be summarised as follows:

(1) The authority will execute a declaration in the prescribed form (Form 1). This may not without the consent of all occupiers be made earlier than two months after the advertisement (ie Form 2) containing the prescribed information. It may also not be executed before the compulsory purchase order has come into operation (including compliance with special Parliamentary procedure).

(2) The authority are to serve the prescribed notice (Form 3) of the making of the general vesting declaration, specifying the land and stating the effect of the declaration:

(a) on every occupier who is not a minor tenant or the holder of a long tenancy about to expire (see below); and

(b) on all those owners and lessees who were individually served with notice of the making of the compulsory purchase order and have responded to the invitation to furnish information to the acquiring authority about themselves and their interests.

(3) Twenty-eight days (the authority may lengthen this period) after the vesting declaration has been executed:

   (*a*) notice to treat is deemed to have been served on the date o execution of the declaration (which cannot be withdrawn) and

   (*b*) the land and the right to enter it vests as if a deed poll has been executed under s 9 of the Compulsory   Purchase Act 1965

but subject to protection for minor tenants and holders of long tenancies about to expire.

3 Minor tenants

The acquiring authority are relieved of any obligation to serve notice of the making of a vesting declaration on certain tenants. These are (ss 2 and 6 of the Act of 1981): yearly tenants and those with lesser interests, eg, quarterly or monthly, and those granted for a longer period than a year but having at the date of the vesting declaration an unexpired period less than the period specified in the vesting declaration. The specified period must exceed one year. See p 71, where these definitions are explained.

The aim is to avoid the acquiring authority having to pay compensation and bother with short tenants who can often be left undisturbed for a period of time—eg, a large built-up area might be required for redevelopment in phases and it would be unnecessary to move immediately all of the residential or business tenants.

When the authority need possession in these cases, they must serve notice to treat and also a 14-day notice of entry. The authority's rights are subject to the tenancies until these notices are served (Act of 1981, s 7 (1)). These provisions do not prevent the termination of the tenancy by notice to quit if the authority prefer to proceed in this way having acquired the freehold. (See also p 68).

The suggested alterations to the wording of the prescribed forms set out in Appendix 5 to Circular 6/85 are now obsolete following the introduction of the new forms.

4 Compensation

Except when dealing with tenants, the acquiring authority will not have to serve notice to treat on owners and lessees, because s 7 of the Act of 1981 puts them in the position of having served such a notice on the date the vesting declaration is made. The authority will apparently have a discretion to serve notice to treat before the date when the vesting declaration becomes operative. In the normal way, they will presumably send a notice of claim to owners for completion and return.

The effect of s 10 of the Act of 1981 is to convert the rights of owners into rights of compensation. Both s 22 of the Compulsory Purchase Act 1965 (omitted interests: see page 62) and the provisions in Sched 2 to that Act (absent and untraced owners: see p 107 above) are accordingly excluded as inappropriate. However, this does not prevent the use of a vesting declaration where there are untraced owners.

If the authority overpay compensation, ie, because an incumbrance is not disclosed or they pay the wrong person, there are provisions in s 11 under which the amount wrongly paid can be recovered as a simple contract debt, and in the case of a local authority applied towards repayment of any debt on or to the account for the land acquisition in question.

Disputed compensation claims must be referred to the Lands Tribunal within six years from the date at which the claimant or his successor in title first knew (or could reasonably have been expected to know) of the vesting.

Compensation will be assessed as at the date of vesting, even if possession is not taken till later (*Mahboob Hussain and others* v *Oldham Metropolitan Borough Council* (1981) 41 P & CR 388). As to the date for the calculation of disturbance following vesting, see *Park Automobile Co* v *Strathclyde Regional Council* (1983) 266 EG 729.

5 Mortgaged property

Section 13 of the 1981 Act enables mortgagors (and tenants) to recover sums mistakenly paid as interest or rent after vesting. If a mortgagor has given additional security by including in the mortgage a second property, not being acquired, there is no provision for apportioning repayments such as s 12 provides in the case of rent charges. Possible hardship may be avoidable by making an advance payment of compensation to the mortgagee in return for the release of the charge on the acquired property.

Chapter 17

Purchase Notices

Most compulsory acquisitions are initiated by the authority having compulsory purchase powers. There are, however, some cases of 'compulsory purchase in reverse' in which an owner can force the acquisition of his interest. These fall into two main classes which can be loosely described as follows:

(a) Where an owner has been refused planning consent to develop his land and considers that his land has no reasonably beneficial use apart from the prospects of development. In this case he may serve a *purchase notice* as outlined in this chapter.

(b) Where an owner-occupier has tried to sell property and failed to do so because of the blighting effect of planning proposals. In this case he may serve a *blight notice*: planning blight is dealt with in Chapter 18.

1 Refusal or conditional grant of planning permission

If permission for development is refused an owner may serve a purchase notice under s 180 of the Town and Country Planning Act 1971 if he claims that the land has become incapable of reasonably beneficial use in its existing state, and that it cannot be rendered capable of reasonably beneficial use by the carrying out of any other development for which planning permission has been granted or for which the local planning authority or the Secretary of State has undertaken to grant planning permission.

The land is to be considered as at the time of the refusal of permission. In practice, most purchase notices follow a straight refusal. Occasionally, however, the authority will say: 'We refuse you permission for *X*, but if you were to apply for *Y* we undertake to grant permission for *Y*'. If they say this, then the prospects of *Y* must be taken into account. In the opinion of the Secretary of State there must be an actual refusal—a deemed refusal is insufficient.

In determining any question as to what is or would in any particular circumstances be a reasonably beneficial use of land, no account shall be taken of any prospective use which would involve the carrying out of new development or contravene the conditions in Sched 18 to the Act of 1971. 'New development' is defined in s 22 (5), which in turn refers to Sched 8 to the Act. The effect is that anything listed in Pt I or Pt II of Sched 8 will not amount to new development and so in effect will be included in the 'existing state'. Part I and Pt II largely deal with rebuilding, enlarging and maintaining existing buildings, whilst Sched 18 sets out the limitations on floor space in the rebuilt or altered building. This rather complicated provision means that when considering whether the land is capable of reasonably beneficial use it is necessary to add to the value of the land in its existing state the extra value of any of the limited developments in Pt I or Pt II of Sched 8. But one cannot compare the value of the existing state with the value of any other possible development, because this will be to take into account the forbidden 'new development'. A purchase notice is not intended to provide a remedy for failure to realise full development potential. The following paragraph from Department of Environment Circular No 13/83 (para 13) is helpful:

In considering what capacity for use the land has, relevant factors are the physical state of the land, its size, shape and surroundings, and the general pattern of land-uses in the area; a use of relatively low value may be regarded as reasonably beneficial if such a use is common for similar land in the vicinity. It may sometimes be possible for an area of land to be rendered capable of reasonably beneficial use by being used in conjunction with neighbouring or adjoining land, provided that a sufficient interest in that land is held by the server of the notice, or by a prospective owner of the purchase notice land. Use by a prospective owner cannot be taken into account unless there is a reasonably firm indication that there is in fact a prospective owner of the purchase notice site. (In this paragraph the word "owner" is used to include a person who has a tenancy of the land or some other interest which is sufficient to enable him to use the land). Profit *may* be a useful comparison in certain circumstances, but the absence of profit (however calculated) is not necessarily material: the concept of reasonably beneficial use is not synonymous with profit.

The following are examples of uses of 'relatively low value' which have been sufficient to render land capable of reasonably beneficial use and thus defeat a purchase notice: use as a sports ground (*General Estates Co Ltd* v *Minister of Housing and Local Government* (1965) EG, 17 April 1965); the grazing of horses on three and a half acres of neglected and semi-derelict land in a residential area of a large town

([1976] JPL 189); and limited agricultural use of wedges of poor land between residential sites ([1977] JPL 256).

Where a case is to be made out for a purchase notice following a conditional grant of planning consent, the owner must show not only that the land is incapable of reasonably beneficial use in its existing state, but that it cannot be rendered capable of such use by the carrying out of the permitted development in accordance with the planning conditions. It is obvious that conditions must be so onerous as virtually to reduce the permission to nil to make a purchase notice a practicable proposition in this type of case.

Land may have become incapable of reasonably beneficial use because of a refusal of planning permission or neglect by the owner, but a purchase notice will not succeed if the condition of the land is due to the carrying out of unauthorised development (*Purbeck District Council* v *Secretary of State for the Environment* (1982) 263 EG 26). However, a purchase notice can be served if there has been unlawful development but, because of the passage of time, it is no longer possible to serve an enforcement notice requiring the owner to restore the land to its previous condition in which it would be capable of reasonably beneficial use (see *Balco Transport Services Ltd* v *Secretary of State for the Environment* [1985] 3 All ER 689).

2 Other cases

A purchase notice may also follow a revocation or modification order, a discontinuance order, a refusal of listed building consent or of consent under a tree preservation order or the Control of Advertisement Regulations (see ss 188–191 of the Act of 1971).

The most usual applications of a purchase notice under s 180 arise when permission is refused for the rebuilding of an existing building, or land is reserved for the functions of a public or local authority, eg, as a school.

In the first case, the site with the existing building will be acquired at a value which will reflect the right to rebuild and extend the cubic capacity and floor space in accordance with Scheds 8 and 18 to the Town and Country Planning Act 1971. In other words, assuming a near-derelict building, the land will be acquired at building site value. In the second class of case, the value will fall to be determined in accordance with normal compensation principles, the price largely turning upon the alternative use which would be permitted if there were no public acquisition proposed (see p 200).

Note that if the application is not for rebuilding but is for the 'enlargement, improvement or other alteration' of a building which was in existence on the appointed day, ie, 1 July 1948, then refusal may give rise to a right to compensation. A purchase notice is the remedy for refusal of development included in Pt 1 of Sched 8 to the Act of 1971: compensation is the remedy for refusal to permit the minor developments in Pt 2 of that Schedule. See p 274.

3 Special grounds for non-confirmation

Under s 184 of the Act of 1971 the Secretary of State need not confirm a purchase notice if it appears to him that the land ought in accordance with a previous planning permission to remain undeveloped or be preserved or laid out as *amenity land* in relation to the remainder of the larger area for which that planning permission was granted. This overrules such decisions as *Adams & Wade Ltd* v *Minister of Housing and Local Government* (1965) 18 P & CR 60. The effect is to prevent a local authority having to buy at residential value open space land included in a layout with the developer's agreement in cases where the planning consent was only granted because of the provision of open space or the like. It may well have been, for example, that the density permitted was increased on the assumption that the open space would be provided as part of the development costs.

4 Procedure

A purchase notice must be served upon the district council (or London Borough Council) concerned even if the planning decision was made by the county council. It must be served within 12 months of the planning decision, but the Secretary of State may extend the period under reg 14 of the Town and Country Planning General Regulations 1976.

The local authority must then within three months: accept the notice itself; or find some other authority, eg, the county council, who will accept the notice; or notify the Secretary of State that the notice is not accepted (s 181). The Secretary of State must then invite representations and decide whether or not to confirm the notice (with or without modifications), or to give permission for the development applied for, or for some alternative development. He can confirm the notice for part and grant planning permission for the remainder if it can be thus made capable of reasonably beneficial use (s 183). If after six months (or after nine months from the service of the notice, if earlier) he has made no decision, he is deemed to have confirmed the notice (s 186).

If the Secretary of State directs that permission be granted for an alternative development which would result in the land being worth less than under the 'existing use' value payable on purchase notice compensation, then the authority must pay the difference between the two values (s 187 (2)).

Department of Environment Circular No 13/83 has a model form of purchase notice.

A purchase notice must relate to the identical land the subject of the planning application, unless part of the application was approved and part refused. The notice can then comprise only the part refused. In the case of listed buildings certain 'inseparable' land (in effect of reasonable curtilage) can be included in the purchase notice besides the listed building itself (see s 190 (3)). The Lands Tribunal have held a purchase notice to be invalid where the claimants subsequently discovered that they did not own the whole of the land the subject of the planning refusal (*Smart & Courtenay Dale Ltd* v *Dover RDC* (1972) 23 P & CR 408).

In *Wain and others* v *Secretary of State for the Environment* (1982) 44 P & CR 289, the Court of Appeal held that if part only of the land, the subject of the purchase notice, is incapable of reasonably beneficial use and another part is capable of reasonably beneficial use, the owner cannot insist on the local authority buying the whole of the land. See also *Bernard Wheatcroft Ltd* v *Secretary of State for the Environment and another* (1982) 44 P & CR 223 as to the powers of the Minister to grant a planning permission for a reduced area to that applied for.

If a notice is confirmed (or deemed to be confirmed), a notice to treat is deemed to have been served and this constructive notice cannot be withdrawn (s 208).

When a purchase notice has been accepted there is a duty on the local authority to negotiate in good faith for the acquisition of the property. Breach of that duty can give rise to a liability for damages (*Bremer* v *Haringey London Borough Council* (1983) *The Times*, 12 May).

Chapter 18

Blight Notices

The term 'planning blight' is used to describe the situation which occurs when prospective purchasers of property are deterred from buying because there is a proposal that a public authority with compulsory purchase powers will acquire it at some future date.

The term is not correctly used to describe the depreciation in values caused by nearby public development, properly called injurious affection, or by the prospect that property may be injuriously affected by future public development.

Statutory provisions designed for the alleviation of hardship caused by planning blight were introduced in the Town and Country Planning Act 1959. They have been amended and extended and are now consolidated in ss 192 to 207 of the Town and Country Planning Act 1971, extended by the Land Compensation Act 1973 and amended principally by the Highways Act 1980 and the Local Government Act 1985.

The basic feature of the blight provisions is that for certain classes of owners and in certain defined circumstances there is a right to force a public authority to acquire the land in advance at an unblighted price. The circumstances are where the owner can show that, as a result of proposals by the authority which would involve their purchase of the land in the future, he cannot currently sell his interest except at a substantially depreciated price. The provisions are based on the principle that the public proposal must have a fair degree of certainty, and they apply to the interests of owner-occupiers (including certain mortgagees) of houses and small businesses, currently not exceeding £18,000 rateable value, and agricultural units.

Part V of the Land Compensation Act 1973 (ie, ss 68–81) extended the statutory classes of blight so as to enable authorities to buy blighted land at an earlier stage. For example, it enabled a notice to be served in respect of land affected by development plans, including structure and local plans; land affected by a proposed compulsory purchase order, by a proposed highway order or land within a slum clearance area. It also enabled personal representatives to serve blight notices and introduce new provisions concerning severed agricultural units.

1 Who may benefit?

(1) *Owner-occupiers of any hereditament which does not exceed the prescribed limit.* In 1973 the prescribed limit was set at a net annual value for rating purposes of £2,250 (SI 1973 No 4250). With the introduction of the new rating system as from April 1990 the limit is now an 'annual value' of £18,000.[1] The claimant must have an 'owner's interest', ie, a freehold or a lease with at least three years to run.

Premises exempt from rates do not qualify for protection (*Essex County Council* v *Essex Incorporated Congregational Church Union* [1963] AC 808). The owners of small shops and businesses will be able to claim under this head. *Sparkes* v *Secretary of State for Wales* (1974) 27 P & CR 545, dealt with the case of a builder's yard owned by the wife of an undischarged bankrupt who used the yard in furtherance of his wife's business. The Tribunal held that the 'practical reality' was that the wife was an owner-occupier. In *Holmes* v *Knowsley Borough Council* (1977) 35 P & CR 119 it was held that because a house was unoccupied when on the market with vacant possession for a period of more than 12 months before the service of the blight notice, the claimant was outside the definition of 'owner-occupier'. For other cases on occupation see *Ministry of Transport* v *Holland* (1962) 14 P & CR 259; and *Segal* v *Manchester Corporation* (1966) 18 P & CR 112. The Act refers to 'a person' so that a limited company can claim. Provision is made in s 204 for partnership firms. 'Hereditament' means a relevant hereditament within the meaning of s 64(4)(*a*)–(*c*) of the Local Government Finance Act 1988.

(2) *Resident owner-occupiers of private dwellings.* There is no limit of value here. A shop or business with living accommodation over would qualify under this heading, whatever the net annual value, provided that both were the subject of a single entry in the valuation list.

(3) *Owner-occupiers of agricultural units*, ie, land occupied as a unit for agricultural purposes, including the farmhouse.

(4) *A mortgagee* entitled to sell an interest in the land and able to give immediate vacant possession (s 201). But a mortgagee cannot

serve where a blight notice served by a personal representative is outstanding (Land Compensation Act 1973, s 78 (4).

In all cases the owner-occupier must have been in occupation for six months: either the six months preceding the blight notice of for six months ending not more that a year before the blight notice; provided that in this event the land has been unoccupied since the end of the six months' occupation. In the case of an owner-occupier of an agricultural unit the requirement as to the land having been unoccupied does not apply. Details are in s 203. The Act in s 200 deals with the position where a claimant dies after serving a blight notice.

(5) *A personal representative* of a deceased person who was at the date of his death an owner-occupier. The personal representative must have tried to sell the interest, but have been unable to do so except at a depreciated price because the land was or was likely to fall within the statutory blight categories. The beneficiary must be one or more individuals, but not any body corporate.

This provision was inserted by the Land Compensation Act 1973, s 78, to avoid a beneficiary being left with a property which he did not wish to occupy (or perhaps was unable to occupy) and which could nevertheless only be sold at a depreciated price. Section 78 makes similar consequential provisions to those contained in s 193 of the Town and Country Planning Act 1971. Briefly these are:

   (*a*) the blight notice by the personal representative must be in respect of the whole of the deceased's interest in the land;

   (*b*) a counter-notice may be served on similar grounds to those set out in s 194 (2) of the 1971 Act adapted as necessary to meet the different circumstances in which a personal representative can serve a blight notice.

2 What gives rise to the right?

The right to serve a blight notice arises in the cases set out in s 192 of the 1971 Act, as extended by Pt V of the Land Compensation Act 1973 and as amended, particularly by the Highways Act 1980 and the Local Government Act 1985. These are as follows:

(1) Land may be shown as being required for the purposes of a government department, local authority or statutory undertakers, or of the British Coal Corporation or a telecommunications operator. This may be an indication in a structure plan in force for the district; an allocation or definition of a site in a local plan in force for the district; if no local plan is yet in force, an allocation or definition in an old-

style development plan (s 138 (1) (*b*) of the Town and Country Planning Act 1962 and Sched 24, para 58, to the 1971 Act); an indication in a unitary development plan in force for the district; or an allocation or definition of a site in a unitary plan.

Where a local plan has been prepared, it will take precedence over the structure plan for the purpose of s 192. Its provisions and not those of the structure plan will determine whether the right arises. This is because the local plan is the instrument of precision which carries into effect the broad intentions of the structure plan. See generally Chapter 2, heads 2 to 6.

(2) Land may be indicated in the structure plan as land which may be included in an action area, ie, an area selected for comprehensive treatment during a prescribed period. If the structure plan was approved prior to 13 November 1980 the local planning authority have a duty to prepare a local plan for any action area designated in it. The duty does not apply to structure plans approved after that date (para 8 (2) of Sched 14 to the LGPL Act 1980) and a local planning authority may prepare an action area plan without any prior designation in the structure plan (s 11 (4A) of the 1971 Act).

Here again, if the local plan has been prepared to indicate the precise proposals for the action area, it is the local plan to which regard must be had to see if there are blighting effects or not (s 192 (2)). In *Bolton Corporation* v *Owen* [1962] 1 QB 470 it was held that the mere fact that land is shown as an area for clearance and redevelopment, without an indication by whom this will be effected, would not bring land within the scope of the previous statutory provision in s 138 of the Town and Country Planning Act 1962. It seemed that this decision might not be followed in view of s 71 of the Land Compensation Act 1973 (below). However, in *Ellick* v *Sedgemoor District Council* (1976) 239 EG 513 the Lands Tribunal applied it in upholding the authority's objection where their outline planning application for redevelopment of the town centre had been withdrawn and no future had been decided for the area. In *Nowell (Executor)* v *Kirkburton Urban District Council* (1970) 21 P & CR 832, a local authority in answer to preliminary enquiries said that a property might be included in a clearance area by reason of the bad arrangement of the house. The Lands Tribunal held that this did not amount to an indication that the property might be included in an action area, because there was no structure plan in being.

(3) Land indicated in a plan approved by a resolution of a local planning authority for development control purposes as land which may be required for the purpose of any functions of a government

department, local authority or statutory undertaker (including a public gas supplier). This category was added by s 71 of the Land Compensation Act 1973. It recognises that land indicated in non-statutory maps may be blighted as surely as if the indication was in a development plan.

A local planning authority's intentions do not only appear in plan form. Section 71 therefore extends the blight provisions to land safeguarded for public development purposes by *resolution*, although not included in any plan. It also covers land similarly safeguarded as a result of a direction to the local planning authority by the Secretary of State, eg, under arts 14 and 15 of the Town and Country Planning General Development Order 1988. There are provisions in s 71 (2) to avoid overlap between this provision and those covering structure plans.

(4) Highway proposals in development plans (unless they fall within the provisions relating to structure local and unitary plans to which reference has been made). In an area in which the new development plan provisions (see p 7) have not been brought into force, the old-style development plan prepared under the Town and Country Planning Act 1947 will continue in force. If this plan shows land as being the site of a highway proposed to be constructed, improved or altered, a blight notice may be served. A diagrammatic representation may be enough (*Williams* v *Cheadle and Gatley Urban District Council* (1966) 17 P & CR 153, and *Smith* v *Somerset County Council* (1966) 17 P & CR 162). See also *Mercer* v *Manchester Corporation* (1964) 15 P & CR 321; and *Bowling* v *Leeds County Borough Council* (1974) 27 P & CR 531.

(5) Highway proposals which have had some formal approval under the procedures in the Highways Act 1980, eg, a special road order under s 16 of the Act of 1980 (see p 11, and *Bone* v *Staines Urban District Council* (1964) 15 P & CR 450). The provision applies to 'land on or adjacent to the line of a highway proposed to be constructed, improved or altered as indicated in an order or scheme which has come into force under the provisions of the Highways Act 1980, relating to trunk roads special roads or classified roads' (see Highways Act 1980, Sched 24, para 20). Other categories of land are covered where a power of compulsory acquisition may become exercisable following other orders or schemes under the Highways Act.

Section 74 of the Land Compensation Act 1973, as amended by the Highways Act 1980, extends s 192 (1) (*d*) of the Town and Country Planning Act 1971 to cases where land is affected by the proposed exercise of powers under s 246 of the Highways Act 1980. Under s 246 land may be acquired for the purpose of mitigating any adverse effect which the existence or use of a new or improved highway may have on the surroundings. The categories of land covered by the blight provisions include land shown on plans approved by a resolution of a local highway authority as land proposed to be acquired under s 246 and land which the Secretary of State has notified the local planning authority that he proposes to acquire under s 246 for a special road or trunk road.

(6) Highway proposals for construction, improvement or alteration which have no better authority than a resolution of the local highway authority, ie, the county council or London Borough Council. Obviously such a resolution may be a preliminary step to the submission and approval of a scheme so that it will later qualify under one of the other headings. Where plans for a road improvement scheme had been disclosed to a prospective purchaser, but had not been approved by a resolution of the highway authority, the Lands Tribunal reluctantly had to accept the validity of the local authority's counter-notice (*Paul* v *Mayor, Aldermen and Burgesses of the Borough of Gillingham* (1970) 21 P & CR 973).

(7) Land notified to the local planning authority by the Secretary of State as the proposed route of a trunk or special road. This notification may precede the making of a formal order under the statutory procedures and is designed to protect the route until the formal order can be made. It brings into play the Secretary of State's powers of direction to prevent development under art 15 (1) of the Town and Country Planning General Development Order 1988.

(8) Land in general improvement areas under Pt VIII of the Housing Act 1985. It is sufficient if this indication rises from information published under s 257 of the Act as being land which the local authority propose to acquire.

(9) Land in a private Act authorising compulsory purchase or lying within the limits of deviation allowed by a private Act to the acquiring authority.

(10) Land in unfinished compulsory purchase orders providing for the acquisition of rights *over* (as opposed to interests in) land. Initially this applied to confirmed orders where the appropriate authority had power to serve but had not served notice to treat.

There was a further extension of powers in s 70 of the Act of 1973, so that the submission of a compulsory purchase order (or preparation of a draft order by a Minister) for the acquisition of rights can trigger off the blight procedure.

This case as originally enacted in s 192 (1) (*g*) of the Town and Country Planning Act 1971 only applied to the acquisition of rights by highway authorities. The Land Compensation Act 1973, s 75, widened the power to cover any acquisition of rights over land, not just highway rights. The power to acquire easements under s 13 of the Local Government (Miscellaneous Provisions) Act 1976 is dealt with at p 89.

(11) Land included in unfinished compulsory purchase order proceedings for the acquisition of interest in land. In the 1971 Act the right arose only after confirmation of the order, ie, when the order was in force but no notice to treat had been served. However the power was extended by s 70 of the 1973 Act in recognition of the fact that even the submission of a compulsory order for confirmation (or its preparation in draft by a Minister) can have a blighting effect. Although there is no certainty that the order will be confirmed, an owner may find it impossible to move because of inability to sell. Section 70 therefore enables a blight notice to be served where a compulsory purchase order has been submitted for confirmation to, or has been prepared in draft by, a Minister and formal notice has been published. The effect of this addition is to give full protection from the time a compulsory purchase order is submitted or prepared in draft to the time when it comes into force, but notice to treat has not been served. However, it is pointed out in Chapter 14 that an owner may be deterred from serving a blight notice because a home loss payment will not be available and because a disturbance claim may be rejected.

(12) Land within a clearance area declared under s 289 of the Housing Act 1985. This addition to s 192 of the Act of 1971 was made by the Land Compensation Act 1973, s 73. The purpose is to enable an owner-occupier of a house or small business in a declared clearance area to serve a blight notice without having to wait for a compulsory purchase order to be made by the local authority. In some cases the authority will make a compulsory purchase order at the same time as they declare the clearance area. In this case an owner-occupier can serve a blight notice under s 70 of the Act of 1973 (see para (11) above) . If there is a delay in making the compulsory purchase order, eg, because of difficulty in establishing all interested parties, the owner-occupier may well be unable to sell. The authority cannot object to a blight notice under s 73 on the ground that they do not propose to acquire any part of the hereditament or that they propose to acquire a part only.

The basis of compensation will be site value (see s 585, Housing Act 1985). A 'well maintained' payment and an 'owner-occupier supplement' will be payable if they would have been payable had the acquisition been by compulsory purchase order under s 290 of the Housing Act 1985 (see p 248).

(13) Section 72 of the Act of 1973 repealed s 11 of the New Towns Act 1965, and brought new town areas within the normal blight provisions. A blight notice may be served, by any person having an interest which qualifies for protection, from the time when notice is published of a draft order describing the area of a proposed new town. Until, after the designation procedure, a development corporation is established the blight notice is to be served on the Secretary of State. Subsequently, the development corporation is the appropriate authority.

(14) Land in a proposed or designated urban development area is brought within the blight provisions by s 147 of the Local Government, Planning and Land Act 1980. Until the urban development corporation is established, notice is to be served on the Secretary of State. Thereafter, the corporation is the appropriate authority.

(15) Section 76 of the 1973 Act brought land affected by new street orders within the blight provisions. This recognises that, even if the local highway authority have no intention of widening the highway in the foreseeable future, owners of dwellings erected prior to the order whose land would be required for the works may be unable to sell in the open market except possibly at a substantially depreciated price. The highway authority are precluded from objecting to a s 76 blight notice on the ground that they do not propose to acquire the hereditament or that they propose to acquire only part of it.

3 When can a notice be served?

The Town and Country Planning Act 1971 allowed a blight notice to be served only when the proposal causing blight had reached an advanced stage. Section 192 refers to structure or local plans 'in force for the district'. Highway proposals again have to be in an order or scheme 'which has come into operation'.

It was recognised for some time that the statutory provisions worked unfairly. As long ago as 1970 Circular No 46/70 issued by the Ministry of Housing and Local Government urged local authorities to use their discretionary powers to buy blighted land where an authority 'has definitely decided what it wants to do'. The guidance of this circular was the basis for an extension of the statutory provisions of

1971 by Pt V of the Land Compensation Act 1973.
The position under ss 68 and 69 of the 1973 Act is as follows:

(a) Structure plans

A blight notice may be served:

(*i*) when a structure plan has been submitted to the Secretary of State for approval;

(*ii*) when proposals for alterations to a structure plan have been submitted to him; or

(*iii*) when the Secretary of State has given notice of modifications he proposes to make in a structure plan or proposals for alterations submitted to him.

(b) Local plans

The procedure for adopting local plans involves the giving of notice inviting objections and the holding of a local inquiry, with similar provisions where the local planning authority propose to make modifications. The 1973 Act advanced the time when a blight notice may be served to the stage when a local plan has been made available for inspection under s 12 (2) of the Town and Country Planning Act 1971, ie, when the public participation stage has been completed and the planning authority have decided upon the content of the plan they wish to adopt.

(c) Development plans

The Secretary of State's approval is needed before proposals for alterations or additions to old-style development plans are submitted to him for approval. Land affected by proposals for public development can be the subject of a blight notice when the amending plan is submitted or the Secretary of State has advertised notice of a modification he proposes to make. However, these provisions are no longer of practical importance, as approval would not be given to alterations or additions to old-style development plans.

There are several consequential provisions in s 68 of the Act of 1973. A blight notice cannot be served after a plan has been withdrawn, for example, because of inadequate publicity. Withdrawal will not invalidate a notice served beforehand—the authority must object that they do not intend to acquire the land if they wish to avoid purchase in this case.

If a blight notice is served on the basis of a submitted plan, the approved plan may throw up a different situation, eg, alter the line of a proposed road. There are, therefore, provisions for a second objection from the authority in this type of case based on the final approved version of the plan.

(d) Highway orders

The statutory blight provisions apply to land in highway orders or schemes submitted to the Secretary of State for confirmation or prepared in draft by him, as soon as formal notice has been published (s 69 of the Act of 1973).

The extended provisions for proposed compulsory purchase orders have already been described (para (11)).

4 Procedure

If satisfied that a client has a case to force a purchase of his interest, his advisers must serve a notice on the authority who are liable to acquire the land. In the case of highways there is a special power for the Secretary of State to determine any difficult question as to which of the several highway authorities should take up notice (Act of 1971, s 205). See *R v Secretary of State for the Environment, ex parte Bournemouth Borough Council* (1987) 281 EG 539 for a case where blight notices were served on two different authorities because of different circumstances.

The notice is to be Form No 1 prescribed by reg 18 of and Sched 1 to the Town and Country Planning General Regulations 1976.

5 Counter-notice

The authority can object to purchasing by serving a counter-notice on any of the grounds in s 194, but they must do so within two months. Again there is a prescribed form—Form 4 in Sched 1 to the 1976 Regulations. The counter-notice must be carefully drafted, for it cannot be amended later (*Essex County Council v Essex Incorporated Congregational Church Union* [1963] AC 808, followed by the Lands Tribunal in *Bryant and Bryant v City of Bristol* (1969) 20 P & CR 742). Any dispute as to the validity of the notice will be settled by the Lands Tribunal. The circumstances relating to the land should be considered as at the date of the counter-notice, rather than at the time the blight notice is served, and so if the authority change their mind after the blight notice has been served, their counter-notice may be valid—see *Mancini v Coventry City Council* (1983) 49 P & CR 127 (zoning for educational purposes replaced by residential after blight notice but before counter-notice).

The grounds for objection are as follows:

(a) That the land is *not within the specified descriptions*. The extensions in the Land Compensation Act 1973 reduce the likelihood of such a counter-notice.

(b) That the authority *do not intend to acquire any part* of the hereditament or, in the case of an agricultural unit, of the affected area,

(c) That the authority *only intend to acquire part*—but not the whole of the claimant's land. The authority do not have to acquire more than the actual parts needed for their proposals. The owner can still force the purchase of the whole area where it would be unreasonably detrimental or inconvenient to take part only (s 202).

(d) That the authority *do not propose to acquire any part* of the hereditament or of the affected area of an agricultural unit for *15 or more years* (Local Government, Planning and Land Act 1980, Sched 15, para 8). The ground is available where the blight notice is served under s 192 (1) (a) and (bb)—land indicated in a structure plan or a unitary developement plan as being required for a public purpose or to be included in an action area, or s 192 (1) (c)—highway proposals in development plans other than structure and local plans. The structure plan is mainly a written statement but is accompanied by diagrams and illustrations. Structure plans may cause blight in cases where more detailed examination will suggest that the land is unlikely to be acquired in the foreseeable future. This ground of objection should not be used if any other ground of objection is available—in other words, it is a ground of last resort and is intended to safeguard authorities where there is a genuine doubt whether or not they will eventually need the land but they are sure that they will not require it for at least 15 years. A counter-notice will not legally preclude the subsequent making of a compulsory purchase order before the 15 years have expired, but the fact that a counter-notice had been served would clearly be an important factor for the confirming Minister to consider if objections had been made to the compulsory purchase order.

The 15-year counter-notice is not available if the land is covered by an order under the Highways Act 1980 relating to trunk roads, special roads or classified roads; the land was shown on plans approved by the resolution of a highway authority as land needed for the construction of a road or for improvement or alteration of the road; or the land was included in a notice served by the Secretary of State on the local planning authority indicating that the land was on the route of a proposed trunk road or special road (ie, paras (5)–(7) on pp 125–6). The reason for these exclusions was that the procedures were thought to involve precision and it should have been possible to say in each case whether or not the land was required.

In order to assist owners successfully served with a 15-year counter-notice a local authority may lend money to a prospective purchaser provided the property does not exceed a certain limit of annual value (s 256). The limit is currently £18,000 (SI 1990 No 465). The hope is that hardship to owners can be avoided by making mortgages available to prospective purchasers. The ordinary building society might be frightened off by the possibility of future compulsory acquisition even if this was clearly unlikely for 15 years or so.

(*e*) *That the claimant had no interest in the land.*

(*f*) *That he had no interest qualifying for protection.* Where a strip of land formerly owned with an adjoining cottage was conveyed into the separate ownership and occupation of the claimant, and there was no separate entry in the valuation list, a counter-notice was upheld as the claimant held no interest in hereditament—see *Dingleside Development Co Ltd* v *Powys CC* (1989) EGCS 135.

(*g*) *That he has not made reasonable endeavours to sell* or that the conditions as to a substantially lower price are not fulfilled.

The Land Compensation Act 1973, s 77, exempts a qualifying owner who has unsuccessfully tried to sell his property before public development proposals have been finalised from having to make further attempts to sell after the land comes within the statutory blight descriptions. But inability to sell must be due to the fact that the hereditament or agricultural unit 'was or was likely to be' comprised in land of one of the specified descriptions at the time when the unsuccessful attempts to sell were made.

If the counter-notice disclaims any present intention (ground (*b*)) or future proposal (ground (*d*)) to acquire, then any existing compulsory purchase order or private Act will cease to have effect (s 199).

6 Reference to the Lands Tribunal

Following a counter-notice an owner has two months to refer the blight notice to the Tribunal. If the authority do not serve a counter-notice, or if they do but it is not upheld, then the notice takes effect. If the authority claim before the Tribunal that they oppose the blight notice on any of the grounds in paras (*b*), (*c*) or (*d*) on p 131, the Tribunal will not uphold the objection unless they are satisfied that it is well founded, ie, the onus of proof will be on the authority. If the counter-notice was on other grounds, they will uphold it when the owner can show that it was not well founded (s 195), ie, the onus of proof will be on the claimant. However, it seems that the Tribunal will not uphold the authority's objection if this will nullify the intention of the Act to protect properties suffering from planning blight (*Rawson* v *Ministry of Health* (1966) 17 P & CR 239). See also *Mancini* v *Coventry City Council* (1983) 49 P & CR 127—the Lands Tribunal must not bring an element of discretion or hardship into their consideration—and *McDermott* v *Department of Transport* (1984) 48 P & CR 351—where the authority had a genuine lack of intention to acquire the premises it was not relevant that severe hardship was suffered by the applicants. As to the onus on the authority to establish their intention not to acquire when they served a counter-notice that they did not propose to acquire any part of the land unless compelled to do so (ie, s 194 (2) (*b*) see *Charman* v *Dorset County Council* (1986) 52 P & CR 88).

Where a notice takes effect, the authority are deemed to be authorised to purchase the land compulsorily and to have served notice to treat which they cannot withdraw. But the owner can withdraw his notice up to six weeks after he has seen what compensation will be payable (s 198), so long as the authority have not gone into possession.

7 Blight notice for whole of agricultural unit

Section 53 (1) of the Land Compensation Act 1973 allows a farmer served with notice to treat for part of the farm to serve a counter-notice requiring the authority to purchase the whole of the agricultural unit. The test is whether what is left to farm after the purchase is capable alone or with 'other relevant land' of being farmed as a separate agricultural unit.

Section 79 (to which ss 80 and 81 are consequential) makes similar provision where the notice to treat is *deemed to have been served* in pursuance of a blight notice.

Section 79 distinguishes between 'the unaffected area' (that part of the farm which does not fall within the blight categories) and 'the affected are' (that part which does). Where a blight notice is served in respect of an interest in the whole or part of a unit the claimant may include in the blight notice:

(a) a claim that the unaffected area is not reasonably capable of being farmed either by itself or in conjunction with other relevant land, as a separate agricultural unit; and

(b) a requirement that the authority shall purchase his interest in the whole of the unit or the whole of that part of the unit in which the claimant has an owner's interest.

'Other relevant land' is defined. It means land comprised within the remainder of the unit and includes land of which the claimant is tenant (or has some similar interest less than that of owner-occupier). It also includes land in any other agricultural unit of which the claimant is owner-occupier (with which the unaffected area might be joined to form an enlarged agricultural unit).

The power to serve a blight notice in s 79 necessitated giving a new power of counter-notice to the authority. This is that the claim (that the unaffected area cannot be farmed on its own or with 'other relevant land') is not justified.

There is a provision in s 80 (2) to ensure that the authority cannot avoid dealing with the claim by saying that they propose to acquire part only of the land in the affected area. The merits of the claim as to the non-farmability of the affected area must be considered.

The powers of the Lands Tribunal are set out in the section. There are three options: to uphold the notice as served so that the affected and the unaffected land will be acquired; to declare it valid in relation to the affected area only; to declare it valid in relation only to that part of the affected area which the authority propose to acquire. Section 195 (5) of the Town and Country Planning Act 1971 dealing with the powers of the Lands Tribunal accordingly becomes unnecessary and s 80 (7) of the Act of 1973 makes it inapplicable to notices served under s 79.

Section 81 of the Act of 1973 modifies and adapts s 196 of the Act of 1971, dealing in detail with each of the different permutations which can arise and providing for each a date on which notice to treat is deemed to be served.

Section 81 (6) provides for the planning assumptions governing the compensation for acquiring the unaffected area or the part of the affected area which the authority did not propose to acquire. It shall be assumed, subject to certain qualifications, that planning permission would be granted for development of the land within existing use, but not for any other development.

The most probable situation is that the remainder of the land may have at most 'hope value'. The claimant should not be entitled to realise this value by selling to the acquiring authority when he could otherwise have realised it only by severing it from his holding. If there is hope value the claimant can only realise it by retaining the land in the expectation of being able to sell it at development value at some future time. The section prevents acquiring authorities from having to pay hope value for land which they do not need for their scheme and whose potential may never be realised.

8 Discretionary powers

A professional adviser may occasionally find himself acting for an owner whose case falls outside the scope of the statutory provisions, eg, the property may have been unoccupied for longer than one year prior to the service of the notice (see p 122) or he may not be an owner-occupier. The Government expressed the hope in Department of the Environment Circular No 73/73 (para 74) and previously in Circular No 15/69 that local authorities will exercise a reasonable discretion in cases of hardship.

9 Disturbance

As to whether a person who serves a blight notice can obtain disturbance compensation see p 99.

---

[1] See Town and Country Planning (Blight Provisions) Order 1990 (SI 1990 No 465). 'Annual value' is defined in s 207, as amended by SI 1990 No 465, as (i) for non domestic premises, the rateable value; (ii) for non domestic premises which include domestic property (or property exempt from non domestic rating) the sum of the rateable value and the 'appropriate value' which, in the case of domestic property, is five per cent of the compulsory purchase value.

Part II

Injurious Effects and Displacement

Chapter 19

Mitigating the Injurious Effect of Public Works

Part II of the Land Compensation Act 1973 implemented certain of the recommendations of the Urban Motorways Committee Report, 'New Roads in Towns'.

These were: a right for householders to claim the expenses of sound insulation measures where the predicted level of noise exceeds a specified level; a power for highway authorities to acquire land compulsorily to improve the environment of areas adjoining roads and for remedial measures such as mounding or planting; a discretionary power to purchase properties subject to severe adverse effects after a road has been brought into use; and a discretionary power to buy property where life would be intolerable during the construction period.

The sound insulation provisions will still be found in s 20 of the Land Compensation Act 1973. The remainder have been re-enacted in the Highways Act 1980, apart from s 26 which applies to public works other than highways.

1 Noise insulation

Section 20 of the 1973 Act provides a regulation-making power for the Secretary of State to impose a duty or confer a power on responsible authorities to insulate buildings against noise caused or expected to be caused by construction or use of public works, or alternatively to make grants towards the cost of insulation.

The Noise Insulation Regulations 1975 (SI 1975 No 1763 as amended by SI 1988 No 2000) were made under these powers and the Department of the Environment issued an explanatory Circular No 114/75. The Regulations impose a duty on highway authorities to provide or pay a grant towards soundproofing measures against excessive traffic noise from new or improved roads. Noise has to be measured in accordance with the technical memorandum 'Calculation of Road Traffic Noise' published by HMSO in 1988 (in some circumstances a 1975 memorandum will still apply—see regs 6 and 15). The *duty* arises in the case of new roads or roads to which a carriageway has been added.

The Regulations give a *discretionary power* if a highway has been altered in regard to its location, width or level of carriageway, ie, some work not so major as an additional carriageway and where a private road is adopted by the highway authority within three years of its being first open to public traffic. There is a further discretion in reg 5 to provide insulation where noise from road construction (as opposed to the use of the road) would be excessive.

Only residential properties can benefit, ie, dwellings, nursing homes and the residential parts of schools and colleges. They must be within 300 metres of the highway. Eligible buildings do not include those to be compulsorily acquired, or the subject of a demolition or closing order or in a declared clearance area. Of more importance is the exclusion of buildings first occupied after the date when the road was first open to public traffic—those who 'come to the nuisance' get no remedy. An occupier cannot get two grants under different statutory provisions, eg, an airport scheme (see below) and a road scheme.

The duty arises if the predicted noise level will, within 15 years, exceed the specified level. When designing a new road, engineers will predict noise levels. Where their predictions show that properties will be eligible for grant, the properties will be shown on maps to be deposited at the offices of the highway authority. In practice it is hoped that these maps will be deposited provisionally during the design stage so that properties can be insulated against construction noise by the authority using their discretionary powers in reg 5. The list of eligible properties must be published within six months of the road being opened to traffic. Any person excluded from the map who considers that he should receive an offer of soundproofing may appeal to the highway authority for reconsideration. Public notice must be given of the right of appeal and an appeal lodged within six months thereof (reg 13).

After publishing a map, the highway authority must make an offer in the prescribed form to the occupier of the eligible buildings or his immediate landlord or licensor. The insulation work offered will usually include double glazing of windows with venetian blinds between glazing of south-aspect windows, ventilator units, and permanent air vents.

The offer of soundproofing falls to be accepted first by the occupier (within three months) and is then extended to the immediate landlord. Provision is made in s 20 (4) to ensure that the owner of property cannot deny his tenant the right to soundproofing, and conversely that a tenant cannot damage the value of the freehold by refusing to allow soundproofing to be carried out.

If the offer of grant is accepted, work must be completed within 12 months from acceptance and be completed in accordance with the relevant specification.

The body responsible for soundproofing is, in the case of roads, the highway authority.

Because they operate similar functions, the soundproofing scheme will probably be administered by the local authority for the area, although the highway authority must determine which properties are eligible unless the agent local authority are also carrying out the road construction scheme (reg 14).

The 1975 regulations provide for noise insulation in respect of highways. Section 20 enables regulations to be made in respect of the construction or use of 'public works' which are defined in s 1 (3) as any highway, aerodrome or other works or land provided or used in the exercise of statutory powers. However the 1973 Act does not provide for soundproofing in relation to aerodromes. Noise from them, or from aircraft using them, must be dealt with by means of a scheme under s 79 of the Civil Aviation Act 1982. Buildings, eg, schools or hospitals, may be covered by an aerodrome scheme. Dwellings near Heathrow and Gatwick airports are covered (see SI 1981 No 651). Some airport owners have made schemes under Private Act powers, eg, Manchester. See p 245 for the position as regards military aerodromes.

2 Remedial works for highways

Two separate powers of acquisition of land are provided for highway authorities to purchase land outside the proposed boundary of a highway in order to reduce the adverse effect of the existence or use of the highway on its surroundings:

(1) *A compulsory power* to acquire land to mitigate the adverse effect of the highway or proposed highway on its surroundings (Highways Act 1980, s 246).

Having acquired the land compulsorily or by agreement, the highway authority may then use it, for example, to erect walls or mounds of earth to act as barriers against noise. They may also plant trees, shrubs or grass on the area (s 282). A wide power is given to develop or redevelop land acquired under s 246 (or other land belonging to them) 'for the purpose of improving the surroundings of a highway'. This will allow landscaping of land left over when works to mitigate noise have been completed: or even the construction of buildings alongside new or improved roads (s 282).

(2) A power *exercisable by agreement only* to acquire land the enjoyment of which is seriously affected by:
  (*a*) the carrying out of works for highway construction or improvement;
  (*b*) the use of a highway which has been constructed or improved by the highway authority.

This power to acquire by agreement is only available if the interest of the vendor is one which falls within s 192 (3) to (5) of the Town and Country Planning Act 1971 (interests qualifying for protection under blight provisions), ie, owner-occupiers of houses, farms and small businesses (see p 122). The power is intended to be used where construction traffic, machinery or equipment makes life intolerable or when a similar situation arises later by reason of noise, fumes, etc, from traffic on the new or improved road. (Section 26 of the Land Compensation Act 1973 extends the power in relation to highway projects to cover the other public works: see head 3 below.)

Department of Environment Circular No 167/74 sets out the basis of valuation adopted by the Department in cases arising under s 22 or s 26 of the Land Compensation Act 1973 and is therefore applicable to cases arising under ss 246 and 282 of the Highways Act 1980.

Where the works of construction are not so permanently damaging to the convenience of life as to justify acquisition by agreement, the authority may choose to pay reasonable expenses incurred by the occupier of a dwelling in providing suitable alternative residential accommodation during the period of construction (Land Compensation Act 1973, s 28). This section incidentally applies to all public works, not just highways. The occupier must reach a prior agreement with the authority before moving himself and his household temporarily.

There are time limits on the exercise of the statutory powers.

Land wanted to mitigate the adverse effects of the existence or use of the road (ie, coming under (1) above) can only be compulsorily acquired if the compulsory acquisition is begun (ie, notice of making advertised) before the road is opened. This really should create no problem because the authority will have a plan for trees, walls, mounds or other sound barriers before it starts work. Of more importance is it to remember that if an owner-occupier wants to secure acquisition by agreement because of the serious effects of construction works (ie, under 2 (*a*) above) the agreement, ie, the contract for sale must be made before the road is opened.

Where an owner-occupier wants to sell because of the serious effects of subsequent use (ie, under 2 (*b*) above) a further period of one year from opening is allowed—in order to allow the effects of use to be properly assessed. A similar extra period of one year from opening covers the case where an owner wants to sell voluntarily (ie, under (1) above) land needed to mitigate the adverse effects of the road on its surroundings.

In addition to these time limits, there are certain other miscellaneous provisions which should be noted:

(1) There are special compulsory powers for acquiring alternative land if a common, etc, is involved (Highways Act 1980, s 246 (5)).

(2) Where the land is compulsorily acquired there are provisions designed to ensure that:

(*a*) compensation is assessed at a price undepreciated by the effect of the highway construction or improvement in question (s 261 (6));

(*b*) there is offset any benefit to other land belonging to the same owner from the highway scheme (s 261 (1)).

Similar provisions apply if rights over land, and not land itself, are required.

(3) Section 282 provides for the planting of trees, shrubs or plants on land *acquired* under s 246, on the land *already owned* by the highway authority, or on an existing or proposed highway There are additional powers in s 253 under which owners of adjoining or nearby *land which is not being acquired* can enter into an agreement with the highway authority to plant or retain trees, etc, and to restrict their use of their land. The agreement, which would have to be with the owner and the tenant for a rented property, is registrable as a local land charge and would bind successive owners.

3 Other public works

No doubt most of the cases where public authorities will acquire land to reduce the damaging effects of statutory schemes will be highway cases. Section 26 of the Land Compensation Act 1973 nevertheless confers a general power on 'responsible authorities' to acquire land to reduce the impact of public works on the surrounding environment. The power is exercisable by *agreement only*, unlike highways, where in one case, s 246 of the Highways Act 1980, the power is exercisable compulsorily. The provisions for highways and public works are very closely parallel, with necessary alterations because of the absence of compulsion and the special need to tie in s 26 with highways legislation.

For example, there is no parallel to s 261 (1) of the Highways Act 1980 designed to avoid a reduced price because of the acquisition being compulsory. As the sale under s 26 must be by agreement, the vendor can ensure a reasonable price is paid.

Statutory undertakers (as defined in s 290 of the Town and Country Planning Act 1971) are excluded from s 26 by virtue of the definition of 'public works' in s 26 (6). This means that local authorities and privatised former statutory undertakers are likely to be the principal bodies who will be concerned with it.

Having acquired land by agreement, the responsible authority have powers in parallel with those given to highway authorities to carry out works on the land acquired or already owned by them. Not only may they plant shrubs, trees, etc, but also dispose of land acquired under s 26.

The power to pay for temporary lodging of persons affected by construction or alteration of works (s 28) applies to public works as well as highways (see head 2 above).

For the position of government departments, see p 245.

Chapter 20

Home and Farm Loss Payments

1 Home loss payment

The Urban Motorways Committee concluded that many people are attached to their house or neighbourhood and that the market value limit to compensation did not recognise the personal inconvenience and distress caused by compulsory acquisition. They therefore recommended the establishment of an additional payment as a solatium for the personal grief of being dispossessed forcibly.

The home loss provisions in Pt III of the Land Compensation Act 1973 entitle certain occupiers of dwellings who have been in occupation for a considerable time (five years or more) to payment based on the formula related to the rateable value of the dwelling with a maximum of £1,500. But the home loss payment is not a return to the pre-1919 situation where a supplement of 10 per cent was customarily added to the compensation on account of the fact that the acquisition was compulsory.

The Housing Act 1974 extended the home loss provisions to oblige registered housing associations to make the payments to persons displaced by their scheme. Further amendments to the provisions have since been made, principally by the Local Government, Planning and Land Act 1980 and the Housing and Planning Act 1986.

(a) Circumstances entitling

Section 29 (1) provides for a home loss payment in five sets of cases of displacement from a dwelling:

    (i) compulsory acquisition of a dwelling;

    (ii) the making of a housing order (ie, a demolition order, closing order or obstructive building order); the acceptance of an undertaking not to use a building for human habitation or the service of an improvement notice under Pt VII of the Housing Act 1985;

   (iii) the carrying out of any improvement to the dwelling or redevelopment of land which was previously acquired by an authority with compulsory purchase powers or appropriated and held for the purpose for which it was acquired or appropriated. This is to meet the case where there is a delay between acquisition or appropriation on the one hand and redevelopment or rehabilitation on the other, or where older housing stock is being dealt with;

   (iv) the carrying out of any improvement to the dwelling or of redevelopment on the land by a housing association which has previously acquired the land and at the displacement date is registered under the Housing Associations Act 1985;

   (v) the making of an order for possession on Ground 10 or 10A in Pt II of Sched 2 to the Housing Act 1985 (landlord intends to demolish and reconstruct; land in an area subject to a redevelopment scheme under Pt V of Schedule). See *Greater London Council v Holmes* [1986] 1 All ER 739 where a claimant was displaced from a mobile home on land owned by the authority and to be sold by them for development; the claimant was rehoused but was entitled to a payment because the land was held for the purpose for which it was acquired and the displacement was part of the redevelopment process. Contrast *R v Cardiff City Council, ex parte Cross* (1982) *RVR* 270 where a tenant displaced from an unfit house owned by the authority, and rehoused, was held not to have been displaced by redevelopment so that no payment was due. 'Improvement' includes alterations and enlargement and 'redevelopment' includes a change of use.

A person must have occupied the dwelling or a substantial part of it as his only or main residence throughout a period of five years ending with the date of displacement. Section 32 (4), as amended by the Local Government, Planning and Land Act 1980, covers the case where a husband and wife or two companions live together in their home for the five-year period, and one party dies after displacement but before being able to make a claim. Provided the survivor is entitled under the will or on the intestacy or as a surviving joint tenant, he or she may make the claim. Section 32 (5) helps the occupier of a furnished or unfurnished bedsitter who may have changed his rooms provided he has remained in the same building.

It is essential to stay in possession until after the confirmation of the compulsory purchase order (s 29 (3)). No home loss payment will be made where a blight notice is served because here the owner is choosing to move voluntarily (s 29 (5)). Displacement must not merely be temporary to allow improvements to be carried out: it must be permanent displacement (s 29 (3A)). If the owner or tenant is rehoused elsewhere he is still entitled to claim.

The only people who are excluded from home loss payments are lodgers, squatters and trespassers.

Section 33 provides for home loss payment to be made to a person residing in a caravan on a caravan site who is displaced from it, provided that no suitable alternative site is available to him on reasonable terms.

Where a landlord sells voluntarily and in consequence the tenant is displaced, the tenant will still be entitled to the home loss payment. There is a discretionary power in s 32 (7) to make a payment to the owner who sells voluntarily (so long as compulsory powers were available). Presumably an owner who would otherwise be entitled will not agree terms for a sale by agreement to an authority possessing compulsory purchase powers unless he receives the equivalent of the home loss payment.

A consultation paper in March 1989 proposed a number of changes to the scheme for home loss payments.

(b) Amount of payment

If the displacement was prior to 16 January 1989 the amount of the payment is three times the rateable value, with a minimum payment of £150 and a maximum of £,1500.

If the displacement occurs on or after 16 January 1989 the amount is ten times the rateable value of the property, subject to a minimum of £1,200 and a maximum of £,1500 (see the Home Loss Payments Order 1989 (SI 1989 No 24)).

The 1989 order was an interim provision. For displacement on or after 1 April 1990 the amount is £1,500 (see SI 1990/776 which adds a new s 30 (1A) to the 1973 Act).

(c) Claims

Claims for home loss payments must be made in writing within six years of the date of displacement (s 32 as amended by the Local Government, Planning and Land Act 1980, s 114).

The claim must contain such particulars as the authority may reasonably require to enable them to determine whether the claimant is entitled to a payment, and if so, its amount.

The payment is to be made within three months from the date of claim (or on the date of displacement if the three months end before displacement).

2 Farm loss payment

The reason for this provision is that farmers who move to a new farm may be faced with temporary unavoidable losses in yield during the familiarisation period. This is because the maximum profit in farming depends to a large extent upon practical knowledge of the special characteristics of individual farms. A farmer who is considering a move at a time of his own choosing can more readily avoid this initial loss of profitability.

(a) Eligibility

To qualify, a claimant must be displaced as a result of the compulsory acquisition of the whole of his owner's interest in the agricultural unit he occupies (s 34 (1)). The interest may be bought following notice to treat for the whole; or the authority may have sought to acquire part only, but have been forced to acquire the whole under ss 53 and 54 relating to the enlargement of notices to treat (see p 76).

'Owner's interest' means a freehold interest or a tenancy for a fixed term of which at least three years are unexpired.

'Agricultural unit' means 'land which is occupied as a unit for agricultural purposes, including any dwellinghouse or other building occupied by the same person for the purpose of farming the land' (s 87, incorporating the definition of s 207 (1) of the Town and Country Planning Act 1971).

Tenant farmers—ie, those who are not long lease holders—are not included in the farm loss payments because they receive payments not made to owner-occupiers. For example, a tenant receives four times the rent to assist in reorganising his affairs under s 12 of the Agriculture (Miscellaneous Provisions) Act 1968. To qualify for a farm loss payment a person must be an owner-occupier or have a lease for a term of years certain of which not less than three years remain unexpired on the date of displacement. Displacement gives rise to a right to the payment only if the owner gives up possession on being required to do so by the acquiring authority on completion of the acquisition or, where the authority permits this, on the expiry of a tenancy or licence.

Sometimes an acquiring authority leave the farmer in possession for a short while (eg, by a 364-day tenancy): if so the three years run from the date he vacates the land. If the short-term arrangement had the legal effect of making the former owner an agricultural tenant, he would not qualify for a farm loss payment, because he would then get compensation under s 60 of the Agricultural Holdings Act 1986 and s 12 of the Agriculture (Miscellaneous Provisions) Act 1968, ie, one or two years' rent for disturbance plus four years' rent for reorganisation.

The claimant must begin to farm another agricultural unit elsewhere in Great Britain not later than three years after displacement.

The claimant must occupy the whole of the new unit as owner or tenant (from year to year, or a term of years). He must himself occupy —he cannot buy a farm with a sitting tenant and still get the payment.

No payment can be made if the acquisition of the interest in the whole or any part of the land is as a result of a blight notice (s 34 (6)).

There is the usual discretionary power to make a farm loss payment in acquisitions by agreement (s 36 (4)).

(b) Amount of payment

The starting point in the calculation is the annual farming profit which the claimant derived from the land acquired.

Because normal operations may have been upset by the prospect of acquisition, profit is averaged out over the three years preceding displacement. If displacement occurs during a farming year, the three-year period is taken to the end of the complete year preceding actual displacement (s 35 (2)).

A 'rent' (calculated in accordance with s 35 (4)) has to be deducted to get at the real farming profit. Non-agricultural business activities are to be disregarded. If, for example, the claimant had a retail business he would only receive compensation for lost of profits from this but not a farm loss payment in respect of the retail activity.

The payment is to be scaled down proportionately if the purely agricultural value of the new unit is less than the purely agricultural value of the land acquired. Broadly speaking this is to be confined to a freehold interest subject to a restriction to agricultural user. Section 35 (7) sets out the basis on which the comparative values are to be assessed. The value of the farmhouses are to be excluded.

Where a claimant is entitled to compensation for development value, he is unlikely to qualify for a farm loss payment. The logic is that he could only realise the value for development if he gave up farming.

In some cases only an insignificant amount of development value may have been included in the compensation. There is provision in s 35 (8) to deal with this sort of marginal case. The machinery is to limit the farm loss payment to the amount by which the average profit plus the compensation assessed on the basis of existing use exceeds the actual compensation paid (which included something for development value). Put in another way, if the farm loss payment plus compensation based on existing use as a farm exceeds the compensation actually paid, the owner can claim the difference as farm loss payment.

Section 36 makes a special provision for partnerships.

A claimant is entitled to reasonable valuation or legal expenses incurred for the preparation and prosecution of his claim. Interest is payable from the date of making the claim until payment.

(c) Procedure for claims

A claimant must put in his claim within one year of the date on which he begins to farm the new unit. As already mentioned, he must begin to farm the new unit not more than three years after the date of displacement. Claims must be in writing and supported by the necessary particulars.

Chapter 21

Disturbance Payments

There were a number of provisions in Acts passed before 1973, permitting an authority to pay compensation for disturbance to persons *who have no interest in the land*. The best-known was that in s 30 of the Land Compensation Act 1961; but there were similar powers in ss 32, 63 and 100 of the Housing Act 1957, s 22 of the New Towns Act 1965, and s 130 of the Town and Country Planning Act 1971. All these provisions were swept away and replaced by a new entitlement to a disturbance payment in s 37 of the Land Compensation Act 1973.

One section which is not repealed is s 22 of the Agriculture (Miscellaneous Provisions) Act 1963, giving a discretionary power in the case of agricultural land. The 1973 provisions accordingly do not apply to any land used for agricultural purposes. They nevertheless apply to land or buildings used for other business purposes.

Paragraph 39 of Sched 13 to the Housing Act 1974 makes it obligatory upon registered housing associations to make disturbance payments to persons displaced by their scheme.

1 Conditions of eligibility

The circumstances giving rise to the right to a payment are the same as those for a home loss payment (see p 145 although ground (v) does not apply). These are displacement by:

(*a*) compulsory acquisition;

(*b*) the making or acceptance of a housing order or undertaking or service of an improvement notice;

(*c*) improvement to 'a house or building or redevelopment of land previously acquired by an authority with compulsory powers;

(*d*) the carrying out of any improvement to a house or building on or redevelopment of the land of a registered housing association.

151

The provision will benefit residential tenants whose contractual tenancy has been brought to an end and tenants holding over from the acquiring authority after their legal tenancy has expired, eg, weekly tenants of business premises who have no security of tenure, and therefore no compensatable interest apart from s 37. Where tenants of shop premises held over after expiry of their annual tenancy following acquisition of the premises by a local authority, it was held that they were entitled under the corresponding Scottish provision to a disturbance payment (*Smith and Waverley Tailoring Co* v *Edinburgh District Council* (*No 2*) (1980) RVR 23).

Lodgers and other licensees, trespassers, and squatters have no legal right to a payment, for they are not in lawful possession. There is, however, a discretionary power in subs (5) to enable authorities to deal with deserving cases.

Section 37 (2) (*b*) excludes any person with an interest in land who is displaced by the acquisition of that land (by an authority possessing compulsory purchase powers) and who is or would be entitled to compensation under any other enactment. The only exception is where the compensation is subject to site value provision (ie, unfit property) and the person is *not* entitled to an owner-occupier's supplement. There is a somewhat similar provision excluding a person displaced by a housing order who is entitled to an owner-occupier's supplement. The object of all this is to avoid a double payment. If an owner-occupier's supplement is payable, the disturbance payment is not. Displacement must be permanent, not temporary to allow housing improvements to be carried out (s 37 (3A)).

In order to qualify a person must have been in lawful possession at a certain point in the procedure:

Compulsory acquisition—when making or preparation of order first advertised.

Acquisition by agreement—when agreement made.

Private Bill—when first published

Housing order, etc—when order made, undertaking not to use for human habitation accepted or improvement notice served.

In *R* v *Islington LBC, ex parte Knight* (1983) 47 PCR 410, the claimant was a secure tenant of a house owned by the local authority. In consequence of improvement works the claimant was allocated a new house and sought a disturbance payment on the basis that the authority had acquired the tenancy by agreement within the meaning of s 37 (3) (*c*). It was held that 'land' did not include the claimant's tenancy but that in any case the interest could not have been 'acquired' since the authority already had the freehold and the claimant's interest had merely been extinguished when it was surrendered. There was no basis for a disturbance payment.

2 Amount of payment

The amount of payment shall be equal to both the reasonable expenses of removal and, in the case of a trade or business, loss by reason of disturbance. In the latter case, regard shall be had to the likely security of tenure of the trader and to the availability of suitable alternative land. Alternative premises are disregarded for traders aged 60 or more who opt for compensation based on total extinguishment (s 46 (7) (see p 222). In *Nolan* v *Sheffield Metropolitan District Council* (1979) 38 P & CR 741 the Lands Tribunal considered what items could be regarded as covered by the words 'the reasonable expenses of removal' for a residential claimant. It was held (following a Scottish case *Glasgow Corporation* v *Anderson* [1976] SLT 255) that the statutory provision must cover not only the immediate costs of physical removal but also those reasonable expenses which flowed naturally and directly from the necessity to remove from the old house and set up in the new one. Increased travel costs attributable to the displacement may be allowable—see *Barker* v *Hull City Council* (1985) 275 EG 157.

Where a dwelling has been modified structurally to meet the special needs of a disabled person, the disturbance payment will cover the cost of reasonably comparable alterations to the new home. The test of eligibility in this case is whether the social services department of the local authority made a grant or assisted towards the cost of the alterations or would have done so if an application had been made to them.

A disturbance payment is apparently not taxable and so differs from compensation for disturbance under the compensation code as amended by the Act of 1973, Pt IV. See p 267.

In *Prasad and another* v *Wolverhampton Borough Council* [1983] 2 WLR 946, the Court of Appeal held that a disturbance claim could be allowed where a person had moved before notice to treat or his land was actually acquired as he was threatened with 'inevitable displacement'.

Note that a person entitled to compensation under s 37 of the Landlord and Tenant Act 1954 must elect either to take that compensation or the disturbance payment. He cannot get both (s 37 (4) of the 1973 Act).

Interest is payable from the date of displacement until payment.

3 Discretionary payments

There is a residual discretionary power to make payments for disturbance, the amount to be determined as if there were a right to a payment, to persons displaced by one of the actions listed in the section (s 37 (5)).

In *Gozra* v *Hackney LBC* (1988) 57 P & CR 211 it was held that the Lands Tribunal has jurisdiction to determine the amount of a discretionary payment under s 37 (5), even though by virtue of s 38 (4) the Tribunal is apparently restricted to disputes as to the amounts of a disturbance payment.

The case of lodgers (persons permitted to occupy but without an interest amounting to legal possession) has already been mentioned.

The power would also cater for cases where the authority had arranged for tenants to move out in advance of their taking one of the listed actions, eg, because alternative accommodation could be made available. Without the discretionary power no payment could be made.

Chapter 22

Rehousing and Relocation Obligations

Those involved with compulsory purchase will often be concerned to know if, quite apart from any question of financial compensation, there is a duty on the acquiring authority to rehouse residential occupiers or to relocate business that are displaced.

Prior to the passing of the Land Compensation Act 1973 there were a number of specific obligations placed on acquiring authorities to rehouse residential occupiers displaced by their schemes. The provisions, however, were considered inadequate and the 1973 Act introduced in ss 39–43 provisions designed to ensure that every person displaced by public action was satisfactorily rehoused. Most of the earlier provisions were repealed by the 1973 Act.

1 Scope of the rehousing responsibility

The relevant authority (usually the local housing authority but including new town development corporations, and the Commission for New Towns in some circumstances) must secure that any person displaced from residential accommodation in their area is provided with suitable alternative accommodation where this is not otherwise available on reasonable terms. The duty is for the authority to do their best as soon as practicable, to find alternative accommodation (*R* v *Bristol Corporation, ex parte Hendy* (1974) 27 P & CR 180). Section 40 applies the duty to caravan dwellers with necessary modifications.

The actions giving rise to the obligation are:

  (*a*) compulsory acquisitions;
  (*b*) housing orders, ie, demolition, closing or obstructive building orders under Pt IX of the Housing Act 1985; orders under s 368 (4) of the 1985 Act relating to lack of fire escapes in multi-occupied houses;
  (*c*) housing undertakings accepted under ss 211, 264 or 368 of

155

the1985 Act in lieu of improvement notices or housing orders;

(d) improvement to a house or building or redevelopment carried out by an authority on land previously acquired or appropriated by them, and held in the meantime for the purposes for which it was acquired. (This applies to acquisitions by development corporations in new towns even if the property has become vested in the New Towns Commission);

(e) the service of an improvement notice under Pt VII of the Housing Act 1985.

Section 39 (6A) reproducing provisions elsewhere in Pt III provides that displacement must be permanent.

A person who serves a blight notice has no right to be rehoused. Nor has a person who has received a mortgage advance from the local authority enabling him to buy alternative accommodation, nor one who is a trespasser, nor one who has been permitted to reside in any house or building on the land pending its demolition (see s 39 (2), (3) and (4)).

2 Qualifying date

Problems have arisen in the past from people moving into redevelopment areas in order to secure that they were rehoused by the authority. Section 39 (6) imposes a qualifying date at which residence is necessary for the section to apply. This date is:

(a) the date when notice of the making of the compulsory purchase order or of the preparation of the order in draft was published;

(b) the date when the agreement to purchase was reached;

(c) the date when clearance, demolition or closing order was made, the undertaking accepted or the improvement notice served;

(d) the date of first publication of any Private Bill in Parliament authorising purchase.

3 Advances repayable on maturity

Section 41 of the Land Compensation Act 1973 enables local authorities to make mortgage advances repayable on maturity ('interest only' loans) to displaced owner-occupiers to whom s 39 applies. 'Owner-occupier' is defined in much the same way as in s 203 (4) of the Town and Country Planning Act 1971, viz, an occupier of residential accommodation who has an owner's interest or an interest with more than three years to run.

The object of the section is to assist owners of low value property who will pay interest only during the life of the loan. The loan may require repayment at the end of a fixed period (s 41 (3)) but advantage may be taken of the provision to extend it for an indefinite period, with a provision for repayment in certain specified events, eg, the death of the mortgagor or the sale of the property. There is nothing to prevent the transfer of the mortgage to a surviving spouse or relative in the case of the death of the mortgagor.

Advances may be made not only for acquisition, but for the conversion of an existing property (s 41 (10)) or for the construction of a new dwelling, in which case instalments may be advanced as the work of construction progresses.

The powers in s 39 are in addition to normal powers to make loans which do not permit the waiver of capital repayments.

4 Repayments by displacing authorities

Section 42 of the Land Compensation Act 1973 requires the displacing authority to make payments indemnifying the rehousing or lending authority against any net loss they suffer in respect of assistance given to displaced persons under the previous sections.

The reason for the indemnity is of course that the cost of rehousing is part of the expenditure on the scheme of the authority by whom the land is acquired or redeveloped and ought not to be reduced by housing subsidies. The indemnity is limited to ten years on the basis that with periodical increases the dwelling should be self-supporting within ten years. Indemnity payments will have to be made by county councils as well as undertakers: but they are not required as between one housing authority and another. The indemnity may be paid in a lump sum or by a series of annual payments.

If the local authority can rehouse a displaced person without providing an additional dwelling within the four-year period mentioned in s 42 (2) no indemnity payment has to be made.

There is a parallel provision where the rehousing obligation is discharged by the granting of a mortgage by the local authority, if this results in a 'net loss' as defined in subs (4). There is power for the Secretary of State to determine a method to be used in calculating net losses.

5 Recoupment of acquisition expenses by tenants

Where a person with no interest or no greater interest than as a tenant for a year or from year to year in the dwelling he occupies is displaced in consequence of the acquisition of the dwelling by an authority possessing compulsory purchase powers, the authority may pay the reasonable expenses (not including the purchase price) incurred by that person in acquiring another dwelling.

The power also arises when the authority take any of the other actions listed in paras (*b*), (*c*), (*d*) and (e) in head 1 above resulting in displacement.

Section 43 of the Land Compensation Act 1973, which makes provision to this effect, overcomes the difficulty that earlier powers only permitted the payment of expenses in acquiring a comparable interest. A tenant with no legal interest or only a minor interest can, with the help of s 43, be helped to acquire a freehold or leasehold property. The making of a payment may avoid the need to provide rehousing under s 39.

The tenant must contract to acquire a reasonably comparable dwelling within one year of displacement if he is to qualify. Trespassers or persons who have moved in after the qualifying date mentioned in s 39 do not qualify for an expenses payment (see s 43 (4) and s 39 (3) and (6).

6 Compensation where occupier rehoused

Section 50 of the Land Compensation Act 1973 prohibits the abatement of compensation, home loss payments, farm loss payments and disturbance payments when a public authority provides or secures the provision of alternative residential accommodation for the person being compensated. This section was designed to stop the practice of some local authorities of reducing compensation where the owner-occupier is rehoused in a council house.

Similarly, where a tenant is provided with alternative accommodation, the compensation to the landlord will not be enhanced on the basis that he has given vacant possession. For the purpose of determining the compensation, the authority is deemed to have taken possession when it is given up by the tenant (s 50 (2) and see pp 55 and 67). The provisions apply also where the general vesting declaration procedure has been adopted.

7 Relocation of businesses

In contrast to the detailed provisions relating to the rehousing of residential occupiers, there are very few obligations in relation to the relocation of businesses.

Section 123 (7) of the Town and Country Planning Act 1971 applies to land which has been acquired or appropriated for planning purposes and is held for the time being for the purposes for which it was acquired or appropriated. The general power of disposal given to principal councils by s 123 of the Local Government Act 1972 is excluded by s 123 (9) of the 1971 Act. In certain cases—in particular, disposals (other than leases for seven years or less) at less than the best consideration that can reasonably be obtained—the consent of the Secretary of State is required.

Section 123 (7) requires the local authority to exercise its powers so as to secure, so far as may be practicable, that persons who formerly lived or carried on business or other activities on the land have an opportunity to obtain accommodation there suitable to their reasonable requirements if they so desire. They must be willing to comply with the requirements of the authority as to the development and use of the land. The terms for the new accommodation are to be settled with due regard to the price at which any of the land has been acquired from them.

The extent of the obligation (under earlier legislation) was considered in *Crabtree (A) & Co Ltd* v *Minister of Housing and Local Government* (1965) 17 P & CR 232. A compulsory purchase order for comprehensive development in a town centre had been confirmed and the owners of part of the area sought to quash the order on the grounds that by entering into an agreement with a development company the local authority had prevented itself from properly exercising its powers as to disposal a required by subs 7. It was held that it is for the local planning authority and the Minister to decide whether or not it is practicable to give an opportunity to the person at present carrying on business to obtain accommodation in the redevelopment area. Such an opportunity was given because under the development agreement retail traders on the site were given first opportunity to take new shops at current market rents. With regard to 'on terms settled with due regard to the price at which any such land has been acquired from them' this was a relic from the time when land was often acquired on terms other than at market value and the words had no real application, except in very exceptional circumstances, to a case where the person dispossessed was entitled to market value.

The duty imposed by the section is therefore of a general character and it would not be easy for a person who wished to be relocated in a redeveloped area for business or commercial purposes to force an issue. Whilst the opportunity afforded to displace owners or occupiers to relocate themselves by agreement with the local authority should not be overlooked, the limitations inherent in s 123 (7) need to be recognised. There is no obligation to provide subsidised accommodation.

Section 18 of the New Towns Act 1981 is in similar terms to s 123 (7) of the 1971 Act but appears to impose a rather wider obligation on the development corporation since the opportunity is available to a displaced occupier who desires to obtain accommodation on land belonging to the corporation. The duty, which appears to arise when any land is sold, does not extend to providing an opportunity of obtaining alternative accommodation for retail businesses selling intoxicating liquor.

Urban development corporations are also obliged to give displaced residents of business occupiers an opportunity to obtain accommodation on land belonging to the corporation, subject to similar provisions to those in s 123 (7) of the 1971 Act and s 18 of the 1981 Act.

Neither a new town nor an urban development corporation is subject to the requirements of s 127 of the 1971 Act or s 123 of the 1972 Act concerning disposal at the best consideration, although neither type of corporation can dispose of land by gift. The wide power of disposal to secure the development of the new town or to secure regeneration of the urban development area suggests that both types of corporation do have the power to provide accommodation to those displaced at less than full market rent—something that a local authority generally cannot do without the consent of the Secretary of State. Also, the obligation on a local authority appears to relate only to the land from which the tenant is displaced, whereas it applies generally to land belonging to a new town or urban development corporation.

Quite apart from any legal obligation to rehouse or relocate, Appendix B to Circular No 6/85 advises that the statement of reasons for a compulsory purchase order should include information which would be of interest to persons affected by the order, eg, proposals for rehousing displaced residents or for relocation of businesses, and addresses and telephone numbers where further information on these matters can be obtained. It is likely that evidence on rehousing and relocation will be required at a public inquiry into objections to an order, and the proposals of the authority will be material when consideration is given to whether the case for acquisition has been made out.

Part III

Compensation

Chapter 23

Historical Note

This chapter outlines the development of the law governing compensation payable on compulsory purchase of land. It deals also with the attempts which have been made in post-war years either to restrict compensation artificially or to introduce special rules governing compulsory acquisitions, some of which affected the way in which compensation was assessed or subjected to taxation.

1 The Lands Clauses Consolidation Act 1845

The first general code to govern compulsory acquisition of land was the Lands Clauses Consolidation Act 1845. It was largely procedural, with detailed provision for the settlement of compensation in the absence of agreement by justices, arbitrators, surveyors or juries. However, the Act contained no guidance or rules as to the basis on which compensation was to be assessed, the assumption apparently being that the parties or their valuers needed no statutory framework within which to exercise their expert professional skills.

Inevitably, judicial interpretation filled the lacuna left in the statute. A series of decisions established the principle that the value to be assessed was the value to the owner of the interest being acquired (*Cedar Rapids Manufacturing and Power Co* v *Lacoste* [1914] AC 569). It thus allowed the courts to take into account the possible loss of profits to the owner (whereas under the law today, prospective profits as such are not compensatable (*George Wimpey & Co Ltd* v *Middlesex County Council* [1938] 3 All ER 781). In practice a figure was arrived at and then 10 per cent was added to cover the forced sale (*Re Athlone Rifle Range* [1902] 1 IR 433). This has been described as 'the added sop (which was in the old days always given in these cases) of 10 per cent to soften the blow of compulsory acquisition'(per Lord Denning in *Harvey* v *Crawley Development*

Corporation [1957] 1 QB 485). As will shortly be seen, the 'added sop' was removed (as long ago as 1919) but the home loss payment and farm loss payment introduced in 1973 look to be very much in the nature of a solatium for occupiers of five or more years' standing. At any rate, these payments are the nearest approach in the modern law to the concept of the 10 per cent addition under the 1845 Act, even if distinguishable from it.

Judicial decision under the 1845 Act also established some other propositions which are still relevant today. Included among these are the following:

(1) There can normally be only one payment of compensation which must cover all damage which the owner may sustain, actual or prospective (*Chamberlain* v *West End of London and Crystal Palace Rail Co* (1863) 2 B & S 617, per Erle CJ at p 638, a case dealing with a claim for injurious affection under s 68);

(2) Although there maybe 'heads of compensation', disturbance is in law treated not as a separate head, but as part of the purchase price or compensation for the land taken (*Inland Revenue Commissioners* v *Glasgow and South Western Railway Co* (1887) 12 App Cas 315). This rule has consequences for stamp duty and taxation. Its existence was also one of the main reasons for the decision in *Horn* v *Sunderland Corporation* [1941] 2 KB 26, where it was held that an owner could not get on top of realisable building value any part of his loss by disturbance in circumstances where building value necessitated removal and disturbance to present use. As was said in that case per Scott LJ at p 42, 'The legislation recognizes only two kinds of categories of compensation to the owner from whom land is taken:

(*a*) the fair value to him of the land taken;

(*b*) the fair equivalent in money of the damage sustained by him in respect of other lands of his held with the lands taken, by reason of severance or injurious affection';

(3) The right to claim under s 68 of the Act of 1845 is in effect preserved by s 10 of the Compulsory Purchase Act 1965. 'Section 68... is a remedy for injuries caused by the works authorized by the Act to the lands of an owner who has had none of his land taken in that locality. The remedy is given because Parliament, by authorizing the works, has prevented damage caused by them from being actionable' (per Scott LJ in *Horn* v *Sunderland Corporation*, above). Section 68 is dealt

with in Chapter 29 together with its modification by the Land Compensation Act 1973.

2 Open market value in 1919

The difficulties caused by the absence of any statutory rules to govern assessment of compensation were increasingly recognised and led to the passing of the Acquisition of Land (Assessment of Compensation) Act 1919. 'The main object of the Act of 1919 was undoubtedly to mitigate the evil of excessive compensation which had grown up out of the theory, evolved by the Courts, that because the sale was compulsory the seller must be treated by the assessing tribunal sympathetically as an unwilling seller selling to a willing buyer' (per Scott LJ in *Horn's* case at p 40). The Act introduced six rules to govern assessment of compensation on compulsory acquisition. The most important was that the value of land was to be taken to be the amount which the land if sold in the open market by a willing seller might be expected to realise. The six rules have stood the test of time and were re-enacted with some additions in substantially the same wording in the Land Compensation Act 1961.

Although 'open market value' is a simple enough concept, it can pose difficult questions for the professional valuer. There is a forced sale to one purchaser and therefore an inability to test the market in the normal way by inviting offers from prospective purchasers. There is also the need to ascertain what planning permissions are in existence or in prospect; here statute has stepped in and ss 14–22 of the Land Compensation Act 1961 deal in detail with the way in which actual, prospective or assumed planning permissions are to be taken into account by the valuers in assessing compensation.

The basis of compensation of open market value continued until 1944 when the first of the 'artificial ceilings' was introduced.

3 Post-war artificial ceilings

The Town and Country Planning Act 1944 introduced a ceiling in order to eliminate scarcity value due to war-time conditions. Compensation was to be assessed on 1939 values which in most cases were lower than in fact obtained in 1944 and the disparity progressively increased.

Then in 1947 came the Town and Country Planning Act, which 'purchased', subject to a global ceiling of £300m, all unrealised development value in land. In consequence the owner could only sell what he had left: and what he had left was the existing use value. Therefore, compensation on a compulsory acquisition was based upon existing use. This phrase was a term of art in the 1947 Act and it included such things as the right to rebuild, certain tolerances as to extensions, and the like. (See Sched 3 to the 1947 Act, re-enacted with some amendments in Sched 8 to the Town and Country Planning Act 1971.) The Act contained temporary provisions for eliminating special value attributable to the right to vacant possession (s 52).

The Town and Country Planning Act 1954 introduced compulsory purchase at existing use value *plus* the value of the admitted claim, if any, on the global fund of £300m. (This was the compensation fund set up by the Government under the 1947 Act on which owners were entitled to claim if they considered their land had development value. The closing date for claims was 30 June 1949. The Central Land Board then settled the claims, which thereupon became 'established' and attached to the land concerned.)

The Act of 1954 was unpopular, because at a time of rising land values it meant that an owner of undeveloped land received less— sometimes much less—on compulsory acquisition than on a private sale. Local and public authorities were understandably often unwilling to exercise compulsory powers because of possible injustice to owners. Owners for their part were unwilling to sell by agreement and prepared to object to compulsory acquisition to the limit of their powers.

In the case of *developed* sites with no prospects of redevelopment the artificial restrictions on compensation were of less importance and the owner in effect obtained open market value from 1949 onwards. This is because the basis of compensation comprised two elements which together equated very closely in most cases to market value. These elements in the case of a developed site were the value of the existing building, and the site value with permission to rebuild (see Sched 3 to the Town and Country Planning Act 1947).

4 The return to market value

Because of the widespread dissatisfaction with the Town and Country Planning Act 1954, it was not surprising that in 1959 compensation on compulsory acquisition reverted to the concept of open market value as it had existed from 1919 until the first of the artificial ceilings was introduced in 1944. The open market value provisions appeared in the Town and Country Planning Act 1959 and were re-enacted in the Land Compensation Act 1961. These provisions continued in force without amendment until 1973, by which time it had become very apparent that compensation provisions were inadequate in the case of many activities of local and public authorities, particularly the building of urban motorways. The Land Compensation Act 1973 sought to put right the main areas of inadequacy or injustice, based on the proposals in the White Paper 'Development and Compensation—Putting People First' (Cmnd 5124) published on 17 October 1972.

The Act conferred a new right to compensation for depreciation in the value of interests in land caused by the use of highways, aerodromes and other public works. It conferred new powers (and in some cases improved duties) to mitigate the injurious effects of such works on their surroundings, for example, by providing sound-proofing for houses affected by noise from new roads. It made new provisions for persons displaced from land by public authorities. These included house and farm loss payments to occupiers of five years' standing, disturbance payments to persons who would not otherwise have been entitled to them, and a right to residential occupiers to be rehoused. In the field of compulsory purchase compensation, the Act widened the scope of compensation payable where an owner retained land which was injuriously affected by the works, thus removing the unsatisfactory previous restrictions based on such cases as *Edwards* v *Minister of Transport* [1964] 2 QB 134. It also extended to farms the provisions enabling an owner to require the purchase of the whole of his lands where the acquiring authority wanted part only, and made a number of useful amendments both to compulsory purchase and planning blight provisions and procedures.

If this historical review were to deal only with Acts which were mainly concerned with compensation on compulsory purchase, it should end at this point. However two Acts, the Land Commission Act 1967 and the Community Land Act 1975, had such an impact on compulsory purchase concepts that some brief words about each seem appropriate. The second and fourth editions of this book were, after all, largely necessitated by the Act of 1967 and the Act of 1975 respectively.

5 The Land Commission Act 1967

The Land Commission Act 1967 did not alter the basis of compensation on compulsory acquisition being assessed at market value. The seller (unless he was exempted under ss 56–58) became liable to betterment levy on the compensation in his hands, unless the acquiring authority was the Land Commission itself. A person who sold to the Land Commission was paid out *net*, ie, levy was deducted first from the statutory compensation.

The Land Commission Act 1967 repealed an unusual provision in the Land Compensation Act 1961—unusual in the sense that it ran counter to the accepted doctrine that there can be only one payment of compensation on compulsory purchase. Under Pt IV of the Act of 1961 a person whose land was acquired compulsorily (or by agreement by an authority possessing compulsory powers) was entitled to additional compensation if within five years of completion planning permission was granted for additional development. The measure of additional compensation was the difference between the compensation on sale and that which would have been payable if the additional planning permission had been in force at the time of sale (see *Lavender Garden Properties Ltd* v *London Borough of Enfield* (1968) 19 P & CR 480). The Act of 1967 (s 86) repealed these provisions on contracts for sale or notices to treat dated after 1 January 1967.

The Land Commission was abolished by the Land Commission (Dissolution) Act 1971. Thus ended the second attempt in 20 years to collect betterment, ie, the value or 'unearned increment' to an owner created by the activity of public or local authorities. The attempt in 1947 was to nationalise, albeit subject to compensation, the development value in land. The compensation to be paid out was to be recouped by the levy of development charges when land received permission for development. Development charges were abolished by the Town and Country Planning Act 1953. But the claims on the compensation fund were retained temporarily, as had been seen, as providing an element in the compensation for compulsory purchase, and permanently as a basis for entitlement to compensation for certain planning refusals and restrictions (see Pt VII of the Town and Country Planning Act 1971). The Land Commission Act 1967 left no such permanent mark on the fabric of ownership and development values. It virtually sank without a trace.

6 The Community Land Act 1975 and its repeal

This Act, which ceased to have effect by virtue of s 101 of the Local Government, Planning and Land Act 1980, was with its associated taxation measure, the Development Land Tax Act 1976, yet another measure aimed at recovering for the community some of the benefits conferred by the grant of planning permission and the provision of infrastructure from public funds. It did not immediately affect the basis of compensation for compulsory acquisition. This was only to come about when circumstances permitted the designation of a 'second appointed day' under the provisions of the Act. On the second appointed day, had it ever been reached, compensation would have been changed to 'current use value'. Basically this meant the value of the land shorn of any value attributable to the hope that development would be permitted. It would have, nevertheless, included any value due to the possibility of carrying out development of any class specified in para 1 of Sched 1 to the Community Land Act 1975 (exempt development) and development of any class specified in Sched 8 to the Town and Country Planning Act 1971.

The taxation provisions of the Development Land Tax Act 1976 provided that public authorities acquiring under the Community Land Act provisions would acquire net of development land tax. (The parallel for this was the provision in the Land Commission Act 1967 under which those who sold to the Land Commission received compensation from which betterment levy had first been deducted.) These 'net of tax' provisions applied until they were repealed by s 112 of and Sched 20 to the Finance Act 1980 on disposals after 16 August 1980. The 1976 Act was repealed in 1985 when development land tax was abolished.

7 The current position

Following the repeal of the Community Land Act 1975, compensation for compulsory acquisition is based on market value, uncluttered by such concepts as the suspension of planning permissions or the need to include 'unsuspended' planning permissions in current use value and so forth.

In the first application under the Mines (Working Facilities and Support) Act 1966 in respect of the exploitation of petroleum, it was held that compensation awarded for the grant of rights ought to be consistent with compulsory purchase compensation. It should be the value of what the owner would lose by the enforced grant, namely, the rights over land having its existing agricultural and forestry use plus compensation for disturbance and injurious affection. (See *BP Petroleum Developments Limited* v *Ryder* (1987) 2 EGLR 233.) The court rejected the submission of the land owners that the compensation should take account of the profits which would be derived from the exploitation of the rights. The basic principles of compensation in compulsory purchase cases therefore prevailed.

Chapter 24

Summary of Compensation Provisions

In the following chapters of this guide, the reader must necessarily be taken through some of the complexities of the compensation provisions on compulsory purchase. However, before becoming involved in details, it may be useful to set out the headings under which an owner can claim compensation, and to cross-reference this bird's-eye view with the later chapters.

1 Purchase money

We have seen that market value has been the prevailing basis of compensation since 1959. Market value has to be assessed in accordance with the rules in the Land Compensation Act 1961, some of which import conceptions inapplicable in the ordinary, 'free' market. The six basic rules and certain statutory modifications of them are dealt with in Chapter 25.

In the case of undeveloped land (or any land with development potential) it is important in the open market to know what permissions for development have been obtained or are obtainable. These permissions set the value. In the case of a compulsory acquisition, there are statutory assumptions which must be made as to the planning position. In certain cases these assumptions will not give an adequate answer and it will be necessary to apply to the local planning authority for a certificate as to the development which would be permitted as an alternative to that proposed by the acquiring authority. All this is discussed in Chapter 26. The right to an advance payment of compensation was dealt with in at p 108. Some special cases where the normal rules for assessing compensation are subject to modification are dealt with in Chapter 30 including—

comprehensive development areas;
action areas in local plans;

buildings of architectural and historic interest;
slum clearance cases;
agricultural holdings;
urban development areas.

2 Injurious affection

If an owner sells *all* his land, he will have no claim under this or
the next heading, which is applicable only where the owner has land
left after the compulsory acquisition. He is entitled not only to the
value of the land taken but also compensation for damage to land
retained caused by the exercise of the compulsory powers. A common
example is where part of a garden is taken. The owner can claim not
only for the value of the land as garden land but for any damage
resulting from its loss, eg, lack of privacy or amenities. Before the
Land Compensation Act 1973 compensation for injurious affection
was restricted to considering what was done by the authority on the
land taken (*Edwards* v *Minister of Transport* [1964] 2 QB 134). The
Act reversed this rule—see s 44 and Chapter 27.

The former difficulty of claiming compensation for injurious
affection to the land of an owner from whom no land is acquired is
dealt with in Chapter 29. This chapter deals fully with the right to
compensation where the value of an interest in land is depreciated by
certain physical factors caused by the use of highways, aerodromes
and other public works in certain circumstances: see Pt I of the Land
Compensation Act 1973.

3 Severance

This claim is similar in many ways to injurious affection. A very
common example is where part of a farm is taken, making the
remainder more difficult to work. It is usual for the acquiring
authority to offer accommodation works in order to minimise the
effect of their acquisition and to reduce the compensation payable.

Examples of the type of claim which is admissible under the
heading of severance will be found in Chapter 27.

Instead of making a claim for severance in the case of agricultural
land an owner or tenant may prefer to take advantage of the
provisions in the Land Compensation Act 1973 allowing owners and
tenants of agricultural units to enlarge the notice to treat or notice of
entry to include the whole of their interest. See p 76.

4 Disturbance

An owner is entitled to the costs of removing plant and machinery to alternative premises, temporary trade disturbance and other incidental costs flowing from the acquisition. The costs of obtaining professional advice form part of the claim for disturbance.

The expenses (legal and otherwise) involved in acquiring alternative accommodation can be claimed under this head by an owner-occupier, but not by an investment owner (*Harvey* v *Crawley Development Corporation* [1957] 1 QB 485).

Compensation is based on the principle of 'equivalence'; broadly speaking, an owner should not be left worse off (apart from any artificial statutory restriction, eg, 'cleared site value' in slum clearance cases: see p 245) than if his land had not been acquired. All the same, he should not gain an undue advantage.

For example, it is not permissible to claim full vacant possession value for building and also disturbance to agricultural operations (*Horn* v *Sunderland Corporation* [1941] 2 KB 26 CA). The income tax position on temporary loss of profits and reimbursed removal expenses following the statements in December 1972 and June 1979 by the Inland Revenue is dealt with in Chapter 33.

Two restrictions on the right to claim should be noted:

(1) *Remoteness:* Claims cannot include hypothetical costs, or loss of hypothetical profits or costs not flowing directly from acquisition. Loss must not be too remote and must be the natural and reasonable consequence of the dispossession.

(2) *Excess rent and rates:* A claim cannot be made, normally, on grounds that alternative accommodation will cost more (to build or rent), as it must be assumed that extra cost will bring increased trade or profits. If a person receives 'value for money', he cannot normally recoup his expenditure as part of his disturbance claim.

See Chapter 28.

5 Legal costs of the conveyance

See Chapter 15.

6 Interest

For interest on the purchase money at the prescribed rate after entry on the land by the acquiring authority, see p 64.

7 Other entitlements

The Land Compensation Act 1973 introduced new entitlements
which, though not strictly in the category of compensation, deserve
mention in this bird's-eye view:

soundproofing grant;

home or farm loss payment;

right to rehousing;

disturbance payments to persons without compensatable
interests.

As to these entitlements, see Chapters 19–21.

Chapter 25

The Six Rules for Assessing Compensation

The Land Compensation Act 1961, s 5, repeats the six basic rules for assessing compensation which were introduced by the Acquisition of Land (Assessment of Compensation) Act 1919. In this chapter we take each rule in turn, and explain its effect, principally by examples based upon decided cases.

1 No special allowance

> *'No allowance shall be made on account of the acquisition being compulsory.'*

This prevents the practice which had grown up under the Lands Clauses Consolidation Act of making such a special allowance, usually 10 per cent (see p 163).

2 Willing seller

> *'The value of land shall, subject as hereinafter provided, be taken to be the value which the land if sold in the open market by a willing seller might be expected to realise.'*

'Open market' does not mean a hypothetical free market but the market upon which a buyer and seller could legitimately have operated at the date concerned (*Priestman Collieries Ltd v Northern District Valuation Board* [1950] 2 KB 398).

That part of the rule referring to a willing seller has been well explained in an Indian case *Vyricherla v Revenue Officer Vizagapatam* [1939] AC 302: 'The disinclination of the vendor to part with his land and the urgent necessity of the purchaser to buy must alike be disregarded. Neither must be considered as acting under compulsion.'

An examination of cases coming before the Lands Tribunal shows that a common approach to the open market value is to produce evidence of comparable transactions in the area at the time at which the value falls to be assessed. Sometimes the acquiring authority will submit particulars of other settlements reached with other owners whose lands are included in the compulsory purchase order, for example other plots acquired to construct a road or similar properties in a clearance area. The Lands Tribunal has said on more than one occasion that it prefers to rely on open market transactions if at all possible, because of the fear that 'some authorities deliberately make settlements with weak claimants on favourable terms and then use those settlements as precedents to compel surveyors acting for impecunious clients to accept terms which they believe to be too low' (*Koch* v *Greater London Council* (1968) 20 P & CR 472 and see *Shaw* v *London Borough of Hackney* (1974) 28 P & CR 477.)

In general the Lands Tribunal has set its face against value being assessed on what is called the 'residual' method of valuation. This involves the valuer in assessing the value (probably on a capitalised rental basis) of a completed development. Deductions are then made for development costs, overheads and profit, leaving a residue which is taken to be the value of the site. If the residual method has been used by valuers in a free market situation and before the possibility of compulsory purchase has arisen, it may nevertheless be acceptable (*Clinker and Ash* v *Southern Gas Board* (1967) 18 P & CR 372 and see *Trocette Property Co* v *Greater London Council* (1974) 28 P & CR 408 CA).

The dictum of Wood VC in *Penny* v *Penny* (1868) 5 LR Eq 227 is often quoted in modern cases as to the basis of valuation. 'The scheme of the Act (of 1845) I take to be this: that every man's interest shall be valued rebus sic stantibus just as it occurs at the very moment when the notice to treat was given'. In a more modern case Lord Buckmaster put it in this way: 'The value to be ascertained is the value to the seller of the property in its actual condition at the time of expropriation with all its existing advantages and with all its possibilities, excluding any advantage due to the carrying out of the scheme for which the property is compulsorily acquired.' (*Fraser* v *City of Fraserville* [1917] AC 187, decided when 'value to the seller' was still the law.)

The time at which values have to be assessed is normally the date of taking possession by the acquiring authority but will be the date of assessment (either by agreement or the Lands Tribunal) if that is earlier (see *Birmingham Corporation* v *West Midlands Baptist (Trust) Association Incorporated*) [1970] AC 874 HL and the cases following it discussed at p 53, et seq). In the case of a general vesting declaration, valuation date is the date of vesting and not the date on which premises are vacated (*Hussain* v *Oldham Metropolitan Borough Council* (1981) 259 EG 56).

In the case of properties subject to a lease or tenancy, the freeholder's compensation will be affected by his ability, at the time of valuation or date of entry, to obtain possession. As has been seen (ante p 158) possession by the lessor arising out of rehousing of a tenant by the acquiring authority will normally be disregarded: the right of renewal to a business tenancy is protected: in addition to this the lessor's right to serve notice to quit on agricultural holding is restricted.

If land or buildings subject to a lease are capable of redevelopment so that the owner and lessee would be likely to work together to achieve the redevelopment value, the so-called 'marriage value' is not to be disregarded in a compulsory acquisition (see *Lambe* v *Secretary of State for War* [1955] 2 QB 612 and *Hearts of Oak Benefit Society* v *Lewisham Borough Council* (1978) 249 EG 967). However, if in the market the buyer would know that the freehold owner was unwilling or unable to assist in creating the 'marriage value' then that fact cannot be ignored (see *Trocette Property Co* v *Greater London Council* (1974) 28 P & CR 408 CA, where the freeholder, the GLC, wanted to reserve the site for a road. Contrast *Mountview Estates* v *London Borough of Enfield* (1968) 20 P & CR 729 where the views of the Lands Tribunal coincide with those expressed in the dissenting judgement of Cairns LJ in *Trocette*).

As to whether the cost of purchasing an access to landlocked land should be deducted from the compensation see *Stokes* v *Cambridge Corporation* (1961) 13 P & CR 77. This case is sometimes quoted as authority for assessing the value of a 'ransom strip' in cases not involving compulsory purchase or indeed involving local authorities. It arose out of the compulsory acquisition of land with assumed planning permission for industrial development, subject to conditions requiring satisfactory access. It was held that no regard should be paid to the fact that the acquiring authority were the owners of the access land, and that the price of that land would be assessed as being one third of the increase in value of the land acquired attributable to the access. In contrast, in *Earl Fitzwilliam's Wentworth Estates* v *British Railways Board* (1967) 19 P & CR 588, the Lands Tribunal rejected a contention by the acquiring authority that the deduction for the cost of acquiring an access road should be 25 per cent of the difference in value of the subject land with and without the access.

As to the effect of an agreement under s 52 of the Town and Country Planning Act 1971 on r 2, see *Abbey Homesteads (Developments) Limited* v *Northamptonshire County Council* (1986) 278 EG 1249. Under the Section 52 Agreement land was to be reserved for school purposes, and the Lands Tribunal was asked whether it should be valued as being freely available for residential development or as subject to a permanent covenant. The Tribunal decided that the restriction was of limited duration and did not preclude a valuation under r 2; the Court of Appeal however held that the reservation did create a permanent restrictive covenant running with the land and the land should be valued on that basis.

3 Special suitability of land

> *'The special suitability or adaptability of the land for any purpose shall not be taken into account if that purpose is a purpose to which it could be applied only in pursuance of statutory powers, or for which there is no market apart from the special needs of a particular purchaser or the requirements of any authority possessing compulsory purchase powers.'*

It is, however, only the speical suitability of *the land* for the purposes of the purchaser which has to be disregarded under this rule. The rule applies only to a use, actual or potential, of the land itself. This rule has no counterpart in normal valuation and the following examples should help an understanding of the way in which it works.

Example 1—The Territorial and Auxiliary Forces Association purchased the unexpired term of a 99-year lease of property in Reading of which they had previously been sub-tenants. In 1951 the War Department set about acquiring the premises compulsorily and notice to treat was served. It was argued that the sitting tenant must be excluded as a potential buyer of the freehold interest, because the freehold interest had a special suitability for the purpose of marriage to the leasehold interest. It was held that this was not a case of special suitability. The fact that the sitting tenant would pay more than a investor, in order not to be turned out, did not clothe the land with 'special suitability' under the rule. The basis of assessing compensation was what the acquiring authority, in a friendly negotiation, would be willing to pay to acquire a freehold interest for their purposes, as though no compulsory powers existed (*Lambe* v

Secretary of State for War [1955] 2 QB 612; see also *London Investment & Mortgage Co Ltd* v *Middlesex Country Council* (1952) 2 P & CR 381, where the same principle was applied by the Lands Tribunal).

Example 2—The Crown acquired land on which there was a limestone quarry. It was purchased for the USA in connection with a naval base which they were erecting nearby: the stone when quarried would have been of special importance to them on account of their special needs. It was held that the land was not clothed with a special suitability within the rule, the value of which had to be ignored. The use of the products of the land elsewhere was not a use of the land (*Pointe Gourde Quarrying & Transport Co Ltd* v *Sub-Intendent of Crown Lands* [1947] AC 565).

Example 3—The Staffordshire Territorial Army Association sought to acquire compulsorily land to the rear of and adjoining the Territorial Army drill hall. The land had garages upon it, and these were attractive to the association, who were very badly off for accommodation for their vehicles. It was held that the association could not be excluded from the category of potential purchasers, nor could the tribunal disregard the enhanced price that the association might have paid to be able to use the garages pending the carrying out of a scheme of development (*Lester and Jones* v *Secretary of State for War* (1951) 2 P & CR 74).

Example 4—Three areas of farm land adjoined an existing waste tip belonging to the National Coal Board. It was claimed that the value of the three areas for tipping purposes must be excluded under r 3, because there were difficulties of access except through Coal Board land, and that, in spite of a great demand for tipping space in the locality, there were areas nearer to the waste to be disposed of. It was held that r 3 did not apply. The market was not circumscribed by the 'needs' of the Coal Board. Although they held the key to the use of the three areas because they could refuse access, there was nothing to prevent another purchaser acquiring access over the Coal Board land—although this was a remote possibility. It could not be said that there was 'no market' under the rule (*Corrie* v *Central Land Board* (1954) 4 P & CR 276).

Example 5—A block of 90 acres of undeveloped land was released for development by an Interim Policy Plan for South Hampshire. The land was in three ownerships at the date of appeal to the Lands Tribunal. A spine road proposed by the plan was aligned through and bisected the 90 acres. The claimant's land lay astride the spine road which had been constructed up to their boundary. The Tribunal considered that the claimant's land possessed a special suitability for the purpose of building a spine road. The market for such a purpose was limited to the acquiring authority or their agent for construction, ie, the company who owned the residential land through which the constructed part of the spine road passed. Rule 3 therefore applied (*Laing Homes* v *Eastleigh Borough Council* (1979) 250 EG 350 and 459).

Example 6—In *Blandrent Investment Developments* v *British Gas Corporation* (1979) 252 EG 267, the House of Lords had to consider whether r 3 applied to the assessment of compensation for the sterilisation of land in which gas mains and pipes had been laid (the 'red land'). This red land was to be jointly developed with other land (the 'blue land') of the claimants. 'The respondents submit that because the red land is specially suitable for development with the blue land, the owner of the blue land has a special need to purchase the red land... Whether or not a particular purchaser has a special need must be a matter of evidence and ...there is no evidence that the owner needed the red in order to develop the blue. A special need must mean some compelling reason peculiar to the purchaser.' 'There was no evidence that the blue land could not be developed without the red. Access over the blue may have been a need of the owner of the red land: but the rule directs attention to the needs not of the seller but the purchaser' (per Lord Scarman). The House of Lords held that the red land had a 'quality' which made it specially suitable for the purpose of a joint development with the blue land, but there was evidence of a market and no evidence as to any special need for the owner of the blue land to purchase the red. Rule 3 therefore did not apply. See also *Barstow* v *Rothwell Urban District Council* (1971) 22 P & CR 942: r 3 inapplicable to purchase of narrow strip of land to be added to other land of the council which had insufficient depth for development on its own.

Example 7—A roundabout was constructed on the order land to effect access to adjoining residential development. The Court of Appeal found that whilst the order land might have been the most suitable land for access to the residential development it was not specially suitable. It might be difficult to obtain planning permission for another access but the order land did not have 'special suitability' and so r 3 did not apply (*Batchelor* v *Kent*

CC (1989) *The Times* 17 August CA).

For value to be excluded under the second leg of r 3 there must be *no* market apart from the special needs of a particular purchaser. It follows that if the acquiring authority want to use the land for the same purpose as the owner, the rule cannot apply, for it cannot then be said that there is no market apart from the authority's needs.

In *Chapman, Lowry and Puttick Ltd* v *Chichester D C* (1984) 37 P & CR 674, the order land was the sole access to adjoining land owned by the authority. There was planning permission both for the access road and for residential development on the authority's land. The Lands Tribunal held that r 3 did not apply to exclude development value since the need for the access was not special to the authority—a hypothetical developer could expect to obtain planning permission as the authority had done and would have the same need as the authority for the access land.

The Lands Tribunal have held that 'particular purchaser' does not mean a particular type or class of purchaser. Therefore the prospect of other market traders acquiring a dilapidated 'market shop' had to be allowed for in the valuation (*Frank Boot Stores Ltd* v *City of London Corporation* (1971) 22 P & CR 1124).

Where land was compulsorily acquired for highway improvements in connection with a large development area and had ransom value, it was held that a member of a consortium of owners could be a 'particular purchaser' but that although there was a need for a road closure outside the order land, private developers can construct and stop up highways so the works were not 'only in pursuance of statutory powers'. Rule 3 did not apply. (*Ozanne* v *Hertfordshire CC* (1989) EGCS 119).

Rule 3 will not be brought into play merely because the land being acquired is not an attactive unit for development on its own, and needs to be considered with other land already owned by the acquiring authority. Provided the claim land has a potential for residential building which would have some value in the open market above existing use value, r 3 will not apply (*Barstow* v *Rothwell UDC* (1971) 22 P & CR 942 concerning allotment land).

4 Land used unlawfully, etc

> 'Where the value of the land is increased by reason of the use thereof or of any premises thereon in a manner which could be restrained by any court, or is contrary to law, or is detrimental to the health of the occupants of the premises or to the public

health, the amount of that increase shall not be taken into account'.

In practice, in the open market a purchaser would discount the purchase price because of any known illegal or restrainable use.

The most usual application of this rule today occurs when land has been used in contravention of planning control. In such cases there may be an operative enforcement notice, or something less, eg, a notice served, but not operative, or merely the possibility that the local planning authority will seek to enforce planning control.

> *Example 1*—A local authority sought to acquire for sea defence two caravan sites. These had been instituted without planning consent and in contravention of previous planning control. It was held that the Tribunal should take into account the possibility of an enforcement notice being served (*Higham* v *Havant and Waterloo Urban District Council* [1951] 2 KB 527).

> *Example 2*—Cardiff Corporation acquired from the British Electricity Authority a house, formerly a dwelling-house, which had later been turned into a private hotel. The premises were occupied by the Authority as offices, but their application under Defence Regulation 68CA for conversion from residential to office use had been refused. The office use was in consequence illegal.The Lands Tribunal accordingly did not take into account any increase in value arising from the office use. The premises were valued as a private hotel (*British Electricity Authority* v *Cardiff Corporation* (1951) 2 P & CR 189).

> *Example 3*—Doncaster Borough Council acquired land used for a scrap business without planning permission. Part of the land was immune from enforcement action because the use commenced before 1963; the remainder was still liable to enforcement proceedings. The Lands Tribunal held that whilst the claimant could not benefit from the unlawful use which was not immune from enforcement, r 4 did not apply to the use which was immune from enforcement because this was not 'contrary to law'. However, the Court of Appeal, applying *LTSS Print and Supply Services Ltd* v *Hackney LBC* [1976] QB 663, held that r 4 applied to the whole of the land (*Hughes* v *Doncaster Metropolitan B C* (1989) EGCS 152).

5 Equivalent reinstatement

> *'Where land is, and but for the compulsory acquisition would continue to be, devoted to a purpose of such a nature that there*

is no general demand or market for land for that purpose, the compensation may, if the Lands Tribunal is satisfied that reinstatement in some other place is bona fide intended, be assessed on the basis of the reasonable cost of equivalent reinstatement.'

This basis of compensation is usually applied to such properties as churches, church halls, schools, hospitals, and the like, but is not limited to charitable uses. *Nonentities Society* v *Kidderminster Borough Council* (1971) 22 P & CR 224 LT, dealt with the position of a theatre acquired for road improvements. It was held by the Lands Tribunal that occasional ventures in the non-educational field of drama and dramatic art did not rob the society of its charitable and educational status. In any case on the evidence it was held that there was no demand outside London and the seaside towns for a commercial theatre. Club premises owned by a limited company controlled by the club trustees were granted reinstatement, although the club premises were let to them on a tenancy from year to year (*Harpurhey Conservative and Unionist Club Ltd* v *Manchester City Council* (1976) 31 P & CR 300). See also *Sparks (Trustees of East Hunslett Liberal Club)* v *Leeds City Council* (1977) 34 P & CR 234, where reinstatement of a social club was allowed even though the club's assets were less than the cost of reinstatement and *Runcorn AFC Ltd* v *Warrington & Runcorn Development Corporation* (1982) 45 P & CR 183 (leasehold for less than a year). Reinstatement need not necessarily be in exactly the same locality (*Aston Charities Trust Ltd* v *Stepney Corporation* [1952] 2 QB 642; and see *Howrah House Trustees* v *London Country Council* (1958) 9 P & CR 483). Compensation may include a sum for a property such as a caretaker's house essential to the running of the main property (*London Diocesan Fund* v *Stepney Corporation* (1953) 4 P & CR 9). It will not matter that the property has a value in the market, eg, as a house, and could be valued according to normal principles (*Incorporated Society, etc, for Destitute Catholic Children* v *Feltham Urban District Council* (1960) 11 P & CR 158—houses used as children's homes the subject of a purchase notice).

The first test is whether the premises are devoted to the special 'non-commercial' purpose.

Example 1—A Methodist chapel was compulsorily acquired, which was subject to a lease to the county council for 14 years for use in connection with the council's school meals service. The Lands Tribunal held that, although the income continued to be applied to ecclesiastical purposes, the land had ceased to be so used, and so r 5 was inapplicable *(Central Methodist Church, Todmorden* v *Todmorden Corporation* (1959) 11 P & CR 32). Contrast *Aston Charities Trust Ltd* v *Stepney Corporation*, supra, where the war had interrupted religious and charitable use, and the court confirmed the view of the Lands Tribunal that r 5 applied. 'The words "devoted to a purpose" introduce a conception of intention and are indicating a different test from that of the *de facto* use at the date of the notice to treat': per Somervell LJ.

Example 2—A homoeopathic clinic, purpose built in 1939, was compulsorily acquired to make land available for redevelopment by Manchester University. It was held by the Lands Tribunal that 'purpose' should be construed to include clinics for medical consultation and diagnosis generally. But even so, there was on the evidence no general market demand for such premises, group medical practices being limited to one per area *(Manchester Homoeopathic Clinic* v *Manchester Corporation* (1971) 22 P & CR 243 LT. Contrast *Wilkinson, Gale and Hall* v *Middlesbrough Borough Council* (1979) 39 P & CR 212: veterinary surgeon's premises not entitled to r 5 treatment. 'I cannot think that r 5 was intended to apply for the purpose of reinstating professional occupiers' per Stephenson LJ.

Example 3—A livestock auction and market was acquired. The Lands Tribunal held that there was evidence of a latent demand for the premises so that r 5 did not apply. However, the House of Lords held that such latent demand was not a general demand within the meaning of r 5—it only occurred in the rare event of market premises being offered for sale with the vendors not intending to open a rival market in the vicinity. Such a rare and intermittent demand did not constitute a general demand and so r 5 was not excluded. (*Harrison and Hetherington Ltd* v *Cumbria CC* (1985) 50 P & CR 596.)

The second test is that there must be a bona fide intention to reinstate. Frequently this presents no problem, eg, the authority may have made a site available and there may be a tender for the work as in *Lane* v *Dagenham Corporation* (1961) 12 P & CR 374.

Example—A light railway was requisitioned during the war and later compulsorily acquired. The claimants failed to satisfy the tribunal that they intended to reinstate. Action taken on counsel's advice which purported to show such an intention was disregarded, and the tribunal sought earlier evidence of a genuine intention to reinstate, but were not satisfied that the course of earlier negotiations proved this (*Edge Hill Light Railway Co* v *Secretary of State for War* (1956) 6 P & CR 211).

In *Trustees of Zoar Independent Church* v *Rochester Corporation* (1975) 29 P & CR 145, the Court of Appeal considered the meaning of the phrase 'devoted to a purpose', in a case where a church was temporarily unusable as the roof had fallen in. Equivalent reinstatement on another site was allowed even though the congregation at the new church would be almost wholly different from that worshipping at the old.

Whether r 5 applies is largely a matter to be decided on the facts, and the tribunal has a discretion whether to award compensation on the basis of the rule or not (*Festiniog Railway Co* v *Central Electricity Generating Board* (1962) 13 P & CR 248).

For a notice of claim to satisfy s 4 of the Land Compensation Act 1961, ie, to prevent withdrawal of the acquiring authority, the notice must do more than indicate that the claim is made under r 5 (*Trustees for Methodist Church Purposes* v *North Tyneside Metropolitan Borough Council* (1979) 250 EG 647).

Where the basis applies the compensation will cover:

(*a*) cost of equivalent alternative site;
(*b*) replacement buildings or works; the cost of a car park required to comply with a planning condition may be admissible (*Lane* v *Dagenham Corporation*, above);
(*c*) architects' and quantity surveyors' fees;
(*d*) other costs.

See, for example, *Cunningham* v *Sunderland Country Borough Council* (1963) 14 P & CR 208, in which a deduction was also made for essential repairs.

Compensation is to be calculated not at the date of notice to treat but at the date when the work of reinstatement might reasonably have commenced (*Birmingham Corporation* v *West Midland Baptist (Trust) Association Inc* [1970] AC 874).

Section 45 of the Land Compensation Act 1973 provides that compensation for the compulsory acquisition of a dwelling which has been constructed or substantially modified to meet the special needs of a disabled person, and is occupied by such a person, shall be assessed as if the dwelling were land devoted to a purpose for which there is no general demand or market if a person whose interest is acquired so elects. This will enable compensation to be based on the reasonable cost of equivalent reinstatement provided the other criteria of the rule are met. These are that, but for the compulsory acquisition, the dwelling would continue to be devoted to the special purpose and that reinstatement is bone fide intended.

The reasonable costs of necessary removal and adaptation of items in the nature of tenants' fixtures and fittings could be claimed as normal disturbance items, and this may meet many cases of homes owned and occupied by disabled people.

Where the disabled person has no interest which is being acquired, he will be entitled to a disturbance payment in respect of removal expenses and certain structural alterations under s 37 of the Act of 1973 (see p 154).

6 Disturbance, etc

> *'The provisions of rule 2 shall not affect the assessment of compensation for disturbance or any other matter not directly based on the value of land.'*

The rule confers no new right to disturbance but preserves the rights under s 7 of the Land Compensation Act 1965 (s 63 of the Lands Clauses Act 1845). 'Any loss sustained by a dispossessed owner (at all events one who occupies his house) which flows from a compulsory acquisition may properly be regarded as the subject for compensation for disturbance provided, first, it is not too remote and secondly that it is the natural and reasonable consequence of the dispossession of the owner', per Romer LJ in *Harvey* v *Crawley Development Corporation* [1957] 1 QB 485.

In *McTaggart* v *Bristol & West Building Society and Avon CC* (1985) 50 P & CR 184, a building society obtained a possession order when the purchaser defaulted on the mortgage. The house was affected by highway proposals and a blight notice was accepted by the local authority. The owner claimed interest payments under the mortgage from the date of service of the blight notice to the acquisition by the authority. It was held that the interest payments could not be claimed under r 6 as the claimant had been dispossessed by the court order not by the deemed compulsory purchase.

In *Hughes* v *Doncaster Metropolitan Borough Council* (1989) (see head 4) it was held that r 4 deals only with open market value under r 2 and does not invalidate a claim for disturbance under r 6 because compensation for disturbance is not part of the 'value of land' within the meaning of r 4.

Disturbance is dealt with in Chapter 28.

7 Modification of basic rules

Sections 6, 7 and 9 of the Land Compensation Act 1961 add three new rules to those in the Act of 1919.

The first is an enactment in statutory form of a principle applied by the courts for many years. That principle was to disregard increases in value occasioned by the scheme of the promoters.

The second introduced into the general law a rule which had appeared in certain special Acts since 1919. Its effect was to provide for a set-off against compensation of betterment caused by the scheme to adjoining land of the claimant.

The third rule is a wider form of s 51 (3) of the Town and Country Planning Act 1947, now repealed. It is aimed at preventing depreciation in value for purposes of compensation as a result of the possible blighting effects of planning proposals.

The remainder of this chapter explains each of these three rules and illustrates them by examples.

(a) Effects of the scheme on values to be disregarded (s 6)

The first rule is usually reduced to the short proposition that 'increases or decreases in value due to "the scheme" are to be disregarded'. This is in fact a summary of some complicated provisions in s 6 of and Sched 1 to the Land Compensation Act 1961. The principle involved is usually referred to as 'the *Pointe Gourde* principle'. In that case, *Pointe Gourde Quarrying & Transport Co Ltd* v *Sub-Intendent of Crown Lands* [1947] AC 565, Lord MacDermott defined the rule in this short, comprehensive and much quoted way: 'It is well settled that compensation for the compulsory acquisition of land cannot include an increase in value which is entirely due to the scheme underlying the acquisition.' Other judges have put the matter in other words: 'The object is to prevent the acquisition of the land being at a price which is inflated by the very project or scheme which gives rise to the acquisition.' (Lord Widgery in *Wilson and another* v *Liverpool Corporation* [1971] 1 WLR 302.)

Originally enunciated as a principle to deal with inflation of value, it is now settled that the *Pointe Gourde* principle also applies to depreciation in value due to the scheme (*Salop County Council* v *Craddock* (1969) 213 EG 633 CA; and *Birmingham City District Council* v *Morris and Jacombs* (1976) 33 P & CR 27 CA followed in *Lawlor* v *Hounslow London Borough* (1981) 41 P & CR 362).

Section 6 provides that no account shall be taken in the various cases set out in the first column of the Schedule of any increase or decrease in value attributable to development of the kind mentioned in the second column of the Schedule if that development would not have been likely if the authority had not acquired the land and if the areas had not been designated as described in the Schedule.

Case 1 in Sched 1 is acquisition for the purposes of development of any of the land authorised to be acquired—not just the 'relevant land' the subject of a notice to treat. Development for any other purposes for which land is acquired is to be disregarded. This assumes that 'the scheme' can be easily discovered. The scheme may be authorised by a private Act of Parliament or may be included in an order or procedure defining the scheme and the area within which it is to operate. The courts have nevertheless not always found it easy to define the scheme, the effects of which are to be disregarded in the valuation.

Sir John Pennycuik in *Birmingham City District Council* v *Morris and Jacombs*, above, said 'A scheme means, I think, no more than a project on the part of the authority concerned to acquire land and of course to acquire it for some purpose for which it is authorised to acquire it'. The most difficult cases have been those where a purchase notice has been served. The local authority is in the same position as if it had made a compulsory purchase order, but the reality is that the owner wishes to be relieved of his interest, so that the authority's 'scheme' may be artificial and hard to define. One can sympathise with Ormrod LJ in the Birmingham case above when he commented: 'There is clearly a danger that the word scheme is acquiring or will acquire a mystique of its own and be used as a starting point for highly elaborate—I almost said sophisticated—argument.'

The following examples will illustrate how the rule and the *Pointe Gourde* principle have been applied so that increases or decreases in value due to the 'scheme' have been disregarded under s 6 of the Land Compensation Act 1961 and Case 1 of Sched 1 thereto.

> *Example 1*—A local authority acquired a large area of land for housing development to meet urgent slum clearance needs. The greater part was acquired by agreement. But there was a large area which was the subject of two successive compulsory purchase order. The Lands Tribunal were satisfied that by the date of the notice to treat in the second compulsory purchase, a purchaser would have known enough about the corporations's scheme to have been able to allow for its effect in deciding what price to pay for the land the subject of dispute. Accordingly the tribunal took the dead-ripe value of comparable adjoining land and made allowances for the increased value owing to the scheme. The Court of Appeal upheld the Lands Tribunal's

approach. It was said by Lord Denning MR that 'a scheme is a progressive thing. It starts vague and known to few, it becomes more precise and better known as time goes on. Eventually it becomes precise and definite and known to all. Correspondingly, its impact has a progressive effect on values. At first it has little effect because it is so vague and uncertain. As it becomes more precise and better known, so its impact increases until it has an important effect. It is this increase, whether big or small, which is to be disregarded as at the time when the value is to be assessed' (*Wilson and another* v *Liverpool Corporation* [1971] 1 WLR 302). Contrast with this *Sprinz* v *Kingston-upon-Hull City Council* (1975) 30 P & CR 273; (1975) 235 EG 225, where a second scheme was treated as an entirely fresh project.

Example 2—Land was declared to be clearance area under Pt III of the Housing Act 1957. Within a month, the local authority resolved to acquire the land compulsorily. It was agreed that the houses on the land were slum houses unfit for human habitation. The area was zoned as residential in the approved development plan. It was within a fairly solid belt of decayed slum areas. For the owner it was argued that the valuation should have regard to the fact that adjoining property was in a clearance area. The price should, therefore, be on the basis that the land could be redeveloped. The House of Lords held that in valuing premises in a clearance area, the likelihood that other premises within the clearance area will be cleared away must be considered on the assumption that the local authority have not acquired and do not propose to acquire them. Since by virtue of s 6 (3) 'development' includes clearance, any clearance by the authority should be disregarded. Only such clearance as would take place apart from the 'scheme' should be taken into account. The test was, in other words, if the corporation did not propose to acquire the land, would redevelopment have taken place by any private developer (*Davy* v *Leeds Corporation* [1965] 1 WLR 445; followed by the Lands Tribunal in *Clapham* v *Norwich Country Borough Council* (1970) 21 P & CR 623).

Example 3—Parts of a former airfield lay within the critical radius of a VOR station—a very high frequency omnidirectional range station sensitive to metal. This formed part of a nationwide network of air navigation installations. Planning permission for broiler houses on four parts of the airfield was refused in order to protect the VOR station, as a result of which purchase notices were served. The tribunal held that the acquiring authority had never formulated or possessed anything which could be dignified by the title of a scheme. Therefore the claimants could not be credited with the benefit of the broiler house permissions they sought and which but for the VOR station they would have obtained. There was no 'scheme' which allowed the refusals of permission to be disregarded (*Packwood Poultry Products Ltd* v *Metropolitan Borough of Solihull* (1976) 31 P & CR 315).

Example 4—A strip of land was reserved for a road scheme between 1951 and 1961, when the scheme was abandoned. A 'nil' certificate of appropriate alternative development was obtained. The tribunal held that the diminution in value owing to the abandoned scheme had to be disregarded. It awarded compensation on the basis that 69 houses would have been built on the land as part of the neighbouring residential development (*Jelson Ltd* v *Blaby District Council* (1974) 28 P & CR 450).

As to disregard of diminution in value (as opposed to disregard of increases) see also *Salop Country Council* v *Craddock* (1969) 213 EG 633, and *Toogood* v *Bristol Corporation* (1973) 26 P & CR 132. In *Morris and Jacombs Ltd* v *Birmingham District Council* (1976) 31 P & CR 305, the *Pointe Gourde* principle was applied to a decrease in value due to the scheme underlying the acquisition. In that case the claimants had been persuaded to reserve a strip of land for back access to terraced houses and, on refusal of consent to develop the strip, had served a purchase notice. The 'scheme' was, therefore, the authority's intention to construct the access road.

If the concept of 'the scheme' is difficult to apply to relatively simple acquisitions, it becomes much more difficult when 'the scheme' may be the creation of a new town, a scheme of town development or some piece of comprehensive development taken under the far-reaching powers in the Planning Acts. Cases 2, 3 and 4 in Sched 1 to the Land Compensation Act 1961 (as amended by the Local Government Planning and Land Act 1980 and the Housing Act 1988) deal with the position where the scheme is harder to identify:

Case 2—Land forming part of an area defined in the current development plan as an area of comprehensive development.

Case 3—Land forming part of the designated area of a new town.

Case 3A—Land forming part of an area designated as an extension to the site of a new town.

Case 4—Land defined in the current development plan as an area of town development.

Case 4A—Land forming part of an area designated as an urban development area under s 134, Local Government Planning and Land Act 1980.

Case 4B—Land forming part of a housing trust area under Pt III of the Housing Act 1988.

The rules which have to be applied in *areas of comprehensive development and urban development areas* are dealt with separately in Chapter 30 on special cases. Although there are today few new town or town development schemes in an active state of development, many of the principles enunciated under Case 3 or Case 4 may be applicable to other cases and are dealt with next.

New Town Cases—The application of the statutory assumptions in the case of new towns was considered by the Lands Tribunal in *Domestic Hire Company Ltd* v *Basildon Development Corporation* (1971) 21 P & CR 299, and *Collins* v *Basildon Development Corporation* (1969) 21 P & CR 318. The tribunal approached its valuation on the assumption that the new town had not and would not come into existence. The tribunal would have to determine what planning permission a potential purchaser might have expected to obtain and what on that basis he would have been willing to pay to a willing seller. In the first case, regard was had to the effect on values which would have resulted from development in the neighbourhood which it might reasonably be supposed would have taken place if there had been no new town (following *Camrose (Viscount)* v *Basingstoke Corporation* [1966] 1 WLR 1100 CA). In the second case, the tribunal distinguished between it and *Halliwell* v *Skelmersdale Development Corporation* (1965) 16 P & CR 305 LT. The new town had diminished the value of the land, and this was to be disregarded under the principle of s 9 of the Land Compensation Act 1961 (see below).

In *Myers* v *Milton Keynes Development Corporation* [1974] 1 WLR 696; (1973) 27 P & CR 518, the Court of Appeal considered whether there was any conflict between the *Pointe Gourde* principle and s 15 of the Land Compensation Act 1961. Section 15 is the section which allows the valuer to assume that planning permission would be granted for development in accordance with the proposals of the acquiring authority. In the case in question, the Development Corporation's proposals were for residential development on the land in question, but only after ten years. This gave some development value, albeit deferred, to the land. The Lands Tribunal had been satisfied that, apart from the new town scheme, planning permission could not reasonably have been expected to be granted. The issue before the court therefore was whether the land had to be valued at existing use value, on the principle that the acquiring authority's scheme must be disregarded. It was held that the assumed permission under s 15 had to be taken into account. The *Pointe Gourde* principle did not affect the interest to be valued—this was a freehold with the benefit of an assumed planning permission. The principle only affected the value of the ascertained interest—the new town proposals had to be disregarded at this point. The question was therefore, according to Lord Denning,'... On 18th March 1970 what price would a willing seller have been prepared to accept, and a willing purchaser to pay, for the Walton Manor estate if there had been no proposal for a new town at Milton Keynes and if the prospects of development on and in the neighbourhood of the Walton Manor estate had then been such as they would have been if there had been no proposals for a new town, but with this one additional circumstance: that the purchaser had an assurance that in March 1980 or thereafter, if he applied for planning permission to develop the Walton Park estate or any part of it for residential purposes, in a manner not inconsistent with the development corporation's proposals, he would be granted it'.

This poses a difficult valuation question. The Court of Appeal appeared to lean towards 'present value deferred ten years' or alternatively 'hope value' as possible alternative approaches.

Town development cases—'The effect of the Schedule is that the valuer is to disregard not only any increase in value of the parcel of land being acquired but any increase due to the development of land other than the claim parcel': per Lord Denning in *Camrose* (*Viscount*) v *Basingstoke Corporation* [1966] 1 WLR 1100 CA. For an application of the principle by the Lands Tribunal in another case of town development, see *Kaye* v *Basingstoke Corporation* (1968) 20 P & CR 417.

Housing Action Trust Area Cases — It is necessary to disregard any development (other than the land the subject of the notice to treat) in the course of the development or redevelopment of the area as a housing action trust area.

(b) Set-off for betterment of adjoining land (s 7)

Section 7 provides that if the owner retains any contiguous or adjacent land, the amount of any increase in the value of that land attributable to the scheme is to be deducted from the compensation otherwise payable. As with s 6, the various cases set out in the First Schedule have to be considered.

Example 1—A road widening scheme for a narrow street bounded by poor properties proves to be the key which unlocks increased site values, based upon the prospects of redevelopment for shops. If the value after the road improvement is more than before, the betterment factor will reduce the compensation to nil: *Grosvenor Motor Co* v *Chester Corporation* (1963) 14 P & CR 478. This case was decided upon the provisions of s 222 of the Highways Act 1959 (now s 261 of the Highways Act 1980) but the principles are the same. (For a case where the availability of drainage into a public sewer laid over land reduced the compensation for laying the sewer to nil, see *Rush and Tompkins* v *West Kent Sewerage Board* (1963) 14 P & CR 469.)

Example 2—Retained land of claimants provided by acquiring authority with service road and rear access. Deduction of £500 made by Lands Tribunal for betterment (*Pepper* v *City of Worcester* (1971) 220 EG 289).

Example 3—Dumping of soil on land for which £6,000 paid during construction of road held not to amount to betterment, but was purely an incident of construction. Compensation for the land in question was not therefore abated (*Cooke* v *Secretary of State for the Environment* (1974) 27 P & CR 234).

Example 4—In *Portsmouth Roman Catholic Diocesan Trustees Registered* v *Hampshire Country Council* (1979) 253 EG 1236) the Lands Tribunal had to consider whether the grant of planning permission for residential development on retained land of the trustees was the kind of benefit to which regard was required under s 222 (6) (*a*) of the Highways Act 1959. There was no doubt that planning permission for the contiguous land would have been refused until the distributor road (which was the purpose of the acquisition) had been constructed on the acquired land. The tribunal held that the kind of benefit to which regard must be had is one which is directly referable to the purpose for which the land is authorised to be acquired, such as where the coming of the road will provide access to the retained land of a new or improved kind (including the creation of a frontage to a widened highway). No betterment was held to arise in the case in question. See also *Laing Homes* v *Eastleigh Borough Council* (1979) 250 EG 350, 459 (see p 178).

(*c*) *Blight caused by news that compulsory acquisition is on foot is to be disregarded (s 9).* This rule provides that no account should be taken of any depreciation of the value of the land attributable to an indication (by way of allocation in the development plan or otherwise) that the land is, or is likely, to be acquired compulsorily.

Example 1—In *London Borough of Hackney* v *MacFarlane and another* (1970) 21 P & CR 342, the Court of Appeal held that the compulsory acquisition of adjacent land was enough to satisfy s 9. It was an 'indication' within the section that the claim land was likely to be the subject of a slum clearance order and to be acquired compulsorily. This indication was not, therefore, to be used to depreciate the value of the property.

Example 2—In *Craven and Craven* v *Castleford Borough Council* (1958) 9 P & CR 390, the Lands Tribunal refused to base its decision upon evidence of previous settlements. Such negotiations were carried out under the shadow of compulsory powers and claimants of this class and financial position are more apt and often obliged to settle for cash than to fight for their rights. This is understandable and natural in view of their circumstances and does not prove that such 'imposed' settlements are a fair guide as to true open market value (per the tribunal).

Section 9 provides that no account shall be taken of depreciation 'attributable to' an indication that compulsory purchase is likely. In *Trocette Property Co Ltd* v *Greater London Council* (1974) 28 P & CR 408, the Court of Appeal considered that the phrase 'attributable to' was used deliberately to ensure greater scope for flexibility in its application than would have been achieved by other phrases such as 'caused by'.

Chapter 26

The Value of Planning Permissions: Certificates of Alternative Development

1 Assessing the value of planning permissions

It is simple enough to say: 'Compensation for acquisitions by local and public authorities shall be the price which the property would obtain in the open market.' Why, then, does the Land Compensation Act 1961 devote so many sections to securing this apparently straight-forward idea?

The answer is that today the value of property cannot be considered without regard to the planning permissions which may be obtainable in respect of it: land is rarely sold in the open market until the planning position has been established. Where land is to be acquired by a local or public authority, it is being withdrawn from the market. The uses to which it will be put after acquisition may well have no commercial counterpart. Nor is it possible to obtain a planning permission for a use other than that proposed by the acquiring body. The planning authority would be bound to refuse any application for an alternative, as it would be safeguarding the planned public use. This is the broad situation with which ss 14–22 of the Act of 1961 attempt to deal. The Act provides that certain assumptions shall be made about the land to be acquired, including assumptions that certain planning permissions exist. Armed with these assumptions, the valuers on both sides can consider what the land would fetch in the open market.

Answering the charge of needless complication, the Minister said in Committee on the Bill: 'The idea of simply leaving it to the arbitrator has caused untold difficulties over a period of 100 years. It was because in the 1845 Act it was not made clear what assumptions the arbitrator was to act upon that the 1919 Act had to be passed and the rules therein were enacted.'

Section 14 itself provides an introduction to the detailed assumptions elaborated in ss 15 and 16. It can be summarised as follows:

(a) Assumed permissions are to be additional to actual permissions in force at the date of notice to treat. Those actual permissions may be conditional or unconditional; in respect of part only of the land; granted in outline only by virtue of a general development order; or be a deemed permission, eg, for development by a local authority under the Town and Country Planning General Regulations 1976, SI 1976 No 1419.

(b) Assumed permissions are not to exclude the possibility that other permissions might be granted. But in making assumptions about those other permissions regard shall be had to any contrary opinion in a certificate of alternative development (as to which see head 5).

There are then three types of planning permission to be considered. They are the actual permissions in force at the date of notice to treat; assumed permissions not directly derived from Development Plans (s 15); and assumed permissions derived from Development Plans (s 16). These are now dealt with in turn.

2 Existing and assumed permissions

As we have seen, s 14 provides that the assumed permissions are additional to the actual permissions. In the first place, therefore, the valuers must take into account any existing permissions in respect of the land. If a local authority buy land for a statutory purpose they will usually do so after they have taken the precaution of obtaining a planning permission for the proposed development. Suppose, for example, that land is being acquired for housing. The authority will often get an outline consent for housing before acquisition. In many cases housing value will be the market value and no further inquiries as to planning permissions will have to be made (1961 Act, s 14 (2)).

Section 15 deals with the case where an acquiring authority have not at the date of notice to treat obtained planning permission for their proposed development. Local authorities must normally get planning permission before they can hope to have a compulsory purchase order confirmed. Government departments, however, are able to develop without the necessity of obtaining planning permission. In this type of case the Act provides (s 15 (1)) for a notional planning permission to be attached to the land such as would permit development of it in accordance with the proposals of the acquiring authority. See *Myers* v *Milton Keynes Development Corporation* in the previous chapter.

Then there is the concept of existing use originally embodied in

Sched 3 to the Town and Country Planning Act 1947 and now to be found in Sched 8 to the Act of 1971. As compensation is no longer related to existing use (see p 166, above) it was necessary to provide specifically that permission should be deemed to be granted for any development mentioned in Sched 3 to the Act of 1947 (1961 Act, s 15 (3)). That Schedule dealt with such matters as the right to rebuild an existing building. The Court of Appeal considered the interpretation of the incidents attaching to a 'right to rebuild' in *Trustees of the Walton-on-Thames Charities* v *Walton and Weybridge UDC* (1971) 21 P & CR 411. References in the Land Compensation Act 1961 to Sched 3 to the Act of 1947 become references to Sched 8 to the Town and Country Planning Act 1971 (see Sched 24, para 2, to the latter Act).

Sometimes a planning authority will grant a personal planning permission, ie, limited to the applicant. These permissions have to be excluded in assessing value because they do not attach to land (s 15 (2)). A deemed permission expressed to be in favour of a county council is not a personal permission (*Williamson and Stevens* (*executors of Walter Williamson dec'd*) v *Cambridgeshire County Council* (1977) 232 EG 369). Temporary permissions on the other hand are merely one form of conditional permission and do not have to be disregarded. *McArdle* v *Glasgow Corporation* [1971] RVR 357 was a decision of the Lands Tribunal in Scotland, where a temporary consent only had been granted for a change of use in premises in view of the probability of compulsory acquisition. It was held that the owner was entitled to compensation for disturbance without restriction.

There are also two cases where compensation has already been paid in respect of the land under some provision in the Town and Country Planning Act 1971. These cases are where an order has been made under s 51 discontinuing an authorised use or where there has been refusal of permission for development included in the definition of existing use in Sched 8, Pt 2 (and see ss 169 and 170). It is necessary in these cases to provide against a double payment of compensation occurring, and the Act of 1961 does this in s 15 (4).

Finally, s 15 (5) provides that if a certificate of alternative development (head 5, below) is granted, the permission mentioned in the certificate shall be taken into account.

3 Land included in development plans

If land is included in a development plan it is a fair assumption that a planning permission will be forthcoming for development in accordance with the plan. The Act of 1961 makes detailed provision in s 16 as to the way in which these assumptions are to be worked out. For example, a plan may allocate the site for a specific purpose, eg, as a school. Here it is to be assumed (s 16 (1)) that planning permission would be forthcoming for the development indicated, although in these cases it may well be necessary to apply for a certificate of alternative development as the planned use for which permission is assumed may have no commercial counterpart.

In the majority of cases, the development plan will not indicate a particular type of development, but will show an area as being allocated primarily for a specific use, eg, residential or commercial. Here it is to be assumed that planning permission would be granted for any development which is for the purpose of the specified use, and is development for which planning permission might reasonably be expected to be granted (s 16 (2)).

The Court of Appeal in *Provincial Properties (London) Ltd* v *Caterham and Warlingham UDC* (1972) 23 P & CR 8, considered the interpretation of s 16 (2) and the earlier case of *Devotwill Investments Ltd* v *Margate Corporation* [1969] 2 All ER 97. In that case Russell LJ had hazarded the view that 'the function of s 16 (2) (*b*) is to resist the *carte blanche* of the rest of the section, but never extinguish its operation'. The Court of Appeal held, however, that not only must the proposed use fit in with the development plan, but also there must be a reasonable expectation that planning consent would be forthcoming. In the *Caterham* case two-thirds of an acre at the top of a hill was zoned for residential purposes, but because of green belt considerations it was perfectly clear that planning consent for building on it would never be granted. Its value was therefore £500 not £10,500.

Sometimes a development plan will allocate land for a range of two or more uses, eg, shops and offices. Here it is not possible automatically to assume permission for the most valuable use, but rather the kind which would be reasonable on the relevant land (s 16 (3)).

There are special rules for areas of comprehensive development which are dealt with at p 239. The relevant assumptions appear in s 16 (4) and (5).

No part of s 16 has caused more difficulty of interpretation than subs (7), which provides in effect that in deciding what permission might be granted one must ignore the compulsory acquisition. This is in line with the general principle that compensation shall neither be increased nor decreased on account of the proposal of the acquiring authority which gives rise to the acquisition.

A very simple example of the operation of the rule will be found in

Richardson's Developments Ltd v *Stoke-on-Trent Corporation* (1971) 22 P & CR 958. Here land that was zoned as residential was required as a children's playground. The Lands Tribunal disregarded its value as a playground in assessing compensation. This can be contrasted with the position in *Margate Corporation* v *Devotwill Investments Ltd* (1971) 22 P & CR 328. Here owners of land allocated for residential use were refused planning permission because part of the land was required for a by-pass. Following confirmation of a purchase notice the Lands Tribunal awarded compensation on the basis that while s 16 (7) prevented an assumption that a by-pass would be built on the land, it was an 'inevitable corollary' that the by-pass would be provided nearby. They awarded compensation on the basis that planning permission might have been expected for immediate residential development of the whole of the land. The House of Lords remitted the case to the tribunal for reconsideration, holding that is was not inevitable that there would be a by-pass elsewhere; the likelihood of some other solution to the traffic problem and the question of what permission might have been expected if the land were not to be compulsorily acquired were questions for the tribunal to determine on the evidence before compensation could be correctly assessed.

Whilst a development plan may give some general guidance as to standards, eg, of density, it will need detailed interpretation in relation to a particular site. Section 16 (6) therefore provides that any planning permission under the section is to be assumed to be granted subject to such conditions as might reasonably be expected to be imposed by the planning authority. A future permission may be assumed, eg, if the programme map indicates that immediate development is not intended.

One of the deficiencies of the section is that there are no statutory means by which an owner can obtain an interpretation of the development plan from the local planning authority. Theoretically, at least, the valuers on each side will have to read the plan provisions and attempt their own solution of the difficult but important question, 'What sort of permission would I get and subject to what conditions? Can I expect permission for ten or 20 houses, etc?'

On this the Ministry's Circular No 48/59 says this to local authorities:

> 'The provision of factual information when requested should present no problems to the authority or their officers. But sometimes officers will in addition be asked for informal opinions by one side or the other to the negotiations. For

example, they may be asked to assist in interpreting the relevant provisions of the development plan in a case falling within [what is now s 16 of the 1961 Act]: or as to the planning permissions which might be assumed in cases where no formal certificate can be applied for, eg, where the land is in a comprehensive development area. It is for authorities to decide how far informal expressions of opinion should be permitted with a view to assisting the parties to an acquisition to reach agreement. Where they do give it the Minister suggests that the authority should:

(a) give any such advice to both parties to the negotiation;

(b) make clear that the advice is informal and does not commit them if a formal certificate or planning permission is sought.'

Any dispute about the interpretation of the development plan and the assumed permission arising will be dealt with by the Lands Tribunal on reference to them of a dispute as to compensation. For an unsuccessful attempt to have matters properly referable to the Lands Tribunal brought before the court on an originating summons, see *Harrison* v *Croydon London Borough Council* (1967) 18 P & CR 486. The court may however be involved if the compensation claim depends upon questions of title or contractual rights (see *Duttons Brewery Limited* v *Leeds City Council* (1980) 42 P & CR 152).

4 What is 'the development plan'?

Section 20 of the Town and Country Planning Act 1971 provides the definition of 'development plan' for use in various statutes including the Land Compensation Act 1961. The structure plan and the local plan, together with any alterations to either, constitute the development plan. However we have already seen (p 9, above) that for some time there will still be old development plans in force. The 1971 Act in Sched 5 sets out the provisions relating to old-style development plans, and in Sched 6 the modifications to be read into the 1971 Act, when the development plan under consideration is of the old style.

As a result of amendments to Sched 7 to the 1971 Act by the Local Government Planning and Land Act 1980, that part of the old development plan which relates to the area covered by a local plan is now automatically revoked on the adoption (or approval) of the local plan unless the Secretary of State makes a specific continuation-in-force order. The Secretary of State still retains his power to revoke the old development plan by order, and this would be applicable in areas with structure plans, but not yet covered by local plans.

The 'development plan' is to be taken to consist of both the structure plan as originally approved or as amended, and any provisions of a local plan for the time being applicable to the district, as adopted by the local planning authority (or approved by the Secretary of State). Where there is a local plan for an area, it will settle in detail the proposed uses of land. It may take time for the whole of an area to be covered by local plans. The Town and Country Planning Act 1971, Sched 7, para 5, accordingly provides for the position where there is a structure plan, but no local plan. For the purposes of the Land Compensation Act 1961 the development plan or the current development plan shall be taken to be either the old development plan, or the new structure plan, whichever gives rise to the more favourable assumptions to the owner as to the grant of planning permission.

Any reference in the Land Compensation Act 1961 to an area defined in the current development plan as an area of comprehensive development is to be construed as a reference to an action area for which a local plan is in force (Act of 1971, Sched 23, Pt I). Here again, in the period before the local plan is adopted the owner can choose whichever assumption is more favourable to him, that the land is either defined in the old development plan as an area for comprehensive development or has been selected by the structure plan as an action area (see p 239). Although the relevant part of para 5 of Sched 7 to the 1971 Act was not amended by the Local Government Planning and Land Act 1980, action area plans are no longer defined in structure plans but in local plans (para 8 of Sched 14 to the 1980 Act) and see p 124.

5 Certificates of alternative development

There are a number of cases in which the approved development plan will offer no guide or no sufficient guide to the planning permissions which might be obtainable. Part III of the Act of 1961 deals with this position by introducing a system of certification. Section 17 allows either of the parties directly concerned—normally this means the acquiring authority or the owner of the land—to apply to the local planning authority (or, on appeal, the Secretary of State) for a certificate to say what development would have been permitted if the land were not proposed to be acquired compulsorily. The value of that permission can then be taken into account (see p 196). If a certificate is refused this is also relevant, see s 14 (3) and p 195, above. Prior to the Community Land Act 1975, the certificate when issued had to state whether permission 'might reasonably have been expected to be granted'. A more positive approach is now made to avoid an unduly theoretical approach as to future development possibilities. The certificate must state that planning permission *would have been given* for development of one or more classes specified in the certificate or that planning permission would not have been given for any development other than that which is proposed to be carried out by the acquiring authority. The procedure introduced in 1975 is continued notwithstanding the repeal of the 1975 Act, by s 121 of the Local Government Planning and Land Act 1980.

The Court of Appeal held that the time at which matters must be considered is that of the notice to treat (actual or deemed) or of the offer to negotiate to purchase (*Jelson Ltd* v *Minister of Housing and Local Government and others* [1969] 3 WLR 282). However it now seems that the facts must be considered as at the date when it was first proposed to acquire (ie, the publication of order, service of notice or making of offer to buy—see s 22 (2)) although planning policies are to be considered at the date of the decision of the authority on the application *Hitchins (Robert) Builders Ltd* v *Secretary of State for the Environment* (1978) 37 P & CR 140).

Certificates are required in three classes of case:
(a) where there is no approved development plan;
(b) where the approved development plan leaves the site without notation, ie, it is not the subject of any planning proposal—this is commonly the case in 'white land' in rural areas on the fringes of towns;
(c) where the site is earmarked on the plan specifically for some public purpose, eg, is shown as a site for a new school, a sewage works, a public library, etc.

A certificate is *not* obtainable if the land is zoned for residential, commercial or industrial use, or is within an area of comprehensive development. Such areas are nowadays defined as action areas in local plans complying with the requirements of s 11 of the Town and Country Planning Act 1971.

Circular No 48/59 has this to say on the approach to be made by local planning authorities to the certificate system:

'4 The Minister thinks it important that the certificate system should be worked on broad and common-sense lines: it should be borne in mind that a certificate is not a planning permission but a statement to be used in ascertaining the fair market value of the land... The Minister would expect the local planning authority to determine this question in the light of the character of the development in the surrounding area and the general policy of the development plan, and to exercise their judgement as planning authority as to what form or forms of development, if any, would be appropriate in those surroundings, excluding only those forms which for some reason or other are inappropriate. Some cases will be simple: for example, where land is surrounded almost entirely by residential development, a certificate of residential use would normally be appropriate. Other cases will be more arguable, and no precise guidance can be given in advance.'

In deciding an application, the planning authority can specify conditions, or that permission would only have been granted at a future time. They can formulate general requirements and they can disregard the provisions of the development plan (1961 Act, s 17 (5) to (7)).

Section 14 (3) of the Act of 1961, as has been already noticed, makes it clear that specific and assumed planning permissions are not mutually exclusive. Value may be affected by the hope of obtaining some other form of planning permission or obtaining permission at some future time.

The mere fact that a planning permission has to be assumed will not give value to the land if the land would be unsaleable in the open market for the purposes permitted by the planning permission (*Manchester Land Securities* v *Denton UDC* (1970) 21 P & CR 430). See also *Pearce and Thorpe* v *Aughton Parish Council* (1973) 26 P & CR 357, and *Bromilow* v *Lancashire Country Council* (1975) 29 P & CR 517.

The authority must assume that there is no public proposal to buy the land and they must also set aside any allocation in the development plan which would necessarily involve public purchase. Where a site was shown on the development plan as public open space, what should be considered was the permission (eg, residential) that could be expected in the absence of an authority possessing compulsory purchase powers and not the public open space use which could only be achieved by the authority (*Scunthorpe Borough Council* v *Secretary of State for the Environment and others* [1977] JPL 653).

However if land owned by a new town development corporation is to be acquired by an education authority to build a school the fact that the plan for the new town allocated the site for educational purposes may be taken into consideration by the local planning authority to which application had been made under s 17 so long as they did not regard it as conclusive. A certificate for playing fields or for an institute in large grounds was valid; even if the school had not been built the area would have remained open (*Skelmersdale Development Corporation* v *Secretary of State for the Environment* [1980] JPL 322). The case was distinguished in *Grampian Regional Council* v *Secretary of State for Scotland* [1983] 1 WLR 1340, where land long identified as school sites was acquired by the education authority for that purpose but certificates under s 17 were given for residential and commercial development. The House of Lords stated that the essential purpose of the certificate procedure is to ensure that when land otherwise available for building development is acquired for a public purpose, compensation should reflect that development value. In the *Skelmersdale* case the land would have remained open because of the planning policy for the area but this was not so in the *Grampian* case.

The Secretary of State has since indicated that in determining what alternative development should be specified in a certificate for land in a new town, the existence of the new town and of any operative master plan for it are material considerations (see [1987] JPL 659). In *Sutton* v *Secretary of State* (1984) 50 P & CR 147, it was held that the Secretary of State should have considered possible development of a larger site including land not owned by the applicant, should not have excluded development because it was of any exceptional nature, and should not have had regard as to whether or not the development was likely to take place.

The following procedural points should be noted:

(1) Certificates can be applied for only by the acquiring authority and a person entitled to an interest in the land (1961 Act, s 22 (1)). The application must be accompanied by a map. If following service of notice to treat or agreement for sale a reference has been made to the Lands Tribunal to determine compensation, a certificate can only be applied for with the consent of the other party or with leave of the tribunal (s 17 (2)).

(2) A copy is to be sent to the other party concerned, and no certificate is issued by the planning authority for 21 days thereafter (to allow the other party to make representations)(s 17 (4)). Two months are allowed to the authority to deal with the application.

(3) A certificate can be applied for when the authority offer in writing to negotiate for the land, or notify the submission of a compulsory purchase order (s 22 (2)).

(4) The onus is on the applicant to state what classes of development (if any) would be appropriate and when. Further the

applicant must state the grounds for the contentions made in his application (s 17(3)).

(5) If the authority gives a certificate for a class of development different from that specified in the application, it must state its reasons and explain how an appeal may be made. Without such particulars (and a statement as to the right of appeal) the certificate will be invalid. (See *London & Clydeside Estates Ltd* v *Aberdeen District Council* (1979) 39 P & CR 549.)

(6) An appeal lies to the Secretary of State within one month of the receipt of the certificate or the failure to issue and within two months of the application. The applicant, the acquiring authority and the planning authority must all be given an opportunity of a hearing before an appointed person (s 18). It is the view of the Secretary of State that he can determine an appeal even if the certificate appealed against is invalid (see [1987] JPL 660). The Secretary of State has a complete discretion to confirm, vary or cancel the certificate and is not bound to adopt the authority's reasons if he upholds, on appeal, its decision on a certificate.

(7) The costs of a successful appeal to the Secretary of State cannot be recovered by a claimant from the acquiring authority (*Hull and Humber Investment Co* v *Hull Corporation* [1965] 2 WLR 161). See however *Tysons (Contractors) Ltd* v *Minister of Housing and Local Government* (1965) 18 P & CR 91, as to the costs of an application to the High Court arising out of a certificate of alternative development.

(8) Any person with an interest in the land can obtain information about the application.

(9) If the owner is absent or cannot be found, special procedures apply(s 19).

(10) If a certificate is granted for an area only part of which is subsequently acquired, the statutory assumption based on the certificate will not apply irrespective of circumstances. However the owner may be able to claim compensation for losses due to the severance of the land acquired (*Hoveringham Gravels Ltd* v *Chiltern District Council* (1977) 35 P & CR 295).

As to the procedure for obtaining, and appealing against a refusal of, a certificate, see the Land Compensation Development Order 1974 (SI 1974 No. 539 as amended by SI 1986 No 435).

As to challenge of a certificate within six weeks in the High Court under s 21 see *Inglewood Investment Co Ltd* v *Minister of Housing and Local Government and Staffordshire Country Council* (1961) 13 P & CR 17; *Parrish* v *Minister of Housing and Local Government* (1961) 13 P & CR 32.

Chapter 27

Severance and Injurious Affection

The right to compensation for severance and injurious affection rests upon the Compulsory Purchase Act 1965, and the statutory provisions are as follows:

(1) Section 7 (which is substantially the same as s 63, Land Clauses Consolidation Act 1845):

In assessing the compensation to be paid... regard shall be had... to the damage, if any, to be sustained by the owner of the land by reason of the severing of the land purchased from the other land of the owner, or otherwise injuriously affecting that other land by the exercise of the powers conferred by this or the special Act.

(2) Section 19 (5) (where part only of the land comprised in a lease for a term of years unexpired is required by the acquiring authority):

Every such lessee shall be entitled to receive from the acquiring authority compensation for the damage done to him in his tenancy by reason of the severance of the land required by the acquiring authority from that not required or otherwise by reason of the execution of the works.

(3) Section 20 (2) (relating to a tenant who has no greater interest than as a tenant for a year or from year to year):

If a part only of such land is required he shall also be entitled to compensation for the damage done to him in his tenancy by severing the land held by him or otherwise injuriously affecting it.

Compensation for the land acquired will be assessed on the basis of the value of the land as severed, not as part of the whole (*Abbey Homesteads Group Ltd* v *Secretary of State for Transport* (1982) 263 EG 983). The compensation is payable where other retained land of the owner is less valuable to him through that retained land being severed from or otherwise injuriously affected by the compulsory acquisition of the land taken. (*Hoveringham Gravels Ltd* v *Chiltern*

District Council (1977) 35 P & CR 295 CA.) It appears to be possible that the consequence of separate assessment of values for both land taken and damage by severance may be to produce an aggregate which is less than the loss suffered by the entire holding.

1 Conditions of claim

Usually a claim is made in respect of contiguous or adjacent land. But contiguity is not essential if several parcels of land are held together in such a way that each contributes to the value of the whole (*Cowper Essex* v *Acton Local Board* (1889) 14 App Cas 153; *University College, Oxford* v *Secretary of State for Air* [1938] 1 KB 648). It is not essential that all the land is held under the same title—see *Oppenheimer* v *Ministry of Transport* [1942] 1 KB 242 where a claimant owned a house but had only an option to purchase the land acquired.

A claim can be made not only when the works and use would amount to a nuisance, if unprotected by statutory powers, but also when the acquiring authority's works and uses would be legal if carried out by a private owner. Provided that injury is sustained, a claim will lie. Where, for example, land was sold at agricultural value for a council housing estate, the Lands Tribunal accepted a claim for injurious affection to residential property retained by the former owner, by reason of the effect of the council estate upon the amenity and character of the neighbourhood, and the possibility of trespass by children and others (*Walker* v *Doncaster Rural District Council* (1955) 6 P & CR 47).

Compensation is claimable both for the construction of works and their use. The courts used to hold, however, that on the wording of s 7 of the Compulsory Purchase Act 1965, regard could be had only to the effect on the land retained by the claimant of the works carried out on the land taken from the claimant himself and not to the whole of the works. The former rule is best exemplified in the case of *Edwards* v *Minister of Transport* [1964] 2 QB 134. In that case the claimant was the owner and occupier of a house with a garden and grounds of about 1.8 acres and also owned an adjacent field of 2.5 acres which was an amenity to the house. The Minister of Transport purchased compulsorily two small pieces of the claimant's land for the construction of a road the use of which injuriously affected the remainder of the claimant's land and the enjoyment of his house. However, most of the injurious affection arose from the use of parts of the road constructed on land not taken from the claimant and the

Court of Appeal held that he was entitled to recover compensation for the injurious affection only in respect of the use of that part constructed on the land taken from him (ie, £1,600, although the total injurious affection to his property due to the construction of the by-pass was admitted to be £4,000).

Section 44 of the Land Compensation Act 1973 reversed the effect of the decision in *Edwards'* case. It provides that where land is acquired from any person for the purpose of works to be situated partly on that land and partly elsewhere, compensation for injurious affection of land retained shall be assessed by reference to the whole of the works and not only the part on the land acquired from the claimant.

Under the principle in *Horn* v *Sunderland Corporation* [1941] 2 KB 26 CA—see p 217, below—an owner cannot get full building value *and* a payment for injurious affection. He would not get both in the open market, and cannot get both from the acquiring authority. He must decide whether the compensation will be greater by reference to development value or by reference to existing use value plus injurious affection and disturbance. Therefore if the acquisition had been at building instead of agricultural value in the *Doncaster* case, quoted above, the owner would probably not have succeeded in his claim for injurious affection. In *Bolton Metropolitan Borough Council* v *Waterworth and another* (1981) 259 EG 625, the Court of Appeal had to consider the depreciation in the value of retained land after severance. The retained land, which would have had residential value if developed with the acquired land, became temporarily incapable of development on its own through lack of access. The arbitrator had deferred the development value of the retained land for seven years from the date of severance based on the forecast date of planning permission made as at the date of severance. Planning permission for residential development of the retained land was in fact given about three and a half years after severance. The Court held that there was no error in law notwithstanding the decision in *Bwllfa and Merthyr Dare Steam Collieries (1891) Ltd* v *Pontypridd Waterworks Co* [1903] AC 426 (which established the principle that an arbitrator should not act upon conjecture if the facts were later established).

The decision in the *Bwllfa* case was also held not to apply in *ADP & E Farmers* v *Department of Transport* (1988) 28 RVR 58. A small area was acquired to form a motorway spur and as a result the development prospects of a much larger area of retained land were damaged. The acquiring authority claimed that alternative means of access were available so that the land could have been developed. A Section 17 certificate was issued for residential development of the land acquired. The tribunal held that the matters which led to the grant of the certificate could be strong evidence in relation to the adjoining land, so planning permission could be assumed for both the land taken and the retained land. The same result would be obtained by applying the *Pointe Gourde* principle and s 6 of the 1961 Act. Also, the method of valuing the land taken and the land retained as two separate interests was to be preferred (see the *Abbey Homesteads* case, p 177) as this accords with r 2 of s 5, with s 7 of the 1965 Act and with the *Stokes* v *Cambridge* principle (see p 176) in determining any ransom payment for an access. The *Bwllfa* principle could not be applied as it would take into account later events which have no bearing on the valuation as at the date of severance.

All future damage must be claimed for, as no subsequent claim can be made by the same owner—this at least is the generally accepted view though it lacks precise authority.

2 Accommodation works

In order to reduce the compensation payable for severance and injurious affection, it is usual for the acquiring authority to agree to do accommodation works. There is no statutory basis for this practice, except in the case of railway acquisitions. The sort of works which may be offered are as follows: new access ways; an underpass to rejoin severed agricultural land; fencing and gates; provision of water supply; and an alternative right of way. In the case of motorways only, it is the Department of Transport's policy to provide a fence or other suitable barrier along the boundaries of the motorway. Such fences are erected on land acquired for the highway, remain the Department's property and are maintained by them.

3 Examples of claim

Motorways which bisect large estates over several miles are among the commonest and most complex examples of today's cases of severance and injurious affection. For a claim which illustrates many points including severance, fencing responsibility, depreciation of fixed farm equipment, injurious affection and injury to sporting rights, see *Cuthbert* v *Secretary of State for the Environment* (1979) 252 EG 921. The tribunal adopted the approach that although a purchaser might well make some calculations under various heads, in the end he would make an overall assessment in deciding by how much he would reduce his bid for the land not taken. This approach was followed in *Wilson* v *Minister of Transport* (1980) 254 EG 875.

The list of examples which follows is based upon cases which have come before the Lands Tribunal. Nearly all involved severance and injurious affection on the acquisition of land. A few, however, have arisen under particular statutes providing for compensation for injury or damage, eg, the Public Health Act 1936 or the Land Drainage Act 1930. (Chapter 34 deals with a number of cases of this kind.)

(1) *Aerodrome*
    (*a*) Harmful effect of noise on sheep; more difficult farming through altered boundaries, etc (*Tory and Tory* v *Secretary of State for Air* (1960) 11 P & CR 458).
    (*b*) Harmful effect of aerodrome on mansion house and estate (*Dunne* v *Secretary of State for Air* (1959) 10 P & CR 157; *Tree* v *Secretary of State for Air* (1958) 9 P & CR 371).

(2) *Agricultural Land*
    (*a*) Difficulty of cultivation from loss of buildings: inaccessibility and inconvenience of buildings retained (*Tollemache* v *Richmond Corporation* (1953) 3 P & CR 331).
    (*b*) Orchard damaged by overflow from soakaway constructed as part of drainage works (*Chambers* v *British Transport Commission* (1962) 13 P & CR 326).
    (*c*) Sewage works causing smell noticeable by those living and working on farm (*Knowles and Geale* v *Droxford Rural District Council* (1961) 12 P & CR 187).
    (*d*) Aerodrome affecting farming and sporting rights (*Bomford* v *Minister of Supply* (1959) 10 P & CR 162).
    (*e*) Acquisition of farmland for naval air station leaves farm with high proportion of heavy wet land, larger buildings than needed and farmhouse unsuited to the holding (*Griffith* v *Admiralty* (1958) 9 P & CR 378).
    (*f*) Laying of sewer leaving clay on surface (*Lucey's Personal Representatives and Wood* v *Harrogate Corporation* (1963) 14 P & CR 376).
    (*g*) Two best fields taken: severance and injurious affection (*Barnes* v *Derbyshire CC* (1971) 212 EG 1179).
    (*h*) Electricity pylons across farm; interference with residential amenity of farmhouse; aerial crop spraying made very difficult (*Pryor* v *Central Electricity Generating Board* (1968) 206 EG 1143).

(3) *Barracks*

Injury to mansion house from use of land as naval barracks (*Brooke-Hitching* v *Admiralty* (1953) 4 P & CR 12).

(4) *Forecourt taken*

(*a*) Of shops (*Caine* v *Middlesex County Council* (1952) 3 P & CR 283).

(*b*) Of house (*Wignall* v *Lancaster County Council* (1953) 4 P & CR 155).

(5) *Housing estate*

(*a*) Effect of housing estate on house and parkland retained by vendor (*Walker* v *Doncaster Rural District Council* (1955) 6 P & CR 47).

(*b*) Housing estate obscuring view of hotel and causing loss of trade (*Holt* (*J*), *Ltd* v *Manchester Corporation* (1958) 10 P & CR 64).

(6) *Land drainage works*

(*a*) Collapse of bridge five years after works carried out by drainage board (*Strutt's Kingston Estate Settlement Trustees* v *Kingston Brook Internal Drainage Board* (1979) 251 EG 577, 677).

(*b*) Injury from flood prevention works on River Thames (*Thameside Estates Ltd* v *Greater London Council* (1979) 249 EG 347).

(7) *Pipe-line or sewer laid*

(*a*) Slight loss of developability arising from laying of water pipe (*Holroyd* v *Huddersfield Corporation* (1953) 4 P & CR 79).

(*b*) Sewer laid under garden of dwelling-house: damage to trees, hedges, etc (*Frost* v *Taunton Corporation* (1957) 9 P & CR 123).

(*c*) Sewer increasing value of land by an amount exceeding damage suffered (*Rush and Tompkins* v *West Kent Sewerage Board* (1963) 14 P & CR 469).

(*d*) See *Lucey's Personal Representatives and Wood* v *Harrogate Corporation*, para 2(*f*), above.

(*e*) Water pipe-line laid: damage to crops: farmer made error of judgement as to time to harvest crop (*Purser* v *Pembrokeshire Water Board* (1968) 205 EG 341).

(*f*) Garage premises blocked by excavations for public sewer: claim under s 278 of the Public Health Act 1936 and para 22 in the Third Sched, Water Act 1945 (*Whitehouse*

(*George*) *Ltd* (*trading as Clarke Bros* (*Services*)) v *Anglian Water Authority* (1978) 247 EG 223).

(*g*) Sewer laid under driveway in 1976 caused subsidence in 1978 and again later. Claim under s 278 of the Public Health Act 1936: the court decided that claim not statute barred as commenced within six years of later subsidence; authority could not escape liability for compensation by arguing that claimants should have sought damages from the sub-contractors who were negligent (*Smith Stone & Knight Ltd* v *City of Birmingham DC* (1988) EGCS 49).

(8) *Pylons*

    (*a*) See *Pryor* v *Central Electricity Board*, para 2(*h*), above.

    (*b*) Electric line and pylon erected over residential building land in course of development. Injurious affection from visual impact; apprehension about television reception and fear of breakage: noise from discharge and access for maintenance (*Turris Investments Ltd* v *Central Electricity Generating Board* (1981) 258 EG 1303).

(9) *Road*

    (*a*) Road widening leaving housing eight feet nearer road (*Clark* v *East Sussex County* (1961) 13 P & CR 93).

    (*b*) Betterment on road widening greater than injury (*Grosvenor Motor Co Ltd* v *Chester Corporation* (1963) 14 P & CR 478).

(10) *Sewage Works*

    (*a*) See *Knowles and Geale* v *Droxford Rural District Council*, para 2(*c*), above.

    (*b*) Effect on farm (*Russell* v *Bradfield Rural District Council* (1957) 8 P & CR 432; *Colman* v *Basingstoke RDC* (1966) 17 P & CR 270, and *Wathall* v *Uttoxeter RDC* (1968) 206 EG 601).

(11) *Severance*

    (*a*) Land intended for garage use severed from adjoining petrol filling station by compulsory acquisition for housing of intervening land (*Brain and Drive Yourself Hire Co* (*London*) v *London County Council* (1957) 9 P & CR 113).

    (*b*) Caravan site and storage land: more difficult access (*Humphries* v *Bracknell Development Corporation* (1962) 185 EG 665).

    (*c*) Land with light industrial consent: six acres severed but sufficient access from claimant's adjoining land (*Freevale Properties* v *Hastings Borough Council* (1961) 178 EG 153).

(*d*) Front land acquired by county council and back land by district council. Both front and back land in the same ownership. The Court of Appeal required the Lands Tribunal to consider whether there was loss arising by the severance of the back land (*Hoveringham Gravels Ltd* v *Chiltern District Council* (1979) 252 EG 815).

(*e*) Backs of houses acquired but tribunal unconvinced of development potential—whether adequate and intelligible reasons were given (*R A Vine (Engineering) Ltd* v *Havant Borough Council* (1989) EGCS 5).

(12) *Soakaway*

See *Chambers* v *British Transport Commission*, para 2(*b*) above.

Chapter 28

Disturbance

As has been seen earlier r 6 in s 5 of the Land Compensation Act 1961 leaves undisturbed the right of an owner to claim compensation for disturbance. The rule reads 'The provisions of Rule 2 shall not affect the assessment of compensation for disturbance or any other matter not directly based on the value of land'. The interpretation of the courts is that disturbance is part of the purchase price not a separate and distinct head of claim (*Horn* v *Sunderland Corporation* [1941] 2 KB 26). However judges are not always able to maintain what seems a rather artificial distinction. Lord Denning for example said in *Bailey* v *Derby Corporation* [1965] 1 All ER 443: 'The only two heads of compensation are these:

(i)   the value of the land: you have to find the value of the land as in the open market between a willing vendor and a willing purchaser;

(ii) compensation for disturbance: you have to find the loss which the claimant suffered by reason of the compulsory acquisition of the land.'

In a more recent case, *Munton* v *Newham London Borough Council* (1976) 32 P & CR 269, Lord Denning has put with great clarity the reasons for treating disturbance separately, and it is helpful to set out a quotation from his judgement in full:

'The second point of law is whether, in order to be binding, there has to be one entire sum agreed that comprises not only the value of the property itself but also the compensation for disturbance. It was decided in 1845 that the injury was only as to the "value of the land," as it was held that in this sum there was to be included the compensation for disturbance; so that only one sum was to be awarded. That seems to be the effect of *Commissioners of Inland Revenue* v *Glasgow & South-Western Railway Co* (1887) 12 App Cas 315 and *Horn* v *Sunderland Corporation* [1941] 2 KB 26. But although only one sum is

213

awarded, it is very proper, in assessing it, to divide it into two parts, (i) the land itself, and (ii) disturbance. Starting with the Acquisition of Land Act 1919 and repeated in the Land Compensation Act 1961, Parliament itself has made a division between the two. In s 5 (6) it says: "The provisions of rule (2)"—that is, about the value of the land—"shall not affect the assessment of compensation for disturbance or any other matter not directly based on the value of land." Since those Acts, the practice always has been for the compensation for disturbance to be assessed separately from the value of the land. That is as it should be. The value of the land can be assessed while the owner is still in occupation, but the compensation for disturbance cannot be properly assessed until he goes out. It is only then that he can tell how much it has cost him to move, such as to get extra premises or to move his furniture. The practice is warranted by two cases in this court: *Harvey* v *Crawley Development Corporation* [1957] 1 QB 485 and *Lee* v *Minister of Transport* [1966] 1 QB 111. In my opinion that is a quite proper view, for the local authority to agree in the first place with the owner on the value of the house itself and to leave till later the compensation for disturbance. That can be assessed later, when the local authority go into occupation and the house-owner moves.'

Whether seen as a separate head of compensation or not, there is no doubt that the disturbance claim is an important element in many cases, particularly those involving the acquisition of commercial or industrial premises. Very often the business interest is leasehold and may attract modest compensation. The disturbance claim for loss of profits, removal expenses, other expenses and professional fees may greatly exceed the sum assessed as compensation for acquiring the legal interest.

A dispossessed owner is entitled to be compensated for his loss due to the acquisition, provided, in the words of Romer LJ, in *Harvey* v *Crawley Development Corporation* [1957] 1 All ER 504 'first that it is not too remote and secondly that it is the natural and reasonable consequence of the dispossession of the owner'.

Compensation is based on the principle of 'equivalence'. Broadly speaking an owner should not be left worse off than if his land had not been acquired. All the same he should not get any undue advantage.

1 Items of claim

It is probably easiest to understand this head of claim by considering some of the items usually claimed under it.

(*a*) Costs of moving stock and machinery to new premises;

(b) Depreciation in value of stock or machinery due to removal;

(c) Costs of notifying removal to clients or customers; new note-paper, bill-heads, etc;

(d) Telephone removals;

(e) Architect's fees on survey of new premises, or preparation of plans for a new building;

(f) Legal costs and stamp duty on purchase of a comparable property; also the surveyor's fees, and the travelling expenses in finding a suitable property. But only an owner-occupier may claim under this heading. An investment owner is not disturbed from the land, and does not qualify (*Harvey* v *Crawley Development Corporation* [1957] 1 QB 485);

(g) Costs of maintaining two sets of premises temporarily during removal including a double payment of rates and other expenses. These costs are often referred to as 'double overheads';

(h) Loss of goodwill;

(i) Temporary loss of profit, eg, resulting from dislocation of business during removal;

(j) Statutory redundancy payments.

A case which illustrates many of the possible items of claim is *Appleby and Ireland* v *Hampshire Country Council* (1978) 247 EG 1183, 248 EG 54, 143, 235 and 326. See also for further illustrations *W J Mogridge (Bristol 1937) Ltd* v *Bristol Corporation* (1956) 8 P & CR 78, and *Jones, Jones and Jones* v *Edmonton Corporation* (1956) 8 P & CR 86 (see p 221).

Each case of disturbance must be considered on its merits. So in *Herrburger Brooks Ltd* v *St Pancras Corporation* (1960) 11 P & CR 390, dispossessed timber merchants were held to be entitled to the costs of a watchman to guard a new site and to the cost of providing it with a fence, as well as for an extra insurance premium.

In *Walkes-Hilliman* v *Greater London Council* (1969) 20 P & CR 736, following *Northwood* v *London Country Council* [1962] 2 KB 411, the Lands Tribunal held that disturbance could not be paid where compensation was based on cleared site value in accordance with s 59 (2) of the Housing Act 1957 (succeeded by s 585 of the Housing Act 1985). But a disturbance payment can now be claimed under s 37 (2) (b) (ii) of the Land Compensation Act 1973 provided that an owner-occupier's supplement is not payable as well.

Claims must not be for items too remote, eg, hypothetical costs and profits or costs incurred not flowing directly from acquisition. In *Rutter* v *Manchester Corporation* (1974) 28 P & CR 443, a tenant successfully claimed increased travel to work costs, the Lands Tribunal holding that it was a natural and reasonable consequence of dispossession, was not too remote and was capable of quantification.

In *Bibby &Sons Ltd* v *Mersey County Council* (1977) 34 P & CR 101, the claimant had taken on lease the whole of an office block of 160,000 square feet to replace 47,500 square feet of office space compulsorily acquired. They had sublet all but two floors. The tribunal held that the move was reasonable but that taking the whole building was not the reasonable and direct consequence of the acquisition. Fees, legal costs and other expenses were accordingly scaled down to what would have been appropriate if two floors only had been taken. This decision was affirmed by the Court of Appeal: (1979) 39 P & CR 53.

In *Bloom (Kosher) & Sons Ltd* v *London Borough of Tower Hamlets* (1977) 35 P & CR 423, the Lands Tribunal held that loss occurring before acquisition could not be compensated. The claim in that case was for professional fees in and about the purchase of alternative premises; losses on non-removable plant and machinery; capital expenditure on alterations to machinery to make it suitable for transfer; costs of altering the new premises, and double overheads. The claimants moved before the compulsory purchase order was made but in the belief that their premises would be acquired in the near future. The tribunal allowed the claim for disturbance, but only for losses occurring after the date of notice to treat. This decision was not followed in *Smith* v *Strathclyde Regional Council* (1981) 42 P & CR 397, and the view of the tribunal in *Bloom's case* appears to be overruled by the decision of the Court of Appeal in *Prasad and another* v *Wolverhampton Borough Council* [1983] JPL 449. This case was admittedly on the wording of s 37 of the Land Compensation Act 1973 (see p 151). However the Court of Appeal accepted that before the 1973 Act made special provision for disturbance claims, the law permitted 'expenses or loss reasonably incurred before being given notice to treat, actual or deemed' to be paid as compensation for disturbance. The test appears to be whether 'a person, threatened with inevitable dispossession because of compulsory acquisition, acts reasonably in moving to other accommodation before being given notice to treat or before his land is actually acquired by compulsory purchase,' per Stephenson LJ.

Where a regional development grant of 22 per cent was payable on items within a disturbance claim, the Court of Appeal held that the amount of the grant should not be deducted from the compensation payable for disturbance. It would be contrary to public policy to lessen the inducement afforded by payment of a grant to relocate in a development area by deducting the amount of the grant (*Palatine Graphic Arts Co Ltd* v *Liverpool City Council* [1986] 2 WLR 185.

Where land has been acquired by general vesting declaration doubts were expressed as to whether the date of assessment for compensation of disturbance should be the same as that for the land, since disturbance was payable for actual loss (see *Park Automobile Co Ltd* v *Strathclyde Regional Council* (1983) 266 EG 729).

2 Disturbance from development land

In *Horn* v *Sunderland Corporation* [1941] 2 KB 26 CA, where a claim for compensation was made on the ground that land was building land, no claim was allowed for business disturbance. It follows that an owner must decide which basis of claim will give him the better compensation, either value at existing use plus a disturbance claim, or value as building land. He cannot have the best of both worlds, for if he sold in the open market to a builder, the latter would not pay him for disturbance and give full building value.

3 Increased rental or improved premises

A word of warning is needed about the possibility of claiming for an increased rental payable for alternative accommodation. In many cases such a claim will not be admissible because it will be a reasonable assumption that the higher rental will be for better premises or greater profitability. 'In so far as the claimant will incur additional expense by way of rent and rates over the rent and rates which might properly have been anticipated as payable for the old premises—such additional expense may be regarded as due to the additional advantages possessed by the new premises': per the tribunal in *Easton* v *Islington Corporation* (1952) 3 P & CR 145. See also *Greenberg* v *Grimsby Corporation* (1961) 12 P & CR 212.

The same reasoning is applied where there is evidence that the claimant has had value for the money he has expended on better alternative accommodation.

In *Bibby & Sons Ltd* v *Mersey County Council* (p 216) the Lands Tribunal disallowed a claim for the fees of an office planning consultant for a report, preparation of plans and supervision of installation because 'this expenditure gave the claimants advantages, including landscaped offices, over and above those which they enjoyed at their old offices and they had value for money'.

In *Smith* v *Birmingham Corporation* (1974) 29P & CR 265, the

Lands Tribunal rejected a claim for structural alterations and improvements to alternative premises as the claimant had received 'value for his money' in the shape of improved premises.

In *Service Welding Ltd* v *Tyne and Wear County Council* (1977) 34 P & CR 228 the claimants built a new factory, thus helping to mitigate loss and there being no alternative factory available. They claimed that the interest and charges on the loan to build the factory should be allowed for in the compensation. The Court of Appeal held that where an owner rehoused himself in alternative accommodation, he was not entitled to recover, by way of compensation for disturbance or otherwise, any part of the purchase price for the alternative (including interest charges) since there was a rebuttable presumption that he had received value for money. As to bank charges and interest, see also *B & T (Essex)* v *Shoreditch Corporation* (1958) 9 P & CR 471, and as to a building loan *Coulson* v *Borough of Bury St Edmunds* (1969) 210 EG 1246. In *Simpson* v *Stoke-on-Trent City Council* (1982) 44 P & CR 226, a householder was refused additional compensation for the interest on a bridging loan, since taking the loan was unreasonable in the circumstances.

In *Bibby's* case (above) in the Court of Appeal, Brandon LJ considered that compensation could be awarded for extra operating costs if there was no alternative and the claimant had no benefit as a result, but this was not the case as the Lands Tribunal had evidence on which it could find that increased cost was offset by resultant advantages.

Where a tenant has an unexpired term of a lease and the rental is less than the current market rents for similar accommodation, ie, is a profit rental, the tenant will be entitled, as part of the purchase money, to the value of the profit rental. Where such a claim is agreed, the tenant is cushioned against the effect of paying more for alternative accommodation. But in such a case he acquires the cushion as part of the value of the lands taken, and not as a disturbance claim.

However, there may still be cases where it can be shown that the alternative premises will cost more and with no equivalent benefit to the claimant. If the compensation including this factor is less than the compensation payable for total extinguishment of the business, then the item could be allowed.

4 Groups of companies

Problems can arise over disturbance claims where a commercial firm carries on business, for tax or other reasons, through separate companies, all interlinked. One may hold the firm's land, another provide the transport and yet another effectively carry on the business on the land of the first company. The legal owner of the land is not disturbed in these circumstances because the land-holding company carries on no business. The business-carrying-on company may have no legal interest in the land, certainly no long-term interest and therefore it may be argued that its disturbance claim can only be the negligible one of an occupier whose occupancy can be brought to an end in a short space of time.

Where compulsory purchase is threatened against a firm operating through wholly owned subsidiaries in this way the prudent course, very often adopted, is for the parent company to ensure that the land is conveyed from the land-holding company to the operating company. No stamp duty would be payable if, as is likely, the transaction were exempt under s 42 of the Finance Act 1930. The operating company would then be able to claim compensation both for the land (of which it would be the owner) and for disturbance, without any problem.

The need to carry out necessary conveyancing of this sort has been reduced by the decision of the Court of Appeal in *DHN Food Distributors (in Liquidation)* v *Tower Hamlets London Borough Council* (1976) 32 P & CR 240. Here three separate companies were treated as one. The 'corporate veil' was pierced to see the commercial realities of the situation. The three companies were 'virtually the same as a partnership in which all the three companies are partners. They should not be treated separately so as to be defeated on a technical point' (per Lord Denning MR). However the corporate veil may be more difficult to pierce in the case of a purchase notice (see *Rakusen Properties Ltd & others* v *Leeds City Council* (1978) 37 P & CR 315). Nevertheless, because it is normally not difficult to rearrange a company's affairs so as to avoid any technical point being taken, it may well be more prudent to do so before notice to treat is served. There should be no conflict with s 4 of the Acquisition of Land Act 1981 (see p 56) which deals with the creation of new interests with a view to obtaining increased compensation.

5 Goodwill and alternative premises

Goodwill is the probability of the continuance of a business connection. If a trader is ejected compulsorily, his goodwill is affected, more or less, depending upon the type of business carried on, the area served, and whether alternative premises can be found or not. In a compulsory acquisition there is no purchase of the goodwill of the business as such. But under the heading of disturbance, compensation is paid for permanent or temporary loss of profits consequent upon the move. See *Park Automobile Co Ltd* v *City of Glasgow District Council* (1975) 30 P & CR 491, as to absence of goodwill in the removal of a petrol filling station to a new site a mile away; no deduction from the compensation was made for any possible recovery of business profits.

Where trade premises are being acquired, the authority very often will make an offer of alternative accommodation, with a view to reducing the claim for disturbance. Each case must be considered on its facts, the test always being whether the premises offered are reasonable, and if they are rejected, whether the claim has acted reasonably in so doing.

For a case of unreasonable refusal, see *Pettingale* v *Stockport Corporation* (1961) 12 P & CR 384; and for ones where the claimant was justified in refusing the alternative offered, see *Tappy and Tappy* v *London County Council* (1954) 5 P & CR 105, and *Line & Sons Ltd* v *Newcastle upon Tyne Corporation* (1965) 6 P & CR 466. In *Knott Mill Carpets* v *Stretford Borough Council* (1973) 26 P & CR 129, it was held that the extinguishment basis (see below) could be claimed if the alternative premises offered were at too high a rental for profitable operation.

Similarly in *Lindon Print Ltd* v *West Midlands County Council* (1986) 283 EG 70, the claimants made 'honest serious and indeed strenuous' attempts to find alternative premises. They had not failed reasonably to mitigate their losses, the onus of proof of such failure being on the authority; accordingly losses would be assessed on the basis of total extinguishment and this was evidently a case to exercise the tribunal's power to assess compensation for loss of goodwill by a robust decision.

Where no alternative premises are available, compensation for disturbance may be based on total extinguishment of the business (*Barlow* v *Hackney Corporation* (1954) 5 P & CR 129; *Mitchell* v *Bristol Corporation* (1956) 8 P & CR 59; *Somers and Somers* v *Doncaster Corporation* (1965) 16 P & CR 323). In a business extinguishment on compulsory acquisition the measure of compensation is 'the value to the claimant' not 'the value in the market'. The loss suffered by an expropriated trader is the ability to derive a future profit out of the premises from which he has been dispossessed. (See *Shulman (J) (Tailors)* v *Greater London Council* (1966) 17 P & CR 244; *Watson and another* v *Warrington Borough Council* (1975) 250 EG 977, and *Afzal* v *Rochdale Metropolitan Borough Council* (1980) EG 512.)

If a claimant becomes ill through no fault of the acquiring authority, he cannot found a claim on the basis of total extinguishment. His state of health is an independent matter and losses flowing from it cannot be the subject of compensation (*Bailey* v *Derby Corporation* [1965] 1 WLR 213). See, however, the special provisions below for traders and businessmen aged 60 and over at the time possession is given up.

Even if a business might have ceased trading for reasons other than the threat of compulsory acquisition this will not prevent a claim for disturbance on the basis of total extinguishment if the threat of compulsory purchase made cessation a certainty (*Wharvesto* v *Cheshire County Council* (1983) RVR 232).

For a case on goodwill and the duty of claimants to mitigate loss by selling a declining business, see *Shulman* (*J*) (*Tailors*) *Ltd* v *Greater London Council* (1966) 17 P & CR 244. In *Bede Distributors Ltd* v *Newcastle upon Tyne Corporation* (1973) 26 P & CR 298, it was held to be reasonable for a company with limited financial liquidity to go into liquidation rather than move to available alternative premises.

An offer of alternative premises by the acquiring authority can be important in other ways than in connection with goodwill. In *Jones, Jones and Jones* v *Edmonton Corporation* (see p 215), the claimants sought to recover for additional transport costs due to the 'extra mileage from the new site over old to customers' factories, etc, for picking up scrap, etc'. The tribunal held that the items were not allowable because the claimants voluntarily chose to occupy the distant site in preference to the alternative offered by the corporation. On the other hand (and somewhat paradoxically) the tribunal held that the claimants were entitled to the costs of removing stock and machinery to the new distant site, and no diminution was made for the fact that an alternative site had been offered nearer. It would seem from this that if an alternative site has been reasonably refused, the claimant will get his costs of stock removal in full, provided that the new site is not an unreasonable distance from the old.

Assessment of compensation for loss of goodwill is essentially a valuation matter. It is usually based on an average of the previous three years' profits, arrived at after deducting rent, interest on capital, labour, material and other expenses. The average profit is multiplied by an appropriate number of years' purchase, in accordance with what the market would pay. This could vary from two to five years' purchase.

For cases on the valuation of goodwill, see *Roy v Westminster City Council* (1975) 31 P & CR 458 (medical practice) and *Tragett v Surrey Heath Borough Council* (1975) 237 EG 423 (sports shop).

6 Extinguishment compensation for persons over 60

Where a trader cannot reasonably reinstate himself, compensation can be paid on the basis of total extinguishment of his business. If, however, the trader chooses not to reinstate his business because of age, he would only be entitled on the basis of the temporary loss he would have suffered if he had moved. The 1973 Act improved the position of traders aged 60 and over in this type of case.

Section 46 of the Land Compensation Act 1973 permits compensation to be assessed on the basis of total extinguishment provided the person has attained the age of 60 when he gives up possession and gives certain undertakings to the acquiring authority. The effect is to enable older traders to elect to give up their business and to be compensated for their actual resulting loss.

Eligibility under the section is, however, limited as in the blight provisions to hereditaments below the prescribed annual value, currently a rateable value of £18,000 (SI 1990 No 465).

The undertakings are to prevent sale of the goodwill or re-engagement in a similar trade or business.

There are provisions for partnerships and small businesses trading as limited companies.

The section also applies to dispossessed business occupiers who have no compensatable interest in the land but receive disturbance payments (see s 46(7)). In practice this seems to cover protected tenants of combined house and shop properties governed by the Rent Acts and business tenants holding over after their tenancy has expired.

7 Tenants

The holders of short tenancies who receive a notice under s 20 of the Compulsory Purchase Act 1965 (see p 68) are entitled to any loss due to disturbance as part of the compensation. If the tenant is allowed to stay on in possession until the end of his tenancy, it is obvious that he will not normally be able to substantiate a claim for disturbance, though he may qualify for a disturbance payment under s 37 of the Land Compensation Act 1973.

Section 39 (1) of the Landlord and Tenant Act 1954 provided that compensation payable on compulsory acquisition should be assessed without regard to the tenant's right to apply for a new tenancy under Pt II of that Act. This provision was considered to be unfair, and s 39 (1) was repealed by s 47 of the Land Compensation Act 1973. The right to a renewal is accordingly taken into account.

In the case of business premises, a 'floor' to the compensation is still provided by s 39 (2) of the Landlord and Tenant Act 1954. Compensation under s 20 of the 1965 Act is not to be below the level which the tenant would have obtained under s 37 of the 1954 Act if the date of obtaining possession had been the termination of the tenancy. The tenant will therefore get at least three times the rateable value (or six times the rateable value in the case of 14-year occupations) (these are the figures under the Landlord and Tenant Act 1954 (Appropriate Multiplier) Regulations 1984 (SI 1984 No 1932) but a new multiplier applies where the rateable value is determined on or after 1 April 1990 (see Landlord and Tenant Act 1954 (Appropriate Multiplier) Order 1990 (SI 1990 No 363)).

8 Disturbance payments

This is the place to give a reminder of the duty which acquiring authorities have under s 37 of the Land Compensation Act 1973. This section is mainly designed to compensate occupiers for disturbance in cases where no legal interest exists. See Chapter 21.

9 Fees

Professional fees which are payable in respect of an alternative premises are payable as part of the disturbance claim, provided that they are reasonable and are not caught by the rule that a claimant may not recover for 'value received'. (*London County Council* v *Tobin* [1959] 1 All ER 649; 10 P & CR 79.) Professional fees, for example incurred before and after notice to treat in examining the possible adaptation of the remainder of the property after acquisition of part, were allowed by the Lands Tribunal in *Smith* v *Strathclyde Regional Council* (1981) 42 P & CR 397.

Fees which are payable as part of the disturbance claim need to be contrasted with fees incurred in formulating a claim for compensation. These fees (normally those of a valuer but perhaps also those of an accountant) are to be regarded as compensation for 'any other matter not directly based on the value of land' under r 6. The effect is that these fees can be the subject of compensation in purchase notice cases where 'disturbance' is excluded from compensation (*Lee* v *Minister of Transport* [1966] 1 QB 111; 17 P & CR 181).

Surveyor's fees on RICS Scale 5 may be limited by the extent to which there is any actual negotiation as opposed to acceptance of proposals for accommodation works (*Mahood* v *Department of the Environment for Northern Ireland* (1985) 277 EG 654).

Chapter 29

Compensation for Injurious Affection Where No Lands Taken

Chapter 27 dealt with compensation for severance or injurious affection of land held with land being compulsorily acquired. This chapter deals with the converse case where the authority's scheme or works cause damage, but where the claimant has had no land taken for the scheme or works. The chapter is in two parts:

(1) the law as it stood before the passing of the Land Compensation Act 1973;

(2) an explanation of the rights conferred by Pt 1 of the Act of 1973 to compensation for depreciation caused by the use of works first brought into use since 17 October 1969.

1 Under the Compulsory Purchase Act 1965

The heading to s 68 of the Lands Clauses Act 1845 provided for 'compensation, where more than £50 claimed, to be settled by arbitration or jury, at option of claimant'. The commencing part of the section reads as follows:

If any party shall be entitled to compensation in respect of any lands, or of any interest therein, which shall have been taken for, or injuriously affected by the execution of the works and for which the promoters of the undertaking shall not have made satisfaction under the provisions of this or the special Act or any Act incorporated therewith, and if the compensation claimed in such case shall exceed the sum of fifty pounds, such party may have the same settled either by arbitration or by the verdict of a jury as he shall think fit.

In spite of the ambiguity of the wording of this section, a long series of decided cases had established that s 68 provided a remedy for injuries caused by the works, or authorised by the Act, to the lands of an owner who had had none of the lands taken in that locality. The remedy was given because Parliament, by authorising the works, had prevented damage caused by them from being actionable, and the compensation was given as a substitute for damages at law.

Section 68 was superseded by s 10 of the Compulsory Purchase Act 1965, which provides in similar terms to s 68 for the assessment of disputed compensation by the Lands Tribunal. The section continues by reaffirming the right to compensation granted by s 68 of the 1845 Act:

This section shall be construed as affording in all cases a right to compensation for injurious affection to land which is the same as the right which s 68 of the Lands Clauses Consolidation Act 1845 has been construed as affording in cases where the amount claimed exceeds fifty pounds.

The present law can therefore largely be ascertained by considering cases decided under s 68 of the 1845 Act. Three such important cases are *Ricket* v *Metropolitan Rly Co* (1867) LR 2 HL 175; *Metropolitan Board of Works* v *McCarthy* (1874) LR 7 HL 243, and *Caledonian Rly Co* v *Walker's Trustees* (1882) 7 App Cas 259 HL.

(a) Conditions of claim

A claim under s 68 of the Lands Clauses Consolidation Act 1845 had to satisfy the following conditions (often referred to as the four rules in *McCarthy's* case) (quoted above). These would apply also to claims made under s 10 of the Compulsory Purchase Act 1965:

  (i) The injurious act must be authorised by the statutory powers. This means that if the damage arises coincidentally and not directly from the exercise of the statutory powers, the person injured will have to rely for a remedy on the general law and not on s 68 (see *Clowes* v *Staffordshire Potteries Waterworks Co* (1872) 8 Ch App 125).

  (ii) The damage must be actionable but for the existence of the statutory powers. (See *Re Penny and South Eastern Railway Co* (1857) 7 E & B 660: loss of privacy not actionable.)

  (iii) The injury must be to land. If the right of action which would have existed would have been merely personal without reference to land or its incidents, compensation is not due under s 68. As a result an owner is not entitled to compensation for damage to his trade or business, or for damage resulting in personal loss or inconvenience, unless such damage is reflected in the depreciation in the value of the land. See the *Argyle Motors* case mentioned under subhead (*b*) below (p 228).

  (iv) When damage arises not out of the execution of the works, but only out of their subsequent use, no case for compensation arises (*Hammersmith and City Ry Co v Brand* (1869) LR 4 HL 171). However, if s 68 is the only provision for compensation, and the statutory powers for the works include construction and maintenance or user, eg, to build a reservoir and maintain a supply of water to it, then compensation may be claimed not only for injury by construction but also for the user of the works after construction (provided that there is some depreciation in the value of the land so that the claim qualifies under condition (iii) above). However, if the special Act makes provision for compensation limited only to injury by 'construction' as, for example, in the case of the Railway Clauses Act 1845, instead of by 'execution' as in the Lands Clauses Consolidation Act 1845, then no claim can be made for injury by use (*Fletcher v Birkenhead Corporation* [1907] 1 KB 205 and *Re Simeon and Isle of Wight RDC* [1937] Ch 525). It seems doubtful whether the extension of the normal rule allowed in this type of case will be of frequent application, and in any event there is less need to have recourse to s 68 in future because of the Land Compensation Act 1973 (see p 228).

(b) Claims rarely admissible

An examination of the proceedings of the Lands Tribunal will show very few cases of claims made under s 68. This is because of the difficulty of bringing a case within the rules, built up over the years, which govern the application of s 68. (See for example *Roberts v Holyhead UDC* (1962) 14 P & CR 358.) Examples of admissible claims are as follows:

(1) *Restrictive covenants*—Where land is purchased subject to a restrictive covenant, the covenantee cannot maintain an action against the acquiring authority, as purchaser, for breach of the covenant; his remedy is compensation under s 68 (see p 94).

(2) *Right of support*—Where there is interference with the support to which the owner of a building is by law entitled, and damage is occasioned, such owner has a right to claim for compensation under s 68 (*Metropolitan Board of Works v McCarthy* (1874) LR 7 HL 243; see also *Till and others v Fnchley Borough Council* (1954) 4 P & CR 362 (removal of support by demolition of adjoining house)).

(3) *Right to light*—If an acquiring authority obstruct a right of ancient lights by building, the adjoining owner has a right to claim compensation under s 68 (*Wigram v Fryer* (1887) 36 Ch D 87).

(4) *Access to highway*—If the physical access to a public highway is taken away or rendered less convenient, and the property is depreciated as a result, compensation is payable. 'The obstruction by the execution of the work of a man's direct access to his house or land, whether such access be by a public road or by a private way, is a proper subject for compensation' (Lord Selborne in *Walker's Trustees* case, quoted above, at p 225, where access was rendered less direct and steeper).

(5) *Private access*—If there is interference with a private right of way, even though only a quasi-easement appurtenant to tenure, compensation will be payable if the value of the interest is depreciated by the interference (*Ford and others* v *The Metropolitan and Metropolitan District Rly Cos* (1886) 17 QBD 12, which concerned a continuous and apparent easement passing with the lease of three rooms in a house).

(6) *Riparian owners*—These owners will be entitled to compensation if there is interference with the natural flow of water (*R* v *Nottingham Old Waterworks Co* (1837) 6 Ad & El 362). However, most cases today are likely to be governed by the provisions of the Water Act 1989 (which replace the statutory code in the Water Act 1945).

(7) *Sporting rights*—Provided that the right is not a mere licence, compensation for interference may be payable (*Bird* v *Gt Eastern Rly Co* (1865) 34 LJCP 366).

Where compensation under s 68 of the Lands Clauses Act or s 10 of the Compulsory Purchase Act is payable, interest will be payable from the date of claim until payment (s 63 of the Land Compensation Act 1973).

On the other hand it has been held that no compensation is claimable in the following events:

(1) *Water rights*—Interference with an underground flow of water, unless there is a prescriptive or other right to it, is not compensatable under s 68 (*New River Co* v *Johnson* (1860) 29 LJMC 93).

(2) *Privacy*—Interference with the privacy of lands through their being overlooked from a road or a railway embankment cannot found a claim under s 68 (*Re Penny* (1857) 26 LJQB 225).

(3) *Stopping-up of highways*—The owner of a filling station was not entitled to compensation for loss of business occasioned by a stopping-up order under s 49 of the Town and Country Planning Act 1947 even though land in the vicinity of the garage was acquired compulsorily for the execution of works (*Jolliffe* v *Exeter Corporation* [1967] 2 All ER 1099). In this case the Court of Appeal

reversed the judgment at first instance. They held that the plaintiff's loss flowed wholly from the closure of the street in which his filling station was sited. He could not be compensated because there was no compensation provided for under s 49 of the 1947 Act. The fact that the stopping-up order was part of a scheme to construct an inner-relief road for Exeter, for which purpose the compulsory acquisition had been made, could not give the land owner a right to succeed under s 68. (There is still no compensation in the successor s 209 of the Act of 1971, although there is provision for compensation in pedestrianisation schemes under s 212.) (See p 284.)

See also *Argyle Motors (Birkenhead) Ltd* v *Birkenhead Corporation* (1974) 27 P & CR 122 HL. In that case a street was temporarily stopped up under a Private Act of Parliament. The Act incorporated s 68 of the Lands Clauses Act 1845. The scheme done under the Act eventually converted the street into a cul-de-sac, and it was held by the House of Lords that the company were entitled to compensation under s 68 for injurious affection to their interest in the land as a yearly tenant but not for damages for loss of profits as such even though the loss might far exceed the compensation for injurious affection.

(4) *Subsequent use*—If the damage arises not out of the execution but only out of the subsequent use of the work, no compensation is payable unless the case can be brought within the sort of special circumstances which arose in *Fletcher* v *Birkenhead Corporation* (see under subhead (*a*) above).

2 Land Compensation Act 1973: depreciatio*-+ caused by use of public works

Because of the severe restrictions placed upon the interpretation of s 68 of the Lands Clauses Consolidation Act 1845 or s 10 of the Compulsory Purchase Act 1965, compensation was not usually payable where depreciation had been caused by the *use of public works constructed on land not taken* from the claimant.

Part I of the Land Compensation Act 1973 remedied this for owners and landlords of dwelling-houses and owner-occupiers of small business premises and of farms. It created a new right to compensation for injurious affection to land not taken from the claimant caused by physical factors arising from the use of new or substantially altered public works. Compensation is payable by the authority responsible for those works to the person making a claim within the time limit specified in s 3.

It has been a basic principle of the law of compensation since 1845 that compensation for injurious affection is only payable where the right of action for nuisance has been taken away by statute. The provisions of the 1973 Act adopt this rule so that they do not apply to works constructed and used in circumstances where statutory powers afford no protection against action for nuisance.

The physical factors which confer an entitlement to compensation are noise, vibration, smells, fumes, smoke, artificial lighting and the deposit of any liquid or solid substance onto the land in respect of which the claim is made. Interference with a view is not included in this list—it may be an obstruction of a right to light, but cannot be the subject of a claim under s 1. A claimant whose property overlooked a new maximum security prison could not claim for loss of a view, but he might claim for the depreciating effect of the security lighting burning throughout the night.

The right to compensation must relate directly to physical factors caused by the use of public works which first came into use or were substantially altered on or after 17 October 1969. The right is for damage caused by personal loss or inconvenience, not for trade loss. If a new motorway results in reduced business, the Act of 1973 does not give a new right to compensation for loss of profits. But compensation will be paid to the extent that the property has depreciated in value due to the physical injurious effects.

(a) New works—types of claim

All highways first used since 17 October 1969 will produce eligibility. If noise is the basis of the claim, the noise must be created by traffic using the length of road near the land in respect of which the claim is made. A general increase in traffic, attributable to an increase in the number of motor vehicles, affecting the new road is not compensatable.

A highway authority is not liable for nuisance caused by the lawful use of a highway whether dedicated to the use of the public or constructed under statute. Highways are therefore included in public works for which compensation is payable without any qualification. But damage caused by a highway or aircraft accident is not covered, (s 1 (7))— although there may be a right of action in any event.

For examples of two unsuccessful claims see *Hickmott* v *Dorset County Council* (1977) 35 P & CR 195 (isolated improvement to sharp bend, involving widening road from 15 feet to 22 feet) and *Streak and Streak* v *Royal County of Berkshire* (1976) 32 P & CR 435 (noise attributable to railway and busy local road and not motorway).

For successful claims see *Barb* v *Secretary of State for Transport*

(1978) 247 EG 473 (two houses in country lane at Gerrard's Cross 630 metres and 730 metres from M40 motorway; depreciation of seven and a half per cent awarded) and *Marchant* v *Secretary of State for Transport* (1979) 250 EG 559 (bungalow in small rural village near Maidstone 597 metres from M20 motorway; £1,000 awarded).

The use of all new aerodromes will produce eligibility. All licensed aerodromes—in effect all the commercial aerodromes in the UK—are covered, ie, not only British Airports Authority or local authority airports, but those privately owned (see Air Navigation Order 1980, SI 1980 No 1965). Unlicensed airports do not acquire immunity from action for nuisance under s 77 of the Civil Aviation Act 1982 and do not need to be covered. Military airports (the section says 'any aerodrome in the occupation of a government department') are not within the section (see p 245).

Compensation is for noise originating in the airport and from aircraft 'arriving at or departing from' as well as on the ground. The intention is to exclude those in normal level flight.

The residual class covered by s 1 is '*Any works or land provided or used in the exercise of statutory powers*'. This includes such things as prisons, sewage works, and incineration plants, provided that the works enjoy immunity from an action for nuisance in respect of their use. For a case involving a refuse tip see *Shepherd* v *Lancashire County Council* (1976) 33 P & CR 296 where the Lands Tribunal found the tip to be unsightly, but was not satisfied that there was measurable depreciation due to the physical factors specified in s 1(2) of the Act of 1973. The tip had a life of six years. The tribunal held that the claim period began one year after the use of tip began and that temporary injury was not excluded from compensation.

It is a cardinal principle of this provision for compensation that it only covers cases where the works have been constructed pursuant to statutory powers which authorise the use and include an intention, express or implied, that the act may be done notwithstanding that it may injure the rights of others so long as the injury is within the contemplation of the statute. Whether there is immunity from an action for nuisance depends upon the circumstances of each case.

Because of the potential difficulty of deciding whether particular statutory provisions do or do not confer immunity from action for nuisance, s 17 provides that a responsible authority cannot affirm and later deny. If they once claim that they have no immunity (so that compensation under s 1 is not payable) they cannot in subsequent legal proceedings plead that in law they have such an immunity.

(b) Altered works

All that has preceded has been in relation to *new works*—new roads, new aerodromes, new public works, some completely new project.

The Act deals with *alterations* to public works and specifies the nature of the alterations which will enable claims to be made in the case of highways and aerodromes (s 9). The basic concept is that the public should only be compensated for what cannot reasonably be foreseen. Therefore intensification of use, eg, by traffic management schemes, or the introduction of more aircraft at an aerodrome, does not qualify for compensation.

When alteration or reconstruction or change of use occurs a claim for depreciation can be made in the same way as if a new work were involved. Section 9 defines what works and changes of use give rise to a claim and applies the earlier provisions of Pt 1 to this type of case. The claim must specify, in addition to the particulars in s 3(1) —as to which see subhead (*c*) below—the alterations or change of use alleged to give rise to depreciation. The provisions relating to betterment are modified so that only betterment caused by the alterations or change of use are taken into account. No claim can be made under Pt I for the alterations or change of use if land is acquired from the claimant. He can therefore claim for injurious affection in the normal way (s 9 (4)).

Highways—The alterations which give rise to eligibility are:
  (i) alterations to the location, width or level of the carriageway (other than resurfacing);
  (ii) the provision of an additional carriageway beside, above or below an existing one.

The alteration must take place after the highway has been open to public traffic—to avoid cases where the authority makes up an unsurfaced road at frontagers' expense. In these cases the 'relevant date' (ie, the date before which the claimant must acquire his interest: see s 2 (1)) is the date on which the highway was first open to traffic after completion of the carriageway alterations.

Aerodromes—In the case of existing aerodromes, eligibility is limited to runway or apron alterations, viz
  (i) a new runway, major realignment of or extension or strengthening of a runway, or
  (ii) a substantial addition to or alteration of a taxiway or apron.

In cases of doubt the Secretary of State can certify whether qualifying works were carried out (s 15). The 'relevant date' here is the date on which the new runway or apron was first used.

Other works—In the case of works other than roads and airports, eligibility arises in the event of

(i)   reconstruction,
(ii) extension,
(iii) other alteration or
(iv) change of use which is not a mere intensification of an existing use.

Works of maintenance are clearly excluded. The 'relevant date' is the date on which the works were first used after completion of the alteration or the date of change of use.

(c) Qualifying interests and claims

The claimant must have acquired his interest before the 'relevant date', viz, the date the highway was first open to public traffic or the public works were first used. (Note that a road may be open to traffic before it is officially opened.) The object of this is to prevent claims by a person who 'comes to the nuisance'—he may have paid a lower price because of the injurious effects anyway. However, those who buy before the start of use but in full knowledge of the scheme to be carried out are not excluded.

In the case of *dwellings*, the claimant must be the owner. He need not occupy the residence himself unless he has the right to do so—his claim is excluded if he has the right to occupy but does not exercise it. The object of this provision is to exclude builders or developers claiming in respect of vacant property. But a person who owns but leases the property has a right to claim, because the lease (or tenancy) excludes his right to possession. Therefore, for dwellings, in general terms owners and landlords can claim. As to property subject to a mortgage or trust or with a right to enfranchise a leasehold, see subhead (f) below.

In other cases, the Act parallels very closely the blight notice provisions of the Town and Country Planning Act 1971 (see p 122). The claimant must be the owner-occupier of *business premises* not exceeding the prescribed limit of rateable value (currently £18,000); or he must be the owner-occupier of an *agricultural unit*. Owner's interest is defined as the fee simple or a lease with not less than three years still to run. Sections 10 and 11 deal with land owned by a trust and occupied by a beneficiary or by persons claiming from personal representatives. A limited company in occupation could claim.

The claimant has to qualify on the date of service of the notice of claim. The claim must not be made before the expiry of 12 months from the opening of the road to traffic, or the works were first used after completion; or later than six years after the first possible date of claim. (See ss 2, 3 and 19 of the Act as amended by the Local Government, Planning and Land Act 1980, s 112.) Section 3 as amended introduces the concept of 'the first claim day', ie, the first day after the expiration of the 12 months' period from 'the relevant date', ie, date of opening or bringing into use (ss 1 (9) and 9 (2)). Responsible authorities must keep a record of 'relevant dates' under s 15 (see subhead (g) below).

However, if property is contracted to be sold or leased to a third party in the first 12 months after the new road or work has been brought into use, the vendor's right to claim is protected. He must in this case submit the claim before disposing of his interest or granting the tenancy. Provided he does so, he can assign his claim to his purchaser—or indeed anyone else who will give money for an uncertainty. There is no prescribed form but the claim must contain the particulars set out in s 3.

The claimant's valuation and legal expenses in preparing and presenting his claim are payable by the responsible authority. When a claim has been made, the authority can enter for survey and valuation purposes on giving reasonable notice.

(d) Assessment of compensation

Compensation is to be assessed by reference to prices current on the 'first claim day' ie, one year and one day after the highway has been open for public use or after the start of use of the works. The theory behind all these provisions is that values may be temporarily depressed during construction and for a period thereafter. Once the highway is properly in use, values are likely to stabilise. Twelve months is regarded as a reasonable period for this settling down process and values will be fixed at the end of this 12 months.

One of the difficult provisions in the 1973 Act is that which requires compensation to take into account any intensification which may reasonably be expected (s 4 (2)). A motorway, for example, may be built in stages. Traffic engineers may calculate that when the second stage is built traffic on the first stage will substantially increase. The physical effects and hence the depreciation on properties fronting the first stage will be based on those calculations. The same sort of thing might happen with a new aerodrome. In *Barb* v *Secretary of State for Transport* (subhead (a) above) the tribunal were satisfied that a prospective purchaser would not take into account a long-term increase in use of the M40.

The claimant in *Dhenin* v *Department of Transport* ((1989) EGCS 57) claimed that projected figures for traffic from a section of the M25 motorway should be rejected in favour of actual traffic flows, ie, the *Bwllfa* principle (see p 207) should be applied. The Lands Tribunal rejected that submission as compensation had to be ascertained at a particular date with any intensification anticipated. However, evidence that post dates the valuation date should not be rejected if it could be helpful in determining the accuracy of the assumptions that have to be made at that date.

Although compensation is fixed by reference to a single date, the nature of the interest and the physical condition of the land are related to the date of service of the claim (s 4 (4) (*a*)). There will be discounted from the valuation any building improvement or extension or any change of use made after the highway or other works were open to public use. In short, no account will be taken of buildings, etc, erected after the start of use (s 4 (5)).

In assessing compensation regard must be had to the availability of sound insulation under Pt II of the Act. Actual completion of the insulation is assumed to have taken place where it could be carried out. This is probably mainly important in relation to aerodromes, where schemes take time to implement. In the case of highways the works should theoretically be completed when the claim under Pt I is made. Other remedial works such as mounds, trees or barriers have only to be taken into account if actually erected by the date of the claim or if the authority has undertaken to provide them. Rules 2–4 in s 5 of the Land Compensation Act 1961(see Chapter 25) are applied (s 4 (4) (*b*)).

Section 5 contains detailed rules as to the *assumptions about planning permission*. Broadly the effect is to restrict the value of an interest in land for the purpose of compensation to its value for the purpose of its 'existing use', ie, its present use plus anything permitted by Sched 8 to the Town and Country Planning Act 1971. This follows logically from the provision limiting eligibility to those who may be suffering hardship in their existing situation: it would be unreasonable to pay compensation for loss of development value in these circumstances. There are the usual provisions to avoid a double payment where compensation has already been paid under planning legislation for loss or restriction of Sched 8 rights.

Rather more difficult to follow are the provisions for reducing compensation where other land is benefited—*the set-off for betterment*. These parallel the provisions in s 7 of the Land Compensation Act 1961 and s 261 of the Highways Act 1980 except that betterment to the land affected may also be set off. On the whole, betterment for the effect of the scheme on the claimant's adjoining land is rarely deducted, although it is logical to deduct for enhancement in value which the owner will realise when the land he retains is sold. If this retained land were subsequently bought compulsorily, the compensation rules for 'disregarding the effect of the authority's scheme' might prevent the owner from realising this enhancement—s 6 (3) and (4) remedy this. So if compensation for Whiteacre is reduced, because the scheme betters Blackacre in the same ownership, then if Blackacre is later acquired (assuming the interest in Blackacre is unchanged: s 6 (4)) the owner will recover the betterment previously set off. Disputed compensation questions will be referred to the Lands Tribunal (s 16).

Interest on compensation is payable either from the date of service of the notice of claim, or from the beginning of the claim period in cases where the property has changed hands and exceptionally the claim has been made before the expiry of the first year from the start of use of works (s 18).

(e) Restrictions on compensation

Compensation will not be paid unless the amount exceeds £50 (s 7).

There cannot be more than one claim from any one interest, but this does not preclude payments to owner and tenant of a dwelling.

Compensation under Pt I will not be payable where the claimant has sold land for the works but retains other land which may be damaged by severance or other forms of injurious affection. He cannot claim under Pt 1 in respect of the retained land but must rely upon his claim for injurious affection made as part of the compensation for acquisition. There would apart from this exclusion be a possibility of double compensation (s 8 (2)).

It will normally pay a claimant to rely on his claim under s 44 of the Land Compensation Act 1973 (see Chapter 27), because injurious affection now covers depreciation due to the construction and use of the whole of works in the scheme. Also under s 44 :

  (i) there is no £50 de minimis rule;

 (ii) there are no restrictions on the types of interest which can benefit;

(iii) depreciation caused by construction and presence of the works is included as well as that caused by their use, eg, visual intrusion can be compensated for and there is no restriction to certain physical factors;

(iv) depreciation is not limited to 'existing use' value.

Where an authority acquire land for public works in circumstances that the vendor retains other land, particulars of the works and the land retained are to be deposited with the district council or London Borough and registered by them as a local land charge (s 8 (4) and (4A)).

If there is a subsequent compulsory acquisition of land which has been the subject of a Pt I claim, the Pt I compensation may become deductible from the compulsory purchase price (s 8 (6)).

If there is eligibility under some other enactment, no compensation under Pt I is payable (s 8 (7)).

(f) Mortgages, trusts for sale, etc

Either a *mortgagor or a mortgagee* can claim under Pt I. The payment will be made to the mortgagee, who may appropriate it towards repayment of the principal, interest and costs secured by the mortgage. Any surplus must be paid to the mortgagor.

In the case of a *trust for sale*, compensation will be held as capital moneys, ie, it will be available for reinvestment but not for income for the beneficiaries. In the rare case of a *strict settlement*, compensation will similarly be treated as capital.

Where a *beneficiary under a trust* occupies land vested in trustees, his occupation will allow them to claim under s 2.

Section 2 excludes people who 'come to the nuisance'. However, those who do so as a result of *inheritance* are in a special position. Section 11 deals with the position of those who acquire their interest as a result of the death of a predecessor in title. Their position needs recognition in that they acquire by gift from a deceased person who would have been in a position to claim if he had lived.

There are also provisions in s 13 dealing with Church of England *ecclesiastical property* where the compensation is payable to the Church Commissioners. Other churches in England will be covered by s 10, as in the case of an ordinary trust.

Section 12 deals with the position where a tenant has a *right to enfranchisement or an extended lease of a house under the Leasehold Reform Act* 1967. The need for this special provision arises because of the provisions in s 2 and s 3 (2) that in order to qualify a claimant must have a qualifying interest before the start of use of the works and still be in possession of that interest when a claim is made. Two cases need to be covered: first, a tenant having three years or more of a tenancy to run may have served a notice under the Leasehold Reform Act and, if he acquires the freehold or an extended lease after the start of use and before a claim can be made, he will have acquired his interest after the relevant date and it will be disqualified by s 2 (1); and secondly, a tenant having less than three years of his lease remaining when the claim was made would be ineligible even though he may be entitled to, and have served a notice of his desire to, have the freehold or an extended lease under the Leasehold Reform Act.

Section 12 therefore provides that where a person is entitled under Pt I of the Leasehold Reform Act 1967 to acquire the freehold or an extended lease of a house by virtue of a tenancy and has given notice, before the start of use of the works, of his desire to have the freehold or an extended lease, but has not yet acquired it, he will be entitled to make a claim under Pt I irrespective of the length of the term of lease remaining unexpired on the date of the claim. Thus a tenancy with less than three years to run would qualify.

The assessment of the landlord's injurious affection will be related to the depreciation in the sum he could have expected to receive on enfranchisement from the holder of the tenancy. The tenant would receive depreciation in the value of his original tenancy before enfranchisement under the claim to be submitted under subs (3) of this section. This value would reflect the benefit of the notice served under the Leasehold Reform Act to purchase the freehold interest or extended lease. If a notice under the Leasehold Reform Act had been served after the start of use of the works and the extended lease or freehold had not been acquired when the claim was made, the assessment of compensation would nevertheless already take account of that notice and the award would reflect this.

(g) Duties of acquiring authorities

The duty under s 8 (4) to register particulars of any case where compensation included something for injurious affection to retained land is dealt with under subhead (e) above.

There is also a duty to keep a record:

(a) in relation to any highway, of the date the road was first open after construction or alterations to the carriageway;

(b) in relation to any public works, of the date of first use after completion or completion of alterations;

(c) in the case of public works other than a highway or aerodrome, of the date on which there was a change of use.

The object is to establish the first claim day and responsible authorities must on request furnish a written statement of what is recorded.

Because aerodromes are extensive and the public do not have

access, there is a special certification procedure to be operated by the Department of Trade. The date of opening of new or reconstructed roads or other works is more readily ascertainable by the public and the record can be checked more easily. There is no need to record dates of opening which occurred before Pt I came into force, even though some provisions are retrospective.

Chapter 30

Special Cases

1 Comprehensive development areas

Comprehensive development areas were defined in old-style development plans: broadly speaking, they were areas which the planning authority considered should be developed or redeveloped as a whole. As has already been seen (p 199) the old-style development plans are being superseded by structure and local plans. An area of comprehensive development has become an action area.

Section 11 (5) of the Town and Country Planning Act 1971 (as substituted by the Housing and Planning Act 1986) provides that 'the local planning authority may prepare a local plan for a part of their area (an "action area") which they have selected for the commencement during a prescribed period of comprehensive treatment by development redevelopment or improvement of the whole or part of the area selected or partly by one and partly by another method'. The prescribed period is ten years from the date of the structure plan approval (Town and Country Planning (Structure and Local Plans) Regulations 1982 (SI 1982 No 555), reg 14). A local plan prepared for an action area must indicate the nature of the treatment selected for the action area.

Action areas had originally to be identified in structure plans, but no structure plan approved after 13 November 1980 may contain a definition of an action area, these now being confined to local plans. Where a structure plan approved before 13 November 1980 designates an action area the local authority remain under a duty to prepare a local plan for the area as soon as practicable.

Whatever the planning machinery for securing that land is dealt with comprehensively, the power of acquisition will rest upon s 112 of the Act of 1971 as amended by the Local Government, Planning and Land Act 1980. This is the section which gives a power of compulsory acquisition of:

(i) any land which is suitable for and is required 'in order to carry out one or more of the following activities namely development, redevelopment and improvement';

(ii) 'land required for a purpose which it is necessary to achieve in the interests of the proper planning of an area in which the land is situated'.

As has been seen (p 186) s 6 and the first Schedule to the Land Compensation Act 1961 provide for the disregarding of any increase (or diminution) in value due to the development or redevelopment of a comprehensive development area in accordance with the plan. To make the compensation provisions fit in with the concept of action areas, the Town and Country Planning Act 1971, s 291 and Sched 23, provide that in the Land Compensation Act 1961 any reference to an area defined in the current development plan as an area of comprehensive development shall be construed as a reference to an action area for which a local plan is in force.

The special provisions for areas of comprehensive development (now action areas) in the Land Compensation Act 1961 are to be found in ss 16 and 17, and are as follows:

(a) No certificate of alternative development is obtainable (Land Compensation Act 1961, s 17 (1) (a)).

(b) The special assumptions as to development plans do not apply (s 16 (1)–(3)).

(c) Instead, the land will get the benefit of one of the range of uses indicated in the plan as the proposed uses of land in the comprehensive development area (s 16 (4), (5)). The particular use to be chosen is to be that which might reasonably have been expected to be the subject of planning permission if there had been no development scheme at all. In other words, the detailed planning provisions of the scheme are out, but the range of uses for the area is in. This range is to be considered in relation to the old layout and not the new proposals in the comprehensive development scheme. Suppose, therefore, that Whiteacre is to become part of a new road in the development proposals. The owner will not lose on this account, for these actual proposals are to be disregarded. Similarly, if Blackacre, lying within an area for commercial redevelopment, is to be the site for a multiple store, its owner will not necessarily get store value: he may have to take something less. The authority will not buy dear because the new use, a store, is lucrative—the Blackacre case; nor will they buy cheap because the new use, a road, has no market value—the Whiteacre case.

It should be noted that only the effect on value of the comprehensive development area as defined in the development plan can be ignored (Land Compensation Act 1961, Sched 1, case 2 explained at p 186). Any subsequent additional area will be in a separate compulsory purchase order and compensation in this additional area will reflect any increase in values created by redevelopment proposed or carried out under the original scheme.

The transition to action areas

As just seen, the Town and Country Planning Act 1971, s 291 and Sched 23, provide as a consequential amendment to the provisions for structure and local plans that any reference in the Land Compensation Act 1961 to an area defined in the current development plan as an area of comprehensive development shall be construed as a reference to an action area for which a local plan is in force. Therefore, when a local plan has been prepared, it will take the place of the definition in the old development plan, and the local plan will then govern the assumptions as to planning consents for valuation purposes. But until the local plan has been prepared, transitional provisions will operate. Because action areas are no longer to be defined in structure plans, the transitional provisions can only affect structure plans approved before 13 November 1980.

These transitional provisions are contained in Sched 7, para 5, to the Act of 1971 and govern the valuation position under the Land Compensation Act 1961 where there is a structure plan in force, but no local plan. The approach is the same as that described above (p 199), of taking whichever plan gives rise to the most favourable assumptions to the owner as to the grant of planning permission. The choice lies between the old development plan on the one hand and the structure plan on the other, in so far as the land is situated within an 'action area' in the structure plan. Until the local plan is prepared, the structure plan (and what is said in it about action areas) will give guidance and information as to the nature of treatment selected. Presumably, the broad outline of treatment for an action area set out in the structure plan may sometimes produce for the owner more favourable assumptions about planning consents than those to be derived from the definition as an area of comprehensive development in the old development plan.

However once a local plan has been prepared for any district, the transitional provisions will cease to apply. The 'current development plan' will be the local plan plus the structure plan, because the old development plan will cease to have effect on the adoption or approval of the local plan (Sched 7, para 5A)—unless exceptionally the Secretary of State keeps some old provisions alive under paras 5B and 5C.

To sum up, once a local plan has been prepared for a district (whether or not it is an action area plan) it will become the current development plan for purposes of the Land Compensation Act 1961. If the local plan contains an action area, ie, an area selected for comprehensive treatment by development, redevelopment or improvement, Sched 23, Pt I to the 1971 Act will operate so that wherever in the Land Compensation Act 1961, the expression 'area defined as an area of comprehensive development' appears, it shall be construed as if it were 'action area for which a local plan is in force'. This imports into action areas in local plans the concept of the 'planned range of uses' described earlier as a determinant of the compensation payable on compulsory acquisition. It follows too that a certificate of alternative development is not obtainable where an action area is defined in an adopted or approved local plan.

2 Buildings of architectural or historic interest

The Town and Country Planning Act 1971 provides that the compensation payable on the compulsory acquisition of a listed building shall normally disregard the fact that the building is listed (s 116). But where it is proposed to use the power in s 114 (compulsory acquisition of listed building in need of repair) and it is shown that the building has been deliberately allowed to fall into disrepair for the purpose of justifying redevelopment of the site, it is possible for the acquiring authority to reduce the compensation which would otherwise become payable to the owner.

The machinery in the Act, s 117, is as follows:

(a) The acquiring authority include in the compulsory purchase order a 'direction for minimum compensation'.

(b) The notice to owners, lessees, etc, must tell them that such a direction has been included and is to explain the meaning of 'a direction for minimum compensation'. It means that planning consent would not be granted for any redevelopment or development of the site and that consent would also not be granted for any works for the demolition, alteration or extension of the building (except development or works to keep it in a proper state of repair).

(c) Compensation will accordingly be assessed without regard to redevelopment site value. The direction for minimum compensation will also prevent an owner claiming anything for the possibilities of raising the value of the building by alterations or extensions. But it would seem that the possibilities of consent to a change of use (not requiring works of adaptation) would not be excluded, and any value which this possibility might have would be reflected in the compensation. So also would the possibility of effecting changes of use under the General Development or Use Classes Orders.

(d) An owner may appeal to a magistrates' court against the inclusion of a direction for minimum compensation. The appeal must be lodged within 28 days of service of the notice of making the order. Either the owner or the local authority can appeal against the magistrates' decision to the Crown Court. It is also open to the Secretary of State to exclude the direction when confirming the order.

3 New town and public development

Section 51 of the Land Compensation Act 1973 is designed to secure that when a new town development corporation comes to acquire land within the new town boundaries, any enhancement of the value of that land may be disregarded if the increase is attributable to the influence of some other specified public works. The machinery is that the Secretary of State may direct to this effect before making the new town designation order—this includes an order extending the site of the new town.

It is not very easy to visualise the circumstances in which this provision may be used. Circular No 73/73 (para 51) states that the section extends the principle of excluding increases or decreases in value due to the scheme of the acquiring authority to the situation where a new town or new town extension is itself a direct consequence of a major public development outside the designated area for a new town which could therefore be regarded as part of the same scheme. Possible examples would be a major power station or an airport outside the new town. The major public development and the new town would really both form part of the same scheme, and will be treated as such for purposes of compensation. Any effect of the new town and the public development on values in the designated area will be disregarded for purposes of assessing compensation.

Public development is defined by relation to the agency carrying it out and includes government departments, statutory undertakers and other bodies having power to borrow money with the consent of a Minister, eg, local authorities.

Section 262 of the Highways Act 1980 seems to be similar in intention to s 51—disregard of enhanced value of land required for service areas, if the land was not included in the original motorway acquisition.

4 Urban development areas

The Secretary of State can designate an area of land as an Urban Development Area if he is of the opinion that it is expedient in the national interest to do so (s 134, Local Government, Planning and Land Act 1980). To regenerate the area he can establish an Urban Development Corporation with wide powers to take over various planning and other functions from the local authorities. The London and Liverpool Dockland Areas were the first two such corporations to be set up.

Section 142 of the 1980 Act gives an Urban Development Corporation powers to acquire land compulsorily if it is in the Urban Development Area, or adjacent to it and required to discharge the corporation's functions, or elsewhere and required for the provision of services in connection with the discharge of functions. New rights can also be acquired compulsorily (s 142 (4)).

Section 145 sets out the special provisions governing the assessment of compensation on compulsory purchase. Land in an Urban Development Area is added to the categories which are listed in s 6 of and Sched 1 to the Land Compensation Act 1961 (see p 190). Therefore compensation is not to be increased or reduced on account of the 'scheme' except insofar as development might have taken place apart from the scheme. Increases or diminutions are not to be ignored merely because they are attributable to development before the designation as an Urban Development Area, to development outside the area, or to development by other authorities.

In *Mersey Docks & Harbour Co* v *Merseyside Development Corporation* (1987) RVR 97 the Lands Tribunal assessed the compensation payable under an arbitration agreement whereby land and buildings were transferred to the development corporation.

There is special provision in s 141 of the 1980 Act for the Secretary of State to transfer to an Urban Development Corporation land vested in a local authority, statutory undertaker or other public body. An order under s 141 has the same effect as a general vesting declaration and s 15 of the Compulsory Purchase (Vesting Declarations) Act 1981 applies the provisions of the 1981 Act subject to the modifications in Sched 2.

It has already been mentioned (Chapter 18) that land affected by designation as an Urban Development Area may give rise to a 'blight notice' (s 147, 1980 Act). Land acquired by the Secretary of State following a blight notice must be transferred to the corporation when set up (s 147 (4)).

5 The Crown and the 1973 Act

The Ministry of Defence acquire land under a special code set out in the Defence Acts 1842–1935. Applying the provisions in Pt I of the Land Compensation Act 1973, ie, ss 1–19 dealing with compensation for depreciation caused by the use of public works (see p 228) would therefore require substantial amendment of the Defence Acts. The government undertook, pending legislation, that 'the substance of the proposals will be put into operation in relation to defence works by administrative action'.

Part I does not apply to any aerodrome in the occupation of a government department, ie, the Ministry of Defence (s 84).

Part I applies to works or land provided or used 'in the exercise of *statutory* powers' (s 1 (3) (*c*)). Defence works, eg, tank training grounds or gunnery ranges, are used in the exercise of *prerogative* powers and Pt I will not apply to them, even if acquired under statutory powers.

Part I will apply to Crown land (other than an aerodrome), whether or not the use is by the Crown, if the works are provided or the land used in the exercise of statutory powers.

The powers in Pt II (mitigation of injurious effects of public works) will be available to the Crown where the Crown is a 'responsible authority' in relation to any public works. For example, the powers in ss 26 and 27 will extend to aerodromes occupied by the Ministry of Defence (acquisition of land and execution of works to mitigate effects of public works: see Chapter 19).

Government departments are on the same footing as other authorities as regards Pt III of the Act (eg, are liable to make home loss payments) and Pt IV, which amends the law of compulsory purchase.

6 Slum clearance

The statutory machinery for dealing with the acquisition of land in clearance areas is contained in Pt XVII of the Housing Act 1985. A clearance area is an area to be cleared of all buildings and is declared by a local housing authority if they are satisfied that the houses in the area are unfit for human habitation or are, by reason of their bad arrangement, or the narrowness or bad arrangement of the streets, dangerous or injurious to the health of the inhabitants, and that the other buildings, if any, in the area are similarly dangerous or injurious and that the most satisfactory method of dealing with these conditions is the demolition of all the buildings in the area (s 289, Housing Act 1985).

There are analogous provisions for dealing with the compulsory purchase of single houses which are unfit. By s 192, where a housing authority has served a repair notice in respect of an unfit house, and the courts on appeal have found that the house cannot be rendered it at a reasonable cost, the house may be acquired compulsorily; and by ss 265 and 300, under certain circumstances a housing authority may compulsorily acquire a house instead of ordering it to be demolished or closed.

(a) Site value

The basic principle governing the compensation to be paid for all such property is that the acquiring authority should not, where the property is unfit for human habitation or dangerous to the health of the inhabitants of the area, pay for any value attaching to the bricks and mortar on the site, ie, the compensation is to be related only to the value of the land as a cleared site. This is a logical extension of r 4 of the statutory compensation code (s 5 of the Land Compensation Act 1961). However, at a date to be appointed by the Secretary of State under the Local Government and Housing Act 1989, the provisions for site value compensation will be repealed (see p 252).

The actual wording of s 585 (1) of the Housing Act 1985 is 'the value at the time when the valuation is made of the site as a cleared site available for development in accordance with the requirements of the building regulations in force in the district'. Any statutory or other restrictions under the Town and Country Planning Acts have to be taken into account, and the usual attempt made to assess what permission would be granted (if any) for the use of the cleared site. In *Walkes-Hilliman* v *Greater London Council* (1969) 210 EG 403, following *Northwood* v *London County Council* [1926] 2 KB 411, the Lands Tribunal held that disturbance could not be paid where compensation was based on cleared site value. However, a disturbance payment can now be claimed under s 37 of the Land Compensation Act 1973 provided that an owner-occupier 's supplement is not payable as well.

An important restriction is the provision as to building regulations. It is this which makes small sites almost worthless. The requirements of the regulations as to the air space around houses, the distance of the front of the house from the footpath or of the rear from the boundary, and other matters often preclude any redevelopment. See, for example, *Preston* v *Leicester Corporations* (1961) 13 P & CR 50.

In assessing redevelopment possibilities, no account can be taken of the fact that the acquiring authority intend to clear the adjoining sites (*Davy* v *Leeds Corporation* [1965] 1 WLR 445). See *Mountview Estates Ltd* v *London Borough of Enfield* (1968) 20 P & CR 729, for the compensation payable for acquiring a leasehold interest where the site had some redevelopment potential. For cases on site value see the following:

> *MacFarlane* v *London Borough of Hackney* (referred to in *Shaw* v *London Borough of Hackney* (1974) 28 P & CR at p 485); *J A & A M Wilson* v *Liverpool County Borough Council* (1968) 21 P & CR 452; *Xerri and Shanks* v *Enfield London Borough Council* (1966) 18 P & CR 117.

Site value not to exceed market value—When market value was reintroduced as the general basis of compensation, it became necessary to make special provisions for the purchase of houses at site value under the Housing Act 1957 (the predecessor of the 1985 Act). Under market value rules, site value would often exceed the value of the site with a house on it. This is because the house is a liability and the costs of demolition have to be taken into account before redevelopment possibilities can be realised (in the case of a house with regulated tenancies the liability would be even greater because possession could not be obtained).

The Land Compensation Act 1961, s 10 and Sched 2, accordingly makes provision that in Housing Act cases compensation on a site value basis shall not exceed the value of the land and the buildings upon it in the open market subject to any tenancy which may affect it. In effect the owner gets whichever is the *less* of the two bases of compensation: cleared site value or market value.

Additional payments—Some attempts to mitigate the hardship which arose from the site value rule have been made from time to time as follows:

(*i*) owner-occupiers of private dwellings now receive an amount of compensation at least equal to the gross rateable value of the premises (Land Compensation Act 1961, Sched 2, para 3);

(*ii*) there are supplements payable for houses which have been well maintained based on 14 times the current rateable value (Housing Act 1985, s 586 and Sched 23—see below);

(*iii*) owner-occupiers will generally be entitled to a supplementary payment, which will bring their compensation up to full market value (Housing Act 1985, s 587 and Sched 24—see below);

(*iv*) allowances for removal expenses and trade disturbance as outlined in Chapter 21 (Land Compensation Act 1973, s 37).

These special allowances in the case of unfit houses require further consideration.

(b) Minimum payment

Where a house is being acquired which was occupied by the 'owner' (ie, any person entitled to receive a notice to treat) at the date of the making of the compulsory purchase order and is so occupied at the date of the notice to treat the compensation shall not be less than an amount equal to the gross rateable value of the dwelling (Land Compensation Act 1961, Sched 2, para 3).

Compensation will include any 'well-maintained payment' (see (*c*) below) and any supplement paid to owner-occupiers (see (*d*) below) but will not include any amount paid for disturbance, severance or injurious affection.

(c) Well-maintained house payment

Schedule 23 deals with well-maintained payments in respect of unfit houses. When a house has been acquired for clearance under s 290, the local housing authority shall, if they are satisfied that the house has been well maintained, make a payment to the owner, if the house is owner-occupied, or to persons liable to repair the house (unless some other person satisfies the authority that the good maintenance is attributable to work carried out by him in which case the authority may make the payment in whole or in part to him).

In clearance area cases, it is not necessary for claimants to apply for payment since the housing authority must serve notice in the prescribed form on every owner, lessee, occupier or mortgagee (so far as it is reasonably practicable to ascertain them) stating whether they are satisfied that the dwelling has been wholly or partly well maintained (para 7, Sched 23). (The prescribed form is in SI 1974 No 1511). Where an owner-occupier's supplement is paid (see below, para (*d*)), the well-maintained house payment will be excluded, unless the supplementary payment is paid in respect of part only of the house (Housing Act 1985, s 588).

The principle is that where money has been expended or works carried out by the tenant, the owner or a mortgagee, in an attempt to maintain the property in a good state of repair, some recompense is justifiable.

The level of payment for good maintenance of tenanted houses is fixed by Ministerial Order by reference to rateable values. If the relevant order was made after 6 July 1982, then the multiplier is to be 14 (Housing (Payments for Well Maintained Houses) Order 1982, SI 1982 No 1112).

There has always been a 'ceiling' proviso to ensure that the well-maintained payment does not exceed the amount by which the full value of the house exceeds its site value. It appears in para 4 of Sched 23 and means that a local authority will not in any circumstances have to pay more for an unfit house than if it had been found to be fit. If the value of the cleared site is as great or greater than the value of the site with the unfit house on it, no payment can be made for good maintenance. Any dispute about this can be referred to the Lands Tribunal for decision.

Payments can be made where a listed building is made the subject of a closing order, or where a house is compulsorily purchased under s 192 of the Housing Act 1985.

Partially well-maintained houses—Paragraph 5 of Sched 23 deals with the partially well-maintained house and provides a remedy where either the interior or exterior has been well maintained, but not both. The most common example is where the tenant has done his best to maintain the interior of his house. But the provision applies if the fabric has been maintained by the landlord, and the tenant has failed to maintain the interior. Where a house does not qualify for a payment as being wholly well maintained but the interior or exterior has been well maintained, the payment is one-half of the amount for a fully maintained house.

Paragraph 6 deals with parts of dwelling, for example flats, or premises used partly for residential and partly for business purposes.

In most cases where houses are let, the well-maintained payment goes to the tenant. It is unlikely that his interest in the site will be worth more than a nominal sum, and the site value goes to the owner. It should be noted that the amount of the well-maintained payment is not affected by the value of the recipient's interest.

A claim for a well-maintained payment should be made as early as possible, preferably before the public inquiry so that the inspector can inspect the house for unfitness and maintenance at the same time. For payment to a person other than the owner, see *Hoggard* v *Worsbrough UDC* [1962] 2 QB 93—duty of local authority to invite representations before deciding to pay person other than owner. The claimant cannot have the amount of the well-maintained payment determined by the Lands Tribunal (*Xerri and Shanks* v *Enfield London Borough Council*

(1966) 18 P & CR 117).

A person aggrieved by the housing authority's decision as to whether a property has been well maintained may make a written representation to the Secretary of State in the same way and time as objection can be made to the compulsory purchase order itself. The Secretary of State can direct the authority to make the appropriate payment (Sched 23, para 8). There is no further appeal as to the merit of the decision.

(d) Supplementary payments to owner-occupiers

Section 587 of and Pt I of Sched 24 to the 1985 Act provided that owner-occupiers should generally be entitled to a supplementary payment which would bring their compensation up to full market value.

There is a separate procedure for unfit houses other than those in clearance areas. With regard to well-maintained houses which are subject to demolition or closing orders, or which are purchased under s 192 or 300 of the 1985 Act, a person must make representations to the housing authority that it has been well maintained and anyone aggrieved by their decision may within 21 days appeal to the county court (Sched 23, paras 1(5) and 2(5)).

Payment of the owner-occupier's supplement is to be made where a house was owner-occupied throughout the qualifying period. This is defined as a period of two years ending with the date on which the authority took action as set out in para 1(2) of the Schedule. The requirement of a qualifying period was included to discourage collusive sales from landlord to tenant in anticipation of clearance merely for the purpose of obtaining higher compensation. For a comment on this provision and the treatment of periods of vacancy in relation to the qualifying period, see *Reeve and others* v *Hartlepool Borough Council* (1975) 30 P & CR 517. As to successive qualifying interests see *Robson & Wood* v *Teesside Borough Council* (1974) 28 P & CR 313. In *Panchal* v *Preston Borough Council* (1978) 36 P & CR 281, the Lands Tribunal held that the supplement was payable to an owner who had moved his wife and children to another house but continued to sleep in the house at nights. In *Mohammed Niaz* v *Rochdale Metropolitan Borough* (1980) 41 P & CR 113 an owner who was absent for some months through the illness of his mother was held nevertheless to have occupied the house vicariously through two friends who had each made a payment towards the purchase price. See also on absence abroad, *Laundon* v *Hartlepool District Council* (1977) 244 EG 885 CA, and *Manzur Hussain* v *Thameside Metropolitan Borough Council* (1982) 43 P & CR 436. In *Patel* v *Leicester City Council* (1982) 43 P & CR 278, the supplement was awarded by the tribunal to an owner who was 'pigging it alone' in the house, his occupation being nevertheless residential in quality.

The Court of Appeal in *Mit Singh* v *Derby City Council* (1982) 43 P & CR 258 held that the supplement was payable to an owner whose son slept in a back bedroom after the owner had moved out. The Court here followed *Hunter* v *Manchester City Council* [1975] QB 877, where an owner let part of the house but continued to occupy one of the upstairs rooms.

In *Heron* v *Sandwell Metropolitan Borough Council* (1980) 40 P & CR 232, it was held that full supplement was payable where a house was jointly owned but one owner lived elsewhere during the week for the purposes of employment, returning to the house only at weekends and for holidays. In *Abdul Aziz* v *Thameside Metropolitan Borough Council* (1982) 43 P & CR 436, the tribunal held that the supplement was payable to an owner who had two houses, the house in question being shared by the owner and staff who worked in his nearby restaurant.

Nothing in Pt I of Sched 24 requires compensation to be assessed by reference to the facts as they existed at the declaration of the clearance area. Therefore where a property was occupied by tenants at the date of entry (which was the valuation date), the normal compulsory purchase code applied and the existence of tenancies reduced the compensation payable; per the Court of Appeal in *Khan* v *Birmingham City Council* (1980) 40 P & CR 412, distinguishing *Hunter* v *Manchester City Council* (above).

An owner-occupier who fails the residence qualification may nevertheless obtain the supplement by proving to the satisfaction of the local authority that he had made reasonable inquiries before he purchased the property and had no reason to expect slum clearance within two years. In such a case the Lands Tribunal have no jurisdiction to substitute their view for that of the local authority (*Mohammed Sagir* v *City of Birmingham District Council* (1980) 39 P & CR 602).

Circular No 68/69 of the Ministry of Housing and Local Government reminds local authorities that their re-housing obligations as a result of slum clearance are in no way affected by the compensation provisions.

Occupation must be by a person entitled to an interest in the house or a member of the family of any person so entitled. There is a definition of 'family' in para 6 of Pt I of the Schedule.

(e) Business premises supplements

Part II of Sched 24 deals with payments in respect of houses used for business purposes. It applies in similar cases to well-maintained payments, except that closing orders are not included. At the 'relevant date' as defined in para 1, and for the two years preceding that date, the house must have been occupied wholly or partly for the purposes of a business, and the person entitled to the receipts of the business must have held an interest in the house, Occupation by an employee is not sufficient (*GE Stevens* (*High Wycombe*) v *High Wycombe Corporation* [1962] 2 QB 547.

Interest does not include a yearly tenancy. See *Morris Marzell* v *Greater London Council* (1975) 30 P & CR 259, as to a business owned by a private limited company, where the Lands Tribunal held that the principal shareholder was not entitled to the receipts of the business so as to qualify for the supplement.

The object of the owner-occupier's supplement has always been to mitigate the hardship suffered by householders who, due to acute housing shortage, had nowhere to live and therefore bought near slum property often at substantial prices. The owners of small businesses carried on in unfit houses were also protected where the unfitness derived from the use of the house as a dwelling rather than from its unsuitability as business premises. The supplement in both cases is the amount by which the 'full compulsory purchase value', ie, the market value of the house as it stands, exceeds the site value (Sched 24, Pt I, para 4 and Pt II, para 4). The effect is to give owner-occupiers the market value of their slum property, recognising that they bought at a time of acute housing shortage or for purposes other than housing.

(f) Local Government and Housing Act 1989

This substantially amends the Housing Act 1985. The concept of the clearance area remains, but the provisions for site value compensation for unfit houses, including well-maintained payments and supplementary payments for owner-occupiers, are repealed (see s 165, Pt IV of Sched 9 and Sched 12). Section 165 is to come into force on a day to be appointed by the Secretary of State—at the time of writing no date had been appointed.

7 Compensation for agricultural holdings

Section 48 of the Land Compensation Act 1973 secures that, in assessing compensation for both landlords and tenants of agricultural holdings, regard is had in both cases to the tenant's security of tenure afforded by the Agricultural Holdings Act 1986 apart from the acquiring authority's scheme.

Under the decisions in *Rugby Joint Water Board* v *Foottit, Shaw-*

Fox and others [1972] 1 All ER 1057 and *Ministry of Transport* v *Pettit* (1968) 20 P & CR 344, a landlord was able to obtain compensation based on the prospects of getting early vacant possession even though the only reason why he could serve a valid notice to quit on his tenant was the acquiring authority's proposals. Section 48 in effect reversed those decisions. The landlord's compensation will be assessed as though there was a protected tenancy. Even if the tenant has left as a result of a notice to quit founded on the authority's proposed use of the land, compensation will be assessed as if the tenant had not left. As to the extent to which, where s 48 applies, it is permissible to take into account any power of the landlord to determine the tenancy under the 1948 Act, see *Dawson* v *Norwich City Council* (1979) 37 P & CR 516, where the Lands Tribunal held that the valuer is not bound to assume that the claimant has indefinite security of tenure.

The converse of this for a tenant is that his security of tenure as provided for under the Agricultural Holdings Act 1986 is to be taken into account unaffected by the proposals of the acquiring authority. Under s 20 of the Compulsory Purchase Act 1965 as affected by the Agriculture (Miscellaneous Provisions) Act 1968 and the Agricultural Holdings Act 1986 the tenant is entitled to:

(*a*) compensation for the value of his unexpired term or interest, based on profit rental value, if any, and loss of profits from the farming of the holding for the period between the taking of possession and the earliest date at which the tenancy could have been brought to an end by notice to quit served on the date when possession is taken, ie, usually between one and two years. The security of tenure can be taken into account unaffected by the proposals of the acquiring authority;

(*b*) any just allowance which ought to be made to him by an incoming tenant, ie, 'tenant right', and compensation for improvements which he could have received under the Agricultural Holdings Act 1986 if his tenancy had been terminated by notice to quit;

(*c*) any loss or injury he might sustain, ie, compensation for actual disturbance losses; a minimum of one year's rent is customary.

The position prior to s 48 of the Act of 1973 may still be relevant since by virtue of s 48 (6) the acquiring authority must make up any shortfall if the tenant's compensation as determined in accordance with s 48 (3)-(5) is less than it would have been if those sub-sections had not been enacted. Section 42 of the 1968 Act (tenant's compensation to be assessed without regard to his prospects of remaining in possession after contractual date) and s 15 (1) of the same Act (effect on tenant's compensation of provision enabling landlord to resume possession for non-agricultural use) are accordingly kept in force for the limited purpose of calculating the minimum compensation.

The effect of all this is that if security of tenure will improve the tenant's position, he will get the benefit of it. But he cannot get less on the new basis than on the old.

Sections 12 and 13 of the Agricultural (Miscellaneous Provisions) Act 1968 remain in force. As a result the acquiring authority is liable to pay additional compensation under s 60 of the Agricultural Holdings Act 1986 as if the tenancy had been determined by notice to quit. The tenant will not get the basic compensation (up to two years' rent) but he will in all cases get four times the rent to assist in the reorganisation of his affairs. This is a non-taxable payment, unlike compensation, which is taxable.

The amount payable under s 12 has to be deducted from compensation assessed on the basis of security of tenure for the tenant. This is because the four-times-the-rent payment had regard to the limited security of tenure embodied in s 42 of the Act of 1968 (now repealed). Therefore, to get a fair comparison of compensation under the old and the new law, the four-times-the-rent payment must be deducted when the new compensation is being calculated.

To sum up, no tenant can do worse under the present law, and some may do better.

8 Farm—choosing notice of entry compensation

A tenant of agricultural land may find that instead of action being taken by the acquiring authority under the compulsory purchase legislation outlined in the previous paragraph, a notice to quit is served by the landlord pursuant to the Agricultural Holdings Act 1986. Possession can be gained by the service of a 12-month notice to quit expiring on the next renewal date of the annual tenancy, on the grounds that the land is required for a use other than for agriculture for which planning permission has been given (Case B in Pt I of Sched 3) or that the land is required for non-agricultural use not falling within Case B and the Agricultural Land Tribunal is satisfied. In such cases s 59 of the Land Compensation Act 1973 gives the tenant the right to opt for compensation to be assessed under the compulsory purchase legislation rather than the agricultural holdings legislation.

In *Dawson v Norwich City Council* (1979) 37 P & CR 516 it was held that s 59 applied equally to the service of a notice by the local authority as to one served by a private landlord, and so where land had been acquired by agreement by an authority possessing compulsory purchase powers, and the authority had then given the claimant notice to quit, the claimant was able to elect under s 59 for compulsory purchase compensation. The Lands Tribunal held that the mischief at which the section aims is the practice of local authorities purchasing by actual or threatened compulsory purchase, then seeking possession from the tenant not as acquiring authority but as landlord, thereby avoiding payment of compensation otherwise than under the 1948 Act. Therefore s 59 applied equally whether the notice to quit was served by the local authority or a private landlord.

It will therefore be helpful to compare the provisions of the two codes.

Under *agricultural holdings legislation*, the tenant is able to continue farming for the remainder of the current year and for a further 12 months and earn profits for that year. On displacement he receives:

Under the Agricultural Holdings Act 1986:

> Basic compensation, being the minimum of one year's and (subject to proof of loss) a maximum of two years' rent for disturbance (s 60 (3)).
>
> Four times the rent tax free to assist in the reorganisation of his affairs (s 60 (4)).
>
> Improvements he has made to the land, including tenant right.

Under *compulsory purchase legislation*, provided the authority serve at least 14 days' notice of entry, they may take possession at any time. In this case the tenant receives (see p 252):

Under the Compulsory Purchase Act 1965 (s 20):

> The value of his unexpired term or interest.
>
> Actual disturbance losses covering removal expenses, forced sale of life and dead stock, etc. No maximum, but one year's rent is generally paid as a minimum.
>
> Improvements he has made to the land including tenant right.

Under s 12 of the Agricultural (Miscellaneous Provisions) Act 1968:

> Four times the rent tax free to assist in the reorganisation of his affairs.

If the tenant opts for compulsory purchase compensation, ie, treats the notice to quit as notice of entry, compensation will be assessed as if it took effect as a compulsory dispossession immediately before the expiry date (ie, the anniversary of the tenancy). He will not, therefore, be compensated for the profits he can continue to earn during the remaining period of his tenancy. But at the end of the year he will have his compensation assessed on the more favourable compulsory purchase basis above. This will include the benefit of s 48 of the 1973

Act (see p 252), which provides that his security of tenure apart from the authority's scheme should be taken into account. He may also be eligible for a home or a farm loss payment (as to which see Chapter 20).

If an authority have to speed up a project and have to serve notice of entry before the expiry of their notice to quit, the tenant will be compensated for dispossession at this earlier date in the normal way.

The election is by notice in writing served not later than the date on which possession is given up.

Section 59 enables a yearly tenant farmer who is entitled to opt for compulsory purchase compensation to benefit from the provisions of s 55, which enables him to enlarge the notice of entry from part to the whole, where the residue is not reasonably capable of being farmed as a separate agricultural unit. An authority who proceed by way of serving notice to quit, rather than notice of entry, will not therefore avoid the provisions allowing the tenant to say 'take the whole'.

Chapter 31

The Lands Tribunal

The Lands Tribunal was set up by the Lands Tribunal Act 1949 and has wide functions in relation to the assessing of compensation for compulsory acquisitions. It is the authority for settling any question of disputed compensation, for determining compensation to absent parties, and for settling compensation where no lands have been acquired from the claimant.

The Tribunal consists of a President and such other members as the Lord Chancellor may appoint. The President is either a person who has held judicial office or a barrister of at least seven years' standing. Other members are barristers or solicitors of like standing or persons with land valuation experience. The jurisdiction of the Tribunal may be exercised by any one or more of its members, and the President may select members with legal or valuation experience according to the type of case.

Of the three types of jurisdiction mentioned above, the settling of the disputed compensation is dealt with at a greater length later in this chapter. With regard to the second type of case in determining compensation to 'absent parties', ie, in accordance with s 5 of and Sched 2 to the Compulsory Purchase Act 1965, the surveyor is selected by the President from the members of the Lands Tribunal. The jurisdiction under this section is strictly his personal jurisdiction and not that of the Lands Tribunal: such cases are, however, for convenience dealt with in the Tribunal's offices. Proceedings in this case are commenced by the acquiring authority sending to the Registrar a request that a member be selected to determine the amount of compensation, together with full information of the land concerned and the steps taken to date. Further information will be requested as necessary.

In the third type of case—ie, where no land has been acquired—the documents referred to in r 16 (2) (ii) of the rules mentioned below are required. The usual type of claim under this heading is for injurious affection.

As was noted in at p 130 the Tribunal is the appropriate authority to determine any dispute as to whether any particular property can properly be subject of a blight notice (see s 195 of the Town and Country Planning Act 1971).

1 The Tribunal's jurisdiction

The Lands Tribunal is not only concerned with cases of disputed compensation. Rating appeals from local valuation courts (valuation and community charge tribunals under the new system) form a large part of its business and it also deals with such matters as applications under s 84 of the Law and Property Act 1925 for relief from restrictive covenants and with applications under the rights of light legislation. It deals with many compensation cases each year and bearing in mind the sensible informality of the proceedings, and that solicitors have a right of audience, it is not surprising that many of the cases are set down for hearing.

The Tribunal will usually consist of a single member, either lawyer or chartered surveyor. Where a case calls for special knowledge, the President may direct that the Tribunal sit with assessors. Cases may be set down for hearing in London or at a provincial centre. The Registrar endeavours to fix the venue as close as possible to the subject land, balancing this with the convenience of the parties and their advisers. As pleadings are delivered through the Tribunal, there is a tendency for the parties to accept delay or a position of stalemate on procedure. It is worth remembering that an application can be made at any time under r 45 of the Rules (see below) to the Registrar to get matters moving. Interlocutory applications are probably not used as much as they should be. Although the proceedings are informal, rather like those at a public inquiry, the Civil Evidence Act 1968 has been applied to the Tribunal with its complicated advance notice of hearsay evidence. The procedure at the hearing is governed by r 52 of the 1975 Rules (see below). The Registrar's office are very helpful over procedure and the forms in use often indicate the next step for the party served by the Registrar to take.

In *Argyle Motors Ltd* v *Birkenhead Corporation* (1971) 22 P & CR 829, it was held that a plaintiff could apply to the court for a declaration to establish his right to compensation under a private Act of Parliament. It was agreed that only the Lands Tribunal could assess the compensation if liability were established by the court. But the mere fact that proceedings before the Tribunal might involve duplication was no ground for the High Court refusing to consider the making of a declaratory order.

The Lands Tribunal has no jurisdiction to decide questions of title. Equally the courts have no jurisdiction to decide matters of compensation: see for example *Harrison* v *Croydon London Borough Council* [1968] Ch 479 where the court refused to consider what planning permissions should be assumed to exist for compensation purposes.

However, the courts will decide contractual relationships between the parties as a matter of law, such a dispute not being within the phrase 'any question of disputed compensation' in s 1 of the Land Compensation Act 1961. See *Duttons Brewery* v *Leeds City Council* (1980) 256 EG 919. In *Munton* v *Greater London Council* [1976] 1 WLR 649 the Court of Appeal considered the effect of the words 'subject to contract' in a case of disputed compensation.

Small claims

In view of the demand for the Lands Tribunal to have a simpler procedure for small claims for compensation on compulsory acquisition under which an oral hearing could be dispensed with, r 33A was introduced. It enables the Tribunal to determine cases without an oral hearing. The consent of the claimant is always needed. While most cases will no doubt arise as a result of a request from a claimant that there should be a direction issued dispensing with a hearing, the Tribunal itself can take the initiative with a procedure to obtain the claimant's consent. Even if a direction has been given for the matter to be dealt with on the written representations of the parties, the Tribunal will be able to insist on a hearing if this seems necessary at a later stage in the proceedings.

2 The Lands Tribunal Rules 1975

The following are some of the more important provisions of the Lands Tribunal Rules 1975 (SI 1975 No 299) affecting proceedings before the Tribunal. The 1975 Rules were amended by the Lands Tribunal (Amendment) and (Amendment No 2) Rules 1981 (SI 1981 Nos 105 and 600) and by SI 1984 No 793 following earlier amendment in 1977.

    1 Any person who wishes to commence proceedings for the settlement of compensation by the Lands Tribunal must send to the Registrar at 48 Chancery Lane, London WC2A 1LX:

(a) a notice of reference in Form 4 in Sched 1 to the Rules;

(b) copies for service upon every other party;

(c) a copy of the notice to treat (if any);

(d) a copy of any notice of claim delivered to the acquiring authority and any amendment to it (note that the absence of a notice of claim may affect costs—Lands Compensation Act 1961, s 4 (1) (b));

(e) the fee of £20 (cheque made payable to HM Paymaster General).

There can be no reference until 28 days after the notice to treat or if there is no notice to treat 28 days after the notice of claim. A reference may be withdrawn by sending the Registrar a written notice of withdrawal signed by all the parties or their solicitors or agents (r 51). If the land is jointly owned, then the reference must be by all the joint owners (see *Williams* v *British Gas Corporation* (1980) 41 P & CR 106). If joint owners do pursue a claim but one is absent abroad and cannot be traced, the Tribunal can decide a binding price in the absence of that owner but cannot make a direction as to the payment of one half of the compensation. The authority may pay the compensation into court and the claimant may then apply for his share (*Peltier & Caddle* v *Manchester Corporation* (1974) 29 P & CR 262).

2 Under r 40 the Tribunal or the Registrar may on the application of any party order the parties to give further and better particulars or to deal with interrogatories, and to deliver a statement of agreed facts or issues. The Registrar may act on his own initiative.

3 A pre-trial review may be held under r 45A either on the application of either party or on the motion of the Tribunal or Registrar. A main objective is to secure that the parties make all such admissions and agreements as ought reasonably to be made by them in relation to the proceedings. The Tribunal or Registrar may give all such directions as appear necessary or desirable for securing the just expeditious and economical disposal of the proceedings.

4 A preliminary point of law may be disposed of on the application of any party to the proceedings and if in the Tribunal's opinion the decision on the point of law substantially disposes of the proceedings it may order that the argument shall be treated as the hearing of the case (r 49).

5 Notice must be given if a valuer or other expert witness is to be called. (Form 4, the notice of reference, provides for a statement to be made as to whether an expert witness will be called.) In the normal way only one expert witness is allowed. An additional expert may be called if there is a mineral claim, or there is a claim for business disturbance, or there has, in other cases, been successful application to the Tribunal. Application may be made to the Registrar pursuant to r 42 (3) and r 45 or may be made to the Tribunal at the hearing for more than one additional expert witness to be called.

6 The expert witness's plan and valuation of the property must be sent to the Tribunal when requested by the Registrar, and a statement of any comparative prices or valuations upon which he relies (r 42 (4)). These documents must be sent within 28 days of the request except that the Registrar on receiving written notice that the parties consent may extend the time by periods not exceeding two months or four months in aggregate (r 48 (1) and (2)). An attempt to rely upon material not so submitted may lead to an adjournment. Copies of the submitted material will be sent to the other party where that party is also calling an expert witness. It is also useful to supply in advance to the Tribunal and the other party any plans that will be produced in evidence at the hearing by persons other than the expert witness, eg, a planning officer.

7 It is usual for the acquiring authority to make an unconditional offer in writing to the claimant of the sum which it is ready to pay as compensation. This can be done any time before the hearing, preferably at least a month beforehand. The amount of the offer is often similar to the expert witness's valuation but may be more. A copy of the offer in a sealed cover marked 'Sealed Offer' should be sent to the Registrar or handed to his clerk at the hearing. It will not be opened by the Tribunal until after its award (see para 9, below).

8 The party claiming compensation will begin the hearing; evidence will usually be given orally, or by consent of the parties or direction of the Tribunal, on affidavit. An application must be made to the President for evidence to be given by affidavit and if granted an order is drawn (r 39 (1)). The Tribunal may order the personal attendance of any deponent for examination and cross-examination but only where his evidence affidavit has been produced as evidence (*Mahboob Hussain* v *Oldham Metropolitan Borough Council*

(1981) 42 P & CR 388). Solicitors have a right of audience. Witnesses are sworn before giving evidence.

9 In general, the Tribunal will only act upon the evidence put forward at the hearing. It will not make its own valuation using its own expert knowledge and it is improper for a Tribunal member 'to give evidence himself' without it being open to cross-examination by the parties (*Hickmott* v *Dorset County Council* (1977) 35 P & CR 195). It is important, therefore, that the party can support by evidence any proposition which is to be argued (see *Dunne* v *Secretary of State for Air* (1959) 10 P & CR 157).

10 A party may ask for a preliminary hearing on any point of law. The Tribunal must state the alternative amount which it would have awarded if it had decided the point of law differently. The procedure is by interlocutory application under r 45.

11 Fees payable will be found in Sched 2 to the Lands Tribunal Rules 1975 (as amended). A hearing fee is payable by the party instituting the proceedings and depends upon the amount involved. The current maximum is £2,000.

12 The decision of the Tribunal must be given in writing and must include reasons, although if there would be no injustice or inconvenience to the parties, the decision and reasons can be given orally. The unsuccessful party has six weeks from the decision in which to ask the Tribunal to state a case on a point of law for hearing by the Court of Appeal. The request is by notice addressed to the Registrar (Lands Tribunal Act 1949, s 3 (4), and RSC, Ord 61, r 1).

3 Costs

By virtue of s 3 (5) of the 1949 Act the Tribunal may order the costs of any proceedings before it to be paid by any other party. Rule 56 of the Lands Tribunal Rules 1975 makes further provision as to costs. However, s 4 of the Land Compensation Act 1961 limits the wide discretion in cases where a 'sealed offer' has been made (see above).

The normal rule in 'sealed offer' cases is that the cost of the proceedings will be payable by the acquiring authority if the Tribunal awards a sum in excess of the sealed offer, and by the claimant —unless there are special reasons—if the award is less than or equal to the sealed offer (s 4, 1961 Act). However even if costs are awarded against the claimant under this provision they are restricted to costs 'so far as they were incurred after the offer was made' and the claimant will still be able to recover from the acquiring authority his costs incurred prior to the date of the sealed offer.

It should therefore be in the interests of the acquiring authority to make the sealed offer at an early date since this would enable them to recover more of their costs—and pay less of the claimant's—should the Tribunal award a sum equal to or less than the sealed offer. Indeed, where an authority delayed making its offer until immediately before the hearing, they were ordered to pay the whole of the costs of the hearing even though the sealed offer exceeded the amount awarded (see *Christodoulou* v *Islington London Borough Council* (1973) 230 EG 233).

Although the 1949 Act and the 1975 Rules give a wide discretion to the Tribunal as to costs, this discretion has to be exercised judicially. In *Pepys* v *London Transport Executive* (1974) 29 P & CR 248 the Court of Appeal held that the Tribunal had erred in ordering the Executive to pay the claimant's costs up to the date of their sealed offer when the Tribunal awarded no compensation at all for injurious affection attributed to the running of trains on the underground Victoria line. It was held that if the Tribunal wished to award costs to a claimant who had failed altogether, there would have to be special reasons which were not present in that case.

The Tribunal may order the claimant to pay the costs of the acquiring authority even though no sealed offer has been made—see *Hood Investment Co Ltd* v *Marlow Urban District Council* (1963) 15 P & CR 299.

4 Interest

The Tribunal may direct that any sum awarded shall carry interest from the date of the award (Arbitration Act 1950, s 14, applied by r 38 of the 1975 Rules). The rate of interest would be the same as on a judgment debt. However there is no provision for interest to be awarded from any earlier date, even though the claim may have been outstanding for a considerable time when the award is made.

Indeed the statutory provisions for the award of interest on compensation are very limited. Mention has been made of the following:

(*a*) Interest on purchase money from date of entry at rate prescribed under s 32, Land Compensation Act 1961 (see p 64, above). In *Simmonds* v *Kent County Council* (1989) EGCS 129 compensation was agreed following the service of a blight notice. The claimant handed the keys of his property to the authority's agent; the Lands Tribunal was asked to determine whether there had been an entry in respect of which interest was payable. It was held that the handing over of the keys constituted an entry but that s 32 did no more than determine the rate of interest and did not provide for its payment.

(*b*) Interest on compensation for injurious affection where no land taken—s 63, Land Compensation Act 1973 (p 227). Interest is to be awarded from the date of claim until payment.

(*c*) Interest on depreciation caused by use of public works, from date of claim or beginning of claim period—s 18, 1973 Act (see p 235).

(*d*) Interest on payment of a farm loss payment—S 36 (6), 1973 Act. Payable from date of claim (see p 150).

(*e*) Interest on disturbance payment for persons without compensatable interests—s 37 (6), 1973 Act. Payable from date of displacement (see p 154). In *Knibb* v *National Coal Board* (1984) 49 P & CR 426, the Court of Appeal decided that the Lands Tribunal had jurisdiction to award interest for a period prior to the date of an award of compensation. In this particular case, which concerned damage to a bungalow caused by mining subsidence, interest was payable from the date when the damage occurred.

There seem to be no other circumstances where interest can be awarded. Also, there are various cases where compensation is payable but where interest cannot be claimed otherwise than from the date of the award as provided for by r 38 (see p 289).

It is understood that the government is reviewing the whole question of the law on interest on land compensation with a view to extending the provisions for the payment of interest.

Chapter 32

Recovery of Compensation from Acquiring Authority

If planning permission is refused for the development of land which has the benefit of an 'established claim', the owner may make a claim on the Secretary of State for the Environment under s 154 of the Town and Country Planning Act 1971 to be paid out, provided he can show (as would normally be the case) that the planning refusal has reduced the value of his land, and that he claims within six months (although the Secretary of State can extend the period). Compensation is also payable for the conditional grant of permission, although there are many exclusions in the s 147 of the Act of 1971. The making of a claim for compensation is dealt with at p 283. This chapter is concerned with circumstances in which compensation already paid under Pt VII of the Act of 1971 may be recovered from an acquiring authority which has used or possesses compulsory purchase powers.

If the Secretary of State accepts the owner's claim, and pays compensation—to the extent to which the established claim is still intact, ie, 'the unexpended balance of established development value' (s 146 of the Act of 1971)—then the fact of payment becomes registrable as a local land charge by the registrar of the district council concerned. Payments of £20 or less are not so registered (s 158).

Where land which has such a compensation payment recorded against it in the local land charges register is subsequently bought by an authority having powers of compulsory purchase, the Secretary of State is entitled under s 257 to recover from the acquiring authority the money he has paid out to the previous owner as compensation. The logic behind this provision is that the authority should buy at a price reduced by the amount of the compensation payment and it is fair that they should repay the Secretary of State after acquisition. The Secretary of State's right to recover:

(a) arises whether or not the compensation notice is registered before or after the notice to treat or contract of sale, provided the planning decision was dated before the notice of contract;

(b) is lost if the land is being acquired for use as a public open space;

(c) is suspended while there is outstanding any fee simple or leasehold interest not vested in the authority.

Whether any land has the benefit of an established claim can be ascertained by inquiry of the Secretary of State under s 145; see also the Town and Country Planning (Compensation and Certificates) Regulations 1974, SI 1974 No 1242.

These provisions for recovery by the Secretary of State are paralleled by the provisions of s 159 applicable to private owners under which compensation paid out to a landowner must be repaid if permission for development is subsequently given.

If the price to be paid by the acquiring authority is based upon the value which the land has for development, then the development will entail repayment of compensation to the Secretary of State under s 159. The market value will take account of this repayment liability. The price to be paid by the acquiring authority where there is a registered compensation notice will accordingly be reduced (*Williams and Williams* v *Plymouth Corporation* (1962) 14 P & CR 171).

Chapter 33

Compulsory Purchase and Tax

When an owner of an interest in land receives compensation for the compulsory acquisition of his interest, normal taxation rules will for the most part apply to the receipt involved. The owner may be liable for income tax or capital gains tax (or corporation tax if a company). This chapter outlines the main provisions which should be borne in mind.

1 Income tax

In *West Suffolk County Council* v *Rought (W) Ltd* [1957] AC 403, compensation included a sum for temporary loss of profits. Because the court assumed that the sum would not be taxable in the hands of the recipient, a deduction was made for the tax which would have been payable if the profit had been earned. In *Stoke-on-Trent City Council* v *Wood Mitchell & Co Ltd* [1980] 1 WLR 254, the Court of Appeal held that the principle in *Rought's* case was only to be applied if it was clear that the compensation would not actually be taxable.

The following statement was then issued by the Inland Revenue (Statement of Practice SP8/79 dated 18 June 1979):

1 The Inland Revenue practice—announced in a statement on December 13, 1972—has been that any element of compensation for temporary loss of profits, which is present in the compensation or price payable by an authority possessing compulsory powers for the acquisition of property used for the purposes of a trade or profession, is included as part of the consideration of the resulting disposal for the purposes of capital gains.

2 The Board of Inland Revenue have reconsidered this practice in the light of the decision of the Court of Appeal in the recent case of the *City of Stoke-on-Trent* v *Wood Mitchell & Co Ltd* (a Lands Tribunal case). In accordance with this decision any element of compensation received for temporary loss of profits in the circumstances described above falls to be included as a receipt taxable under Case I or II of Schedule D. Compensation for losses of trading

stock and to reimburse revenue expenditure, such as removal expenses and interest, will be treated in the same way for tax purposes.

3 The practice described in paragraph 2 will also apply in compensation cases where no interest is acquired (eg compensation due to damage, injury or exploitation of land, or to the exercise of planning control).

4 The new practice will appy to all cases in which the liability had not been finally determined at the date of the Court of Appeal's judgment (July 28, 1978).

The effect of this statement is that any amount of the compensation included for temporary loss of profits, losses on trading stock or to reimburse revenue expenditure such as removal expenses and interest will be treated as trading receipts in all cases not finally determined on 28 July 1978, and not as capital gains—the practice prior to 1979.

Although compensation is regarded as a single payment, for tax purposes it may be apportioned between capital and income; and any sum liable to be taxed as income is to be excluded from the assessment of the capital gain.

In *Pennine Raceway Ltd* v *Kirklees MBC* (1988) EGCS 168 the Lands Tribunal made a deduction in respect of capital gains tax when awarding compensation for depreciation arising from an Article 4 Direction (see p 277). The Court of Appeal held that the compensation was subject to capital gains tax, as claimed by the Inland Revenue, and so the tribunal had been wrong to award a net sum.

(a) Interest

Interest payable after entry will be subject to a deduction of tax at a basic rate (Income and Corporation Taxes Act 1988, s 349 (2) (*a*)). It will generally be treated as income of the recipient in the year of assessment in which it is received.

In *Parkside Leasing Ltd* v *Smith* (*Inspector of Taxes*) [1984] 1 WLR 310 a haulage contractor ceased trading when its premises were compulsorily acquired. Disturbance compensation, with interest, was received on 9 April; the cheque was presented on 11 April and the company began a new trade on 10 April. It was held that the payment of interest was not chargeable to tax until actually received and that delivery of the cheque was not to be treated as the receipt of the sum so as to give rise to liability to tax.

(b) Special cases

The fact that a sale is to an authority with compulsory powers of acquisition will usually allow a tax payer to defeat a claim that he has been carrying on the trade of dealing in land or that he purchased the land with a view to realising a profit on its disposal (see ss 18 and 776 of the 1988 Act).

2 Capital gains tax

(a) Rollover relief

If an owner applies the compensation received on a sale to an authority with compulsory powers towards purchasing alternative land, he can claim rollover relief by virtue of ss 111A and 111B of the Capital Gains Tax Act 1979. This does not apply if the new alternative premises is a dwelling-house to which the main residence exemption applies. The new land must be acquired in the period beginning 12 months before and ending three years after the disposal (or such longer period as the Inland Revenue Commissioners may allow) (Capital Gains Tax Act 1979, s 115). The normal treatment of severance compensation as dealt with in the next paragraph is excluded. The compensation is treated as additional compensation for the acquired land.

(b) Sales of part only

Two provisions in the capital gains tax legislation apply only when there is a sale of part of an owner's land so that he is left with part, and may have received compensation for injurious affection.

If the market value of the land acquired is small (5 per cent is the usual Revenue figure) in relation to the value of the whole, the owner may elect to defer payment of tax until the next disposal of the retained land occurs. He does this by electing to treat the compensation as a deduction from the allowable expenditure. Because the deductible expenditure is reduced, the tax bill on the later disposition will obviously be increased (Capital Gains Tax Act 1979, s 108).

Where part only is sold and there is a severance compensation claim, there will normally be two compensation figures, one for the land acquired and the other for the injury to the retained land. For capital gains tax, each can be treated as a part disposal (see Capital Gains Tax Act 1979, s 110 (2)).

Where compensation includes payments for goodwill and other items, the owner may apportion the compensation as between the land itself and the disturbance and other items of claim (Capital Gains Tax Act 1979, ss 43 (4) and 110 (1)).

3 Disposal date

The date of disposal for capital gains tax where land is acquired compulsorily is either the date of settlement of compensation (whether reached by agreement or laid down by the Lands Tribunal) or the date of entry on the land, whichever is earlier (Capital Gains Tax Act 1979, s 111). However, if the owner sells by contract, albeit under threat of compulsory purchase, ordinary rules apply—that is the date of unconditional exchange of contracts will be the date of disposal: Capital Gains Tax Act 1979, s 27.

4 Inheritance tax

Section 197 of the Capital Transfer Act 1984 (also known as the Inheritance Tax Act) provides that where a notice to treat is served before or within three years from death, the provisions of the Act apply even though the acquisition may occur after the expiry of the three year period. Losses on sales are taken into account but not gains.

Section 198 deals with the date of sale. The general rule is that the date of sale is regarded as the date of contract. With regard to compulsory acquisition the date of sale is the date when compensation is agreed or determined, except when the acquisition is by general vesting declaration. In that case, the date of sale is taken to be the last day of the period specified in the declaration.

5 Value added tax

The sale by compulsory purchase may attract VAT. It cannot do so unless the sale is (VATA 1983, s 2):

(a) by a 'taxable person', that is someone who is or ought to be registered for VAT (note that the sale itself will sometimes make registrable a person who was not before);

(b) in the course or furtherance of a business carried on by him. However, HM Customs interpret this phrase widely (see also VATA 1983, s 47 (5), (6)), and broadly seem to take the view that any disposal of a business asset (including a capital business asset) by a taxable person falls within the phrase. However a sale of a dwelling by an owner-occupier is certainly not caught.

If so then the sale will be standard-rated for VAT if (and only if):

(i) the property consists of a freehold new building or freehold new civil engineering work: VATA 1983, Sched 6, Group 1,

Item 1(*a*). This broadly means a building or work which is under construction or which is not more than three years old;

(ii)   the acquiring authority happens to be the vendor's immediate landlord (VATA 1983, Sched 6, Group 1, Note (1));

(iii) the vendor has elected to 'waive exemption' in respect of the land or building in question, under VATA 1983, Sched 6A, paras 2, 3;

(iv)   in a few other special cases, for example where a significant part of the value of the land stems from fishing or sporting rights.

It seems likely, on the analogy of the stamp duty position (see p 110), that, where the sale attracts VAT, the element of the price which is for disturbance, severance, loss of profits and so on is also part of the price for VAT and will attract VAT. A vendor making a standard-rated sale must provide the authority with the proper VAT invoice within 30 days of the time of supply of the sale: VAT (General) Regulations 1985, r 12.

The acquiring authority will want to obtain a refund from HM Customs of the input VAT it has had to pay on the purchase, if it possibly can. On this see VATA 1983, s 20 and HM Customs' Notice 749. In very brief outline the position as regards a local authority is as follows:

(*a*) if its purchase is for non-business purposes, the authority is entitled to a refund of the input VAT;

(*b*) if the purchase is for business purposes, but that business is a standard-rated or zero-rated business so far as the authority is concerned, the authority is entitled to a refund of the input VAT;

(*c*) if the purchase is for the purpose of a business activity by the authority, but that business activity is exempt from VAT, then the authority is entitled to a refund of that input VAT if and only if the whole of its input VAT for the year relating to exempt business activities is less than 5 per cent of its *total* input VAT for the year;

(*d*) if (*c*) does not apply, then the authority is not entitled to a refund of input VAT incurred by it in relation to exempt business activities.

Therefore it seems likely that if, for example, a local authority incurs input VAT for the purpose of a property development project in which the authority will be involved for essentially commercial reasons, for example to derive a rental income or make a profit on the resale of the land to the developer, then it would not be entitled to a refund of its input VAT unless either (*c*) applied on the facts of the case, or the authority itself elected to waive exemption in relation to the development land.

6 Other cases

A home loss payment does not appear to be taxable: nor does a disturbance payment made under s 37 of the Land Compensation Act 1973. Payments to tenant farmers under s 12 of the Agriculture (Miscellaneous Provisions) Act 1968 are non-taxable.

Chapter 34

Compensation in Various Cases Where there is no Land Acquisition

Most of this book has been concerned with the procedures for compulsory acquisition by a public authority and with the ways in which compensation for that acquisition can be assessed and claimed. Consideration has also been given to two types of 'compulsory purchase in reverse', ie, the purchase notice (Chapter 17) and the blight notice (Chapter 18). In those cases it is not the local authority which initiates the purchase, but the owner who can compel acquisition of his interest because of some action taken by the authority. There are also cases where compensation can be claimed to mitigate the injurious effects of public works.

There is a further group of cases in which problems of compensation may arise even though there has been no acquisition of land by a public authority. It is likely that those involved with the acquisition and development of land will come across at least some of these cases from time to time and so it seems appropriate to set out in this chapter an outline of the circumstances in which compensation may be payable as a result of planning restrictions and other actions of public authorities, without the authorities acquiring any interest in the land concerned. These are dealt with under the following headings:

1 Eighth Schedule rights
2 Article 4 directions
3 Revocation or modification orders
4 Discontinuance orders
5 Historic buildings
6 Ancient monuments
7 Tree preservation orders
8 Advertisement regulations
9 Stop notices
10 New development; unexpended balance of established development value
11 Pedestrianisation orders
12 Stopping up orders
13 Access to highways
14 Other highways orders
15 Sewers
16 Land drainage
17 Minerals

The list is not intended to be exhaustive but rather to draw together various statutory procedures where a liability to compensation may arise either in association with or separate from compulsory purchase.

There will be many occasions when a private practitioner will be asked by clients affected by the actions of a public authority whether any compensation can be claimed if, eg, their trade is adversely affected or they find that they cannot carry out some improvement to their homes. Similarly, those advising local authorities may well need to draw the attention of officers or committee members to the fact that compensation may be payable if planning permission is refused in certain circumstances or if other restrictions are imposed. This chapter deals with cases where provision is made by statute for the payment of compensation in defined circumstances. It does not deal with the cases where damages may be claimed against a local authority because of any alleged negligence in the performance of its statutory powers or duties, or because of any trespass or nuisance that might occur in the discharge of those functions. The reader should however bear in mind that a remedy in damages may be available even in cases where no statutory compensation can be claimed. On the other hand, if the statute does contain a specific provision for the payment of compensation then this may be the only remedy. It may be that an injunction or damages would not be possible because the fact that a compensation clause has been included may indicate that only a statutory remedy in compensation is available: see *Marriage* v *East Norfolk Rivers Catchment Board* [1950] 1 KB 284.

1 Eighth Schedule rights

This term is frequently used to describe the situation in which, while planning permission for certain types of development is still required, compensation may be payable if it is refused. There are no 'rights' to develop but since planning authorities will be reluctant to incur a liability to pay compensation, in practice it will often be found that an owner can count on getting permission for these classes of development.

Section 169 of the Town and Country Planning Act 1971 applies where the Secretary of State, either on appeal or on a reference of an application to him for determination, refuses permission—or grants it subject to conditions—for development of one of the classes specified in Pt II of Sched 8 to the Act. A person can claim compensation equal to the reduction in the value of his land as a result of the refusal or conditions.

The first point to note is that a claim for compensation can only be made following a decision by the Secretary of State. A refusal by the local planning authority is not sufficient. The next point to consider is whether the refusal or conditional grant of permission comes within the scope of Sched 8. The Schedule is entitled 'development not constituting new development' and is divided into two parts. Detailed consideration of the various classes of development is not within the scope of this book but Pt I—development *not* ranking for compensation—consists of Class I, ie, rebuilding so long as the cubic content of the original building is not exceeded by more than one-tenth (or the greater of one-tenth or 1,750 cubic feet in the case of a dwelling-house), and Class II, ie, the use of a single dwelling-house as two or more dwelling-houses.

If planning permission is refused for development within Classes I or II the only remedy for an owner is to serve a Purchase Notice (see Chapter 17).

Part 2 of the Schedule—development which *does* rank for compensation—includes six further classes of development. Class III is perhaps the one which is most frequently considered in relation to compensation claims. It covers the enlargement, improvement or alteration of a building by up to one-tenth of the cubic content (the greater of one-tenth or 1,750 cubic feet in the case of a dwelling-house). The extent of the development for which compensation can be claimed has since been modified by s 278 (1) of and Sched 18 to the 1971 Act, to which reference is made later. Class IV covers building or other operations for agricultural or forestry purposes on land which was agricultural or forestry land; Class V is the working of minerals on land held with agricultural land; Class VI is the use of land for a purpose within a use class if used for another purpose within the same class as set out in the Town and Country Planning (Use Classes for Third Schedule Purposes) Order 1948, SI 1948 No 955; Class VII covers the use of an additional part of a building or land for a purpose for which part is already used, and Class VIII covers the deposit of waste materials or refuse in connection with the working and minerals.

As a result of the further modifications introduced by s 278 and Sched 18, the increases permitted by Classes III and VII *do not* apply to a building erected or rebuilt since 1 July 1948. Also, in the case of a pre-1948 building, the increase will be restricted to one-tenth of the gross floor area in addition to the limit on the increase on the cubic content.

Therefore no compensation can be claimed if permission is refused for the extension of a building erected or rebuilt after 1 July 1948, and in the case of older buildings the extension is subject to a 10 per cent limit on both the cubic content and the floor space. The Court of Appeal has held in *Camden London Borough Council* v *Peaktop Properties (Hampstead) Ltd* (1983) 45 P & CR 177, that the addition of a floor to a block of flats, thus creating additional flats to be occupied as dwellings, came within Class III of Sched 8 but since the gross floor space would be enlarged by slightly over one-tenth, the developer was not entitled to any compensation. The Lands Tribunal had previously held that a compensation claim was possible even though the development exceeded the amount permitted by the Schedule, and that only the excess should be disregarded. The Court of Appeal, however, held that any excess disqualified the claim entirely. Developers seeking to extend buildings must therefore ensure that their proposals do not exceed the limits if they are seeking to convince the local planning authority that permission cannot be refused because the payment of compensation would be inevitable. The *Peaktop* case established that the 10 per cent enlargement was available for a building as a whole, rather than simply the individual flats within it. The decision led to the passing of the Town and Country Planning (Compensation) Act 1985 which amends s 169 of the 1971 Act so as to provide that the Eighth Schedule is to be construed as not extending to any works which would increase the number of flats in a building or increase the cubic content of any flat by more than one-tenth.

The 1985 Act had effect in relation to applications made after 23 January 1985. See *ADC Estates Ltd* v *Camden LBC* (1989) EGCS 134 for a case where an application was posted on 22 January 1985 but where lessees had not been served with notice so that correct certificates were not submitted until later. The Lands Tribunal held that the incorrect certificates were irrelevant and that the application was made before the new Act came into force.

There is no provision for the repayment of any compensation should permission be given later for the development for which compensation was paid. Also, there is no necessity for the person claiming compensation to show either the intention or ability to implement the proposal in respect of which compensation is claimed.

In *Richmond Gateways Ltd* v *Richmond upon Thames LBC* (1989) EGCS 61 the Court of Appeal held that the Lands Tribunal was entitled to adopt a residual valuation and that it was not necessary to deduct a sum for developer's risk and profit.

In *Church Cottage Investments Ltd* v *Hillingdon LBC* (1989) EGCS 133 another case concerning a proposal to construct flats on the roof of residential blocks came before the Court of Appeal. The Court upheld the decision of the Lands Tribunal that because proposed extensions would not receive building regulations' approval unless outer walls were rebuilt, the cost of that rebuilding should be taken into account.

2 Article 4 Directions

By virtue of art 3 and Sched 2 to the Town and Country Planning General Development Order 1988 (SI 1988 No 1813) planning permission is deemed to be granted for 28 types of 'permitted development'. The best known is Pt I—development within the curtilage of a dwelling-house. If however the local planning authority or the Secretary of State wish to withdraw the rights to permitted development, a direction may be made under art 4 that development of any of the classes should not be carried out in any particular area unless planning permission is obtained.

Section 165 of the 1971 Act provides for compensation to be payable where permission granted by a development order is withdrawn either by the revocation or amendment of the development order itself, or by the issue of an Article 4 Direction. Where permission is withdrawn an application for planning permission has to be made and if this is refused or granted on conditions, compensation may be claimed. If permission for the development is subsequently granted then the compensation can be recovered by the authority (s 168).

For recent cases concerning the liability of a local planning authority to pay compensation following an Article 4 Direction see *Jones* v *Metropolitan Borough of Stockport* (1982) 45 P & CR 419 (erection of a piggery on agricultural land) and *Pennine Raceway Ltd* v *Kirklees MBC* (1988) EGCS 168 (airfield used for temporary drag racing). In *Carter* v *Windsor and Maidenhead RBC* (1988) 57 P & CR 480 the claimant divided land previously used for producing hay crops into 15 paddocks. The claimant had arranged to sell the land but when the Article 4 Direction was made the sale fell through, as did sales of individual plots. The Lands Tribunal considered alternative valuations based on a sale in lots and as a single unit. The tribunal held that the land could be valued as individual plots.

3 Revocation or modification orders under s 45 of the 1971 Act

A local planning authority can revoke or modify a planning permission, provided that the development has not yet been carried out. A revocation or modification order has to be confirmed by the Secretary of State unless it is an 'unopposed' order under s 46. By virtue of s 164, compensation is payable where permission is revoked or modified (unless it is pursuant to an 'unopposed order). The claimant must have an interest in the land and must show abortive expenditure, eg, on the preparation of plans or some other loss or damage directly attributable to the revocation or modification. Loss of future profits can be the subject of a claim (*Hobbs (Quarries)* v *Somerset County Council* (1975) 13 P & CR 286) but the claim must not be too remote.

A 'person interested in the land' can claim under s 164 even though he has only an enforceable contractual right to the use of the land rather than a legal or equitable interest (*Pennine Raceway Ltd* v *Kirklees Metropolitan Borough Council* (1982) 45 P & CR 313).

4 Discontinuance orders

Section 51 of the 1971 Act enables a local planning authority to require the discontinuance of any use of land or the alteration or removal of any buildings or works. The power can be used whether the building or the use of land is lawful or unlawful. However, compensation is payable by virtue of s 170 of the 1971 Act if it is shown that any person has suffered damage in consequence of the discontinuance order, whether by depreciation of the value of interest in land or by disturbance in the enjoyment of the land. Compensation can be claimed for loss of trade (*Harrison* v *Gloucester County Council* (1953) 4 P & CR 99). Expenditure on works in compliance with an order can be recovered. Compensation can be claimed for plant purchased after a discontinuance order had been made but before it had been confirmed since it is expressly provided that an order shall not take effect until confirmed (see *K & B Metals* v *Birmingham City Council* (1976) 33 P & CR 135, a case involving a scrap metal dealer). If development is subsequently permitted, there is no provision for repayment of compensation.

5 Historic buildings

Compensation may be claimed:
(*a*) for refusal of consent to the alteration of a listed building (s 171);
(*b*) where listed building consent is revoked or modified (s 172);
(*c*) where loss or damage is caused by the service of a building preservation notice (s 173).

In addition a listed building purchase notice may be possible under s 190 (see p 118).

For compensation to be payable under s 171, it is necessary to show that listed building consent has been refused by the Secretary of State (not just by the local planning authority) for works of alteration or extension to a listed building. Compensation is not payable for refusal of consent for demolition. Also, either the works must not constitute 'development' under s 22, or if they do it must be development permitted by a development order.

Since internal works will not usually constitute 'development' it may well be that compensation can be claimed for refusal of consent to internal alterations. In the case of a proposed extension to a listed building within the limits of the Eighth Schedule rights described earlier in this chapter, it may be that although the local authority could not refuse planning permission without running the risk of having to pay compensation, they can refuse listed building consent—and thus prevent the extension being built—because compensation would not be payable for a refusal for a scheme involving 'development' which was not permitted development.

The right to claim compensation for the revocation or modification of listed building consent is set out in s 172 and is similar to the provisions of s 164 (revocation or modification orders). Compensation can also be claimed under s 172 for the revocation or modification of a consent granted for the demolition of an unlisted building in a conservation area (Town and Country Planning (Listed Buildings and Buildings in Conservation Areas) Regulations 1987 (SI 1987 No 349), reg 10.

Section 173 provides for compensation following the service of a building preservation notice if the Secretary of State decides not to list the building or after six months has taken no decision. Compensation can be claimed by any person interested in the building in respect of any loss or damage directly attributable to the effect of the notice. This can include any sum payable in respect of breach of contract caused by having to discontinue works as a result of the building preservation notice.

If the Secretary of State does decide to list the building then a claim can be made under s 171 as just described. It is also possible to apply for listed building consent whilst the building preservation notice is in force, ie, before the Secretary of State has made his decision. If such a claim is successful the compensation will not become payable until the building is actually listed.

Compensation is not payable as an automatic consequence to the listing of a building or the service of a building preservation notice, and so unless it is possible to establish a claim under ss 171–173 it may mean that an owner finds that a development cannot be commenced or completed, even though planning permission has been obtained, because a building is listed or a building preservation notice is served at a late stage. For this reason it is worth considering whether application should be made for a certificate that a building is not intended to be listed (s 54A, 1971 Act).

6 Ancient monuments

The Historic Buildings and Ancient Monuments Act 1953, s 12, provided for compensation for injurious affection as a result of a preservation order. In *Hoveringham Gravels Ltd* v *Secretary of State for the Environment* (1975) 30 P & CR 151, the Court of Appeal considered the relevance of refusal of planning consent in a claim for injurious affection under s 12.

With the repeal of that section and the coming into force of Pt I of the Ancient Monuments and Archaeological Areas Act 1979, compensation can be claimed under s 7 of the 1979 Act for the refusal of scheduled monument consent. Compensation is payable by the Secretary of State to an owner who suffers loss or damage in consequence of the refusal or conditional grant of consent but only in respect of works which are needed to implement a planning permission granted before the monument was scheduled, or which do not constitute development (or which are permitted by a development order) or which are necessary for the continuation of the existing use of the monument. If planning permission is granted for some other use or development, compensation will not be payable if scheduled monument consent is refused. There are further provisions for the recovery of compensation on the subsequent grant of consent (s 8, 1979 Act) and for compensation where works affecting a scheduled monument which were previously authorised cease to be authorised because consent has been revoked or modified (s 9).

Part II of the 1979 Act introduced new arrangements for 'rescue archaeology'. In a designated area of archaeological importance (only five historic centres have so far been designated), a person proposing to carry out operations which would disturb the ground has to give six weeks' notice and this gives rights initially for inspection and observation during a six-week period. If the investigating authority serve notice of intention to excavate they can have a further four and a half months to excavate the site. By s 46, any damage caused to the land or to any chattels on it as a result of the entry, investigation or excavation, gives rise to a claim for compensation from the Secretary of State or any other authority on whose behalf the powers were exercised.

Any disputed compensation claims under the 1979 Act are to be referred to the Lands Tribunal (s 47).

7 Tree preservation orders

Trees, groups of trees or woodlands may be the subject of orders under ss 60 or 61 of the 1971 Act. Orders must be made in (or substantially in) the model form set out in the Schedule to the Town and Country Planning (Tree Preservation Order) Regulations 1969, SI 1969 No 17. The model order provides for the payment of compensation to any person who suffers loss or damage in consequence of the refusal or conditional grant of consent under the order (arts 9–12) except that compensation is not payable if the authority certifies under art 5 that the refusal or condition is in the interests of good forestry or that the trees (other than trees comprised in woodlands) have an outstanding or special amenity value.

Section 174 of the 1971 Act deals with compensation in respect of tree preservation orders although it does not directly state that compensation will be payable. Instead it provides that an order may make provision for compensation. However, as the order must be substantially in the form set out in the regulations, it may be assumed that compensation will be payable.

As to the basis of compensation, see *Bell* v *Canterbury City Council* (1988) EGCS 31. The claimant wished to clear the trees and convert the land to agriculture. The woodland was subject to a tree preservation order and consent to fell was refused, the authority indicating that had they consented they would have imposed a replanting direction. The Court of Appeal held that the measure of compensation was the diminution in the value of the land (so long as this was not too remote) and not just the loss of the value of the timber. The date of valuation was the date of refusal of consent.

If consent is given under a tree preservation order and a direction requiring replanting of a woodland area is made, s 175 of the 1971 Act provides that compensation may be payable if the Forestry Commission decide not to make any advance (by grant or loan) in respect of the replanting because they consider the direction has frustrated the use of the woodland area or the growing of timber for commercial purposes, ie, that it has required replanting on an amenity rather than commercial basis.

Compensation may also be payable if the Forestry Commission refuse a felling licence under s 11 of the Forestry Act 1967. Claims can be made for any depreciation in the value of trees which is attributable to deterioration in the quality of the timber as a result of the refusal of the licence.

8 Advertisement regulations

Only in very limited circumstances can a claim for compensation be made in connection with restrictions on advertising. Section 147 (1) (b) of the 1971 Act states that no compensation is payable in respect of a decision on an application under s 63 for consent to display advertisements. The limited circumstances in which compensation may be claimed are set out in s 176 which provides for the payment of reasonable expenses incurred in complying with an order made under the Town and Country Planning (Control of Advertisements) Regulations 1989 (SI 1989 No 670), for the removal of an advertisement which was being displayed on 1 August 1948, or for the discontinuance of the display of advertisements on a site used for that purpose on that date.

Also, if consent for the display of advertisements is revoked or modified under reg 17 of the 1989 Regulations, compensation may be claimed for abortive expenditure or for other loss or damage sustained which is directly attributable to the revocation or modification, although compensation for the depreciation in value of any interest in land is excluded.

9 Stop notices

Local authorities may be deterred from using the stop notice procedure under s 90 of the 1971 Act because of the compensation provisions set out in s 177. A stop notice is used in conjunction with an enforcement notice in order to prohibit the activity at an earlier date than would be possible under the latter. However, compensation may be claimed if the stop notice is withdrawn or if the enforcement notice ultimately does not take effect because it is:

(a) quashed on grounds other than that planning permission ought to be granted;

(b) varied (other than on that ground) so that the breach no longer includes the activity;

(c) withdrawn (other than following the grant of permission for the activity).

If the stop notice or the enforcement notice are found to have been a nullity, then no compensation is payable because the notice could not be withdrawn, quashed or varied (see *Clwyd County Council* v *Secretary of State for Wales* [1982] JPL 696).

The claimant must have an interest in or occupy the land and he is entitled to be compensated in respect of any loss or damage directly attributable to the prohibition contained in the stop notice (or so much of the prohibition as ceases to have effect by virtue of a variation of the enforcement notice).

Of particular importance to a local authority contemplating the use of a stop notice is the provision in s 177 (5) that the loss or damage for which compensation is payable shall include a sum in respect of any breach of contract caused by the taking of action necessary to comply with the prohibition. If an authority serve a stop notice in a case where work is being carried out under a building contract, and the notice is subsequently withdrawn, quashed or varied, the compensation claim may include any sum due from the owner to the building contractor in respect of the cessation of work.

Compensation is not restricted to the diminution in the value of the land. In *J Sample* (*Walkworth*) *Ltd* v *Alnwick District Council* [1984] JPL 670 compensation was awarded in respect of such things as the cost of keeping the work force idle and for the cost of temporary accommodation. In *Graysmark* v *South Hams DC* (1989) 3 EG 75, the Court of Appeal disallowed some heads of damage as being too remote but allowed interest payments on the development which had been stopped and deferment of the profits.

The compensation may be reduced where the entitlement is attributable to the failure of the claimant to comply with a notice served under s 284 requiring information about the land or to any misstatement made in response to such a notice.

10 New development: unexpended balance of established development value

Section 146 of the 1971 Act gives a right to compensation where planning permission for the carrying out of 'new development' (ie, any development other than developments specified in Pt I or Pt II of the Eighth Schedule to the 1971 Act) is refused or granted subject to conditions. However, the right only arises if the claimant is at the time of the decision entitled to an interest in the land, there is an unexpended balance of established development value, and value of the claimant's interest if depreciated as a result of the decision.

Various other restrictions on the right to compensation are imposed by ss 147–149 of the Act and there are further provisions in ss 38 and 39. The measure of compensation is dealt with in ss 152 and 153; the method of claiming is set out in s 154 (and see the Town and Country Planning (Compensation and Certificates) Regulations 1974 (SI 1974 No 1242)). Sections 155–163 set out various further provisions as to the determination of claims, payment of compensation, apportionment of registration, the recovery of compensation on subsequent development, and on the calculation of value for the purposes of Pt VII of the 1971 Act.

The earlier provisions of Pt VII (ie, ss 135–145) deal with the definition of the 'unexpended balance of established development value' and the ascertainment of its amount.

Mention has been made of compensation claims under the Eighth Schedule for development which does not constitute new development. Claims for development which does constitute new development are made under Pt VII but the combined effect of the requirement for an unexpended balance of established development value, and the various exclusions of ss 147 and 148, together with the other provisions mentioned, is that only rarely will a claim for compensation be possible under Pt VII. It is therefore not proposed to deal in detail with the relevant statutory provisions. Chapter 32 explains how compensation may have to be repaid if the land is sold to an authority with compulsory purchase powers.

11 Pedestrianisation orders

Under s 212 of the 1971 Act the Secretary of State may, on the application of the local planning authority, make an order to provide for the extinguishment of vehicular rights over a highway, ie, to convert the highway into a footpath or bridleway. The order may provide for the use on the highway of specified descriptions of vehicles or for particular persons or vehicles to use the highway in specified circumstances. This is particularly useful to enable a highway to be converted into a pedestrian precinct, with provision for service vehicles to use the precinct at specified times.

Section 212 (5) provides that anyone who at the time of the coming into force of the order had an interest in land having lawful access to the highway, can claim compensation in respect of any depreciation in that interest which is directly attributable to the order and in respect of any other loss or damage. Any claim must be made within six months from the date of the decision giving rise to it and must comply with reg 14 of the Town and Country Planning General Regulations 1976 (SI 1976 No 1419).

It will usually be more satisfactory for a trader likely to be adversely affected by a pedestrianisation order to object to it and then seek agreement with the local authority for alternative rights of access (eg, a new service road) or for provision to be made in the order allowing him access, rather than to take no action and then claim compensation for depreciation.

Local authorities may achieve similar results, without incurring a liability to pay compensation, by using the appropriate road traffic legislation, ie, a traffic regulation order or an experimental traffic order under the Road Traffic Regulation Act 1984.

12 Stopping up orders

Mention has already been made (p 228) that no compensation can be claimed in respect of an order under s 209 of the 1971 Act for the stopping up or diversion of a highway. Financial provisions can be included since s 209 (3) (*a*) allows the Secretary of State to include in the order a provision requiring any authority or person to pay for or contribute towards the cost of any work provided for by the order or for any increased expenditure attributable to the doing of such work. However, this provision is more likely to be relevant to those directly involved in the development scheme giving rise to the order.

There is no provision for the payment of compensation when the magistrates' court authorise the stopping up or diversion of a highway under s 116 of the Highways Act 1980.

However if a public footpath or bridleway is stopped up or diverted as a result of an extinguishment or diversion order made under ss 118–119 of the 1980 Act, then compensation will be payable under s 28 (as applied by s 121) for depreciation in the value of an interest in land or for disturbance in the enjoyment of land.

13 Access to highways

The possibility of making a claim for injurious affection when the physical access to a public highway is taken away or rendered less convenient has been dealt with at p 228. There are also statutory provisions concerning the stopping up of private rights of access. The highway authority has power under ss 124–125 of the Highways Act 1980 to stop up any private means of access from a highway to premises if the access is likely to cause danger to or interfere unreasonably with traffic or if the premises adjoin a trunk road, special road or classified road. A claim for compensation can be made by any person who suffers damage by depreciation of an interest in premises to which he is entitled or for disturbance in the enjoyment of the premises (s 126 (2)).

14 Other highways orders

A highway authority can make a 'public path creation order' under s 26 of the Highways Act 1980. Any person having an interest in land which is depreciated in value or who otherwise suffers damage by being disturbed in the enjoyment of land is entitled to claim compensation under s 28; the claim is to be in accordance with the relevant regulations.

If an improvement line is prescribed under s 73 of the 1980 Act compensation can be claimed by a person whose property is injuriously affected. Similar provisions apply where a building line is prescribed (s 74).

In *Westminster Bank Ltd* v *Minister of Housing and Local Government* [1971] AC 508 the House of Lords decided that the powers of a local planning authority to refuse planning permission were wide enough to enable them to refuse permission for the extension of a bank on the grounds that it was desirable for the street to be widened, even though alternative machinery was available to prescribe an improvement line under the Highways Acts. The authority could choose to refuse planning permission—which should not carry with it the risk of compensation—rather than use the improvement line procedure and face a claim for compensation.

There are various other powers in the Highways Act 1980 which enable highway authorities, eg, to alter levels (s 77), prevent obstruction of views at corners (s 79), etc. The use of these powers frequently carries with it a liability to pay compensation to those who suffer damage or incur expenditure.

15 Sewers

By virtue of s 15 of the Public Health Act 1936 a water authority may construct a public sewer through private land simply by serving reasonable notice on the owners of the land concerned. There is no land acquisition involved although the sewer itself will be the property of the water authority. However, an owner can claim compensation under s 278 of the 1936 Act, which provides that a local authority shall make full compensation to any person who has sustained damage by reason of the exercise by the authority of any of their powers under the Act. Disputes are to be settled by arbitration, but if less that £50 compensation is claimed the magistrates' court may determine the dispute. If compensation is claimed in respect of damage sustained by the construction of a sewer or laying of a water main over the claimants' land, then any betterment shall be taken into account by the arbitrator.

See the section entitled 'examples of claim' in Chapter 27 for cases where compensation was claimed following the laying of sewers etc.

16 Land drainage

Section 17 (5) of the Land Drainage Act 1976 provides that where injury is sustained by any person by reason of the exercise by a drainage authority of any of their general drainage powers, then the authority shall be liable to make full compensation to the injured person. In the case of dispute the amount of compensation is to be determined by the Lands Tribunal. This compensation provision is also applied in relation to other provisions of the 1976 Act (see s 33 (4), s 39 (4) and s 44 (3)).

17 Minerals

The Town and Country Planning (Minerals) Act 1981 introduced various modifications to the compensation provisions if orders are made to modify planning permissions for the working of minerals or to use the discontinuance order procedure to impose restoration and after-care conditions upon existing mineral workings. The provisions are set out in s 45 subss (5)–(7) and ss 51–51F of the 1971 Act.

The 1981 Act inserted a new section, 164A, in the 1971 Act, providing for a special basis for reduced compensation raised in respect of modification orders in relation to mineral permission. Similarly, new ss 178B and 178C made provision for compensation in respect of the discontinuance orders, prohibition orders, suspension orders and supplementary suspension orders which can be made under the new ss 51 to 51F. There are detailed provisions setting out preconditions for payment of the special rates of compensation.

18 Procedures and timetable for compensation claims

Section 178 of the 1971 Act applies the rules set out in s 5 of the Land Compensation Act 1961 to claims for compensation for revocation or modification (s 164) withdrawing permission for a development order, ie, Article 4 Directions (s 165); Eighth Schedule development (s 169); and discontinuance orders (s 170). This means that compensation for disturbance will be payable in all those cases.

Sections 178A–C set out the basis for compensation in respect of mineral working compensation orders.

Tree preservation orders (s 174), replanting directions (s 175) and stop notices (s 177) are specifically excluded from the provisions of s 178. That section will also not apply to compensation claims involving historic buildings (ss 171 and 173), or to ancient monuments, but it does apply to claims involving pedestrianisation orders (s 212 (7)).

Section 179 of the 1971 Act provides that (unless it is otherwise provided by a tree preservation order or by any regulations made under the Act) any question of disputed compensation under Pt VIII of the 1971 Act shall be referred to the Lands Tribunal. The tribunal will therefore normally determine the compensation in connection with revocation or modification orders, Article 4 Directions, Eighth Schedule rights, discontinuance orders, tree preservation orders (except as otherwise provided) and advertisement regulations claim. It will also deal with pedestrianisation order claims.

In most cases the procedure and timetable will be in accordance with reg 14 of the Town and Country Planning General Regulations 1976 (SI 1976 No 1419). Claims have to be made within six months of the relevant decision and shall be in writing and served on the appropriate authority. Forms are not prescribed.

In the case of claims concerning listed buildings (ie, ss 171–173) claims should be made in accordance with reg 9 of the Town and Country Planning (Listed Buildings and Buildings in Conservation Areas) Regulations 1987 (SI 1987 No 349). Again, this should be made within six months and should be submitted in writing.

Claims under s 174 in connection with Tree Preservation Orders should comply with art 11 of the model form set out in the Town and Country Planning (Tree Preservation Order) Regulations 1969 (SI 1969 No 17). The relevant period is 12 months from the date of decision. Claims relating to replanting directions under s 175 should be made within 12 months—see s 175 (4) of the 1971 Act.

Claims under the Advertisement Regulations should be made in accordance with regs 17 or 20 (as appropriate) of the Control of Advertisements Regulations 1989 (SI 1989 No 670).

Claims raised to the refusal of permission for 'new development', ie, involving an unexpected balance of established development value, should be made in accordance with the provisions of s 154 of the 1971 Act. A claim must be made within six months of the relevant planning decision.

19 Interest on compensation

It has already been explained (at p 263) that the Lands Tribunal can direct that a sum awarded by them shall carry interest from the date of the award. In *Hobbs (Quarries)* v *Somerset County Council* (1975) 30 P & CR 286, it was held that interest could not be awarded where planning permission had been revoked. This principle would seem to extend to modification orders, discontinuance orders and the other types of compensation payable under the 1971 Act and described in this chapter.

In the *Hobbs* case the tribunal commented that since they could award interest if sitting as an arbitrator behind closed doors, it seemed to verge on the absurd that they could not do so when sitting in open court. The law concerning interest on compensation is under review at the time of writing.

Appendix 1

Acts Conferring Powers of Compulsory Acquisition

1 Alphabetical table of principal Acts

ACT	MAIN PURPOSES	PARTS OR SECTIONS
Airports Act 1986	Purpose of airport operator	59
Ancient Monuments and Archaeological Areas Act 1979	Preservation of ancient monuments	10
Telecommunications Act 1984	In connection with the establishment or running of a public telecommunications operator's system	34
Caravan Sites and Control of Development Act 1960 Caravan Sites Act 1968	For provision of caravan sites and accommodation for gypsies	24 (of Act of 1960) 6 (of Act of 1968)
Civil Aviation Act 1982	Provision of aerodromes by local authorities For functions of Civil Aviation Authority	30 42
Coast Protection Act 1949	Coast protection	14, 27
Countryside Act 1968	For country parks, camping and picnic sites	4, 7, 9, 10

ACT	MAIN PURPOSES	PARTS OR SECTIONS
Education Acts 1944–1988	Land required for a school, college or education purposes, including transport, meals, recreation facilities	90 (Act of 1944)
Electricity Act 1989	Any purpose connected with authorised activities of holder of license to generate or supply electricity	10 & Sched 3
Fire Services Act 1947	For the purposes of the functions of a fire authority	3,8
Food Act 1984	For the purposes of the Act	110
Forestry Act 1967	Land for afforestation or forestry purposes	40
Gas Act 1986	Acquisition of land by a public gas supplier	9 & Sched 3
Highways Act 1980	For construction or improvement of a highway For constructing roads in accordance with special roads orders Other wide powers: see part 2 of this appendix	238–246
Housing Act 1985	For provision of housing accommodation and acquisition of clearance areas and unit houses	17, 192, 290, 300
	Housing action areas	243
	General improvement areas	255

ACT	MAIN PURPOSES	PARTS OR SECTIONS
Housing Associations Act 1985	Power to Housing Corporation to acquire for sale or lease to registered housing association or providing dwellings	88
Housing Act 1988	Housing action trusts	77
Industrial Development Act 1982	Power for Secretary of State to provide premises in development or intermediate area	14
Land Compensation Act 1973	Mitigating adverse effects of highways and other works	22
Land Drainage Act 1976	Functions of internal drainage board Drainage works against flooding	37, 98
Local Government Act 1972	For any purpose for which a principal council, a parish council or community council, is authorised to acquire land, unless expressly limited to purchase by agreement	121, 125
Local Government (Miscellaneous Provisions) Act 1976	Acquisition of 'new rights'	13
Local Government, Planning and Land Act 1980	Powers for Land Authority for Wales and urban development corporations	104, 142
Local Government and Housing Act 1989	Improvement of a renewal area	93

ACT	MAIN PURPOSES	PARTS OR SECTIONS
National Health Service Act 1977	By Minister or local social services authority for the purposes of the Act	87
National Parks and Access to the Countryside Act 1949	In connection with national parks, long distance routes, open air recreation and derelict land	12, 13, 17, 18, 21, 53, 54, 76, 77, 89 103
New Towns Act 1981	Land designed as site of New Town, adjacent land and land for services	16
Pipe-Lines Act 1962	Pipe-lines in land	11, 12–14
Police Act 1964	For the purpose of functions of a police authority, including functions in relation to traffic wardens	9
Post Office Act 1969	Purposes in connection with powers of Post Office	55
Prison Act 1952	Provision of prisons	36
Public Health Act 1875	Provision of public walks and pleasure grounds	164
Refuse Disposal (Amenity) Act 1978	Disposal of abandoned vehicles and refuse	7
Road Traffic Regulation Act 1984	Provision for parking places	40
Small Holdings and Allotments Act 1908	Allotments	25
Social services–Local Authority Social Services Act 1970	Transferred functions of local authorities under various enactments	2 (1), Sched 1
Telecommunications Act 1984	Establishment or running of telecommunications system	34

ACT	MAIN PURPOSES	PARTS OR SECTIONS
Town Development Act 1952	Purposes connected with town development	6
Town and Country Panning Act 1971	For development and other planning purposes	112
	By Secretary of State for Environment of land necessary for the public service	113
	Listed buildings in need of repair	114
	In connection with highway orders	218
Water Act 1989	Purposes of National Rivers Authority or water or sewage undertaker	151

2 Table of land acquisition powers for highways purposes

STATUTORY POWER TO BE CITED	PURPOSE OF PROPOSED ACQUISITION
Road Traffic Regulation Act 1984—s 40	(a) Provision of off-street parking places, including means of access and buildings or other facilities necessary to their use, by county councils, London Boroughs and district councils. [NOTE: s 186(1)(a) of the Local Government Act 1972 empowers both county and district councils to provide off-street parking but under s 39(3) of the 1984 Act the latter cannot exercise their powers without the consent of the county council. Where off-street parking places are to be provided by county councils, s 39(1) of the 1984 Act provides that they shall consult the district council concerned]. (b) provision of means of access to premises adjoining or abutting on to such parking places.
s 57	Provision of facilities similar to those in (a) and (b) above by parish councils (but subject to the consent of the county council).

STATUTORY POWER TO BE CITED	PURPOSE OF PROPOSED ACQUISITION
	[Note: The power to acquire land compulsorily for such purposes is exercised by the district council on behalf of the parish council under the provision of s 125 of the Local Government Act 1972].
Highways Act 1980— s 4	The execution of side road works in pursuance of an Agreement with a local highway authority under s 4.
s 239	(*a*) Construction of a new highway or improvement of an existing highway; (*b*) executing works authorised by an order under s 14 of the 1980 Act (such works can, by virtue of s 125 of the 1980 Act, include the provision of new means of access to premises and, by virtue of s 108 of the Act, the diversion of navigable watercourses); (*c*) the provision of maintenance compounds or other buildings or facilities in connection with all-purpose trunk roads; (*d*) the improvement of a highway included in the route of a special road but not yet transferred to the special road authority; (*e*) the purposes of an Order under s 18 of the 1980 Act (side roads and private accesses in connection with special roads); (*f*) the provision of service areas or maintenance compounds or other buildings or facilities in connection with special roads; (*g*) provision of exchange land where common land, etc, is to be acquired for the purposes of (*a*) to (*f*) above; (*h*) the improvement or development of frontages to a highway or land adjoining or adjacent thereto.
s 240	(*a*) The provision of private means of access to premises; (*b*) use of land in connection with the construction or improvement of a highway or with the carrying out of works authorised by an order under ss 14 or 18 of the Act or under s 108 of the Act [eg, for working space or for provision of access to a working site, the acquisition of parts of severed buildings]; (*c*) the diversion of an non-navigable watercourse or carrying out works to watercourses under s 110;

STATUTORY POWER TO BE CITED	PURPOSE OF PROPOSED ACQUISITION
	(*d*) the provision of a trunk road picnic area;
	(*e*) the provision of a public sanitary convenience under s 114;
	(*f*) the provision of a lorry area under s 115;
	(*g*) the provision of exchange land where common, etc, land is required for any of the purposes in (*a*) to (*f*) above.
s 241	Vacant land between improvement line and boundary of street.
s 242	Works in connection with certain bridges.
s 243	Providing, altering or improving cattle-grids.
s 244	Providing or improving a road-ferry.
s 245	Provision of a depot or other facility for a local highway authority.
s 246 (1)	The mitigation (in certain circumstances) of adverse effects of highways or proposed highways on their surroundings.
s 248	The acquisition of land in advance of requirements in the circumstances mentioned in subs (3) of s 248.
s 250	The acquisition of rights by the creation of new rights and the acquisition of exchange land where common, etc, land is to be burdened with new rights.
s 260	The inclusion of land, already acquired by agreement, in a compulsory purchase order so as to override the effects of a restrictive covenant or other third party right.

Acquiring Authority's Checklist for Compulsory Purchase Order Proceedings

Preparatory

1 Complete owners and occupiers list.
2 Obtain authority for dispensation from individual service of notices under s 6 (4) of the Acquisition of Land Act 1981 if reasonable enquiries fail to disclose owner.
3 Obtain planning consent for development proposed by the acquiring authority.
4 Prepare statement of reasons for making order.
5 Have six plans prepared for submission and deposit purposes with extra copies for office use and informal deposit purposes.
6 Check minute (or other authority) for making order.
7 Check that the land does not fall within any special category referred to in Pt 3 of the 1981 Act (see Chapter 11).
8 Check whether any building is listed or of list quality, subject to a building preservation notice or in conservation area. Prepare certificate as required by DOE Circular No 6/85, Appendix H.
9 Consider draft of statement of purpose of acquisition.
10 In complicated case, submit draft order to confirming Ministry for comment.

Making order

11 Prepare order in Form No 1 in the Compulsory

ITEM

Purchase of Land Regulations 1990 and seal two orders and two maps.

12   Arrange for a copy of the order and map to be placed on deposit in some place in locality for at least 21 days. If possible arrange for display in public libraries, Citizen's Advice Bureaux, etc, in the area as well as formal places of deposit.

13   Prepare certificate in respect of order submission—see Appendix D in Circular No 6/85.

14   Prepare certificate regarding building preservation (if necessary) or submit nil return in covering letter—see Appendix H in Circular No 6/85.

15   Certificate whether or not order contains (a) any consecrated land or (b) any land in a conservation area—see Appendix H Circular No 6/85.

Notices

16   Prepare press notice—Form No 7 in 1990 Regulations.

17   Send press notice to at least one local paper for advertisement in two successive weeks and order copies.

18   Prepare individual notices for owners, lessees, occupiers. Omit monthly, weekly or statutory tenants from service list. Use Form 8 or 9, as appropriate, in 1990 Regulations.

19   Enclose statement of reasons with the notice.

20   Serve notices personally; or by recorded delivery; or by registered post (see p 16 above for procedure where dispensation from individual service authorised).

21   Register making of order as local land charge if this is required by statute.

22   Inform local land charges registrar (to enable conveyancing enquiries form to be answered).

Submission of order

23   Submit order to Secretary of State for the Environment (or other confirming Minister) as soon as notices and advertisements have been issued.

Enclosure check list

(a) One sealed order and two sealed maps.

(*b*) Four additional unsealed copies of the order and two additional unsealed copies of the map.

(*c*) Certificate in support of order submission (Item 13) confirming: service of the notices (stating the date and method of service); unknown owners and whether individual service dispensed with; that the copy, order and map have been duly deposited; service of the statement of reasons on: owners lessees and occupiers; other residents and applicants for planning permission.

(*d*) Two copies of the statement of reasons for acquisition and that of any document referred to in it. The statement of reasons must include a statement of the planning position.

(*e*) Certificate regarding building preservation, or nil return (Item 14).

(f) Certificate regarding consecrated land or conservation area (Item 15).

(*g*) In highway cases where a distance limit is applicable, confirm that the plots are within 220 or 880 yards as appropriate from the relevant centre line (s 249 and Sched 18, Highways Act 1980; para 82 of Circular Roads No 1/81).

(*h*) In highway cases quote scheme title, Departmental reference number and pro-gramme year, and indicate whether the compulsory purchase order covers all outstanding land requirements for the complete scheme.

Confirmation

24 Make copies of the order as confirmed for service and official use.

25 Prepare press notice in Form No 10 in the 1990 Regulations.

26 Send press notice to at least one local paper (one publication only) and order copies. Inform confirming Department of date of first publication.

27 Serve notice in Form No 10 individually on all those served with notice under Item 18 (owners, lessees, etc) and enclose a copy of the order as confirmed.

ITEM

Notice to treat

28   Serve notice to treat on all owners.
29   Take instructions as to which lessees and tenants
      are to receive notice to treat (see p 57)

[*or alternatively*]

General vesting declaration

30   Serve prescribed notice (Form 2 in SI 1990 No
      467) on all owners, lessees and occupiers either
      with notice of confirmation or later (but before
      notice to treat). Claim form is incorporated in the
      notice.
31   Advertise in local newspaper (once).
32   Register as local land charge.
33   After two months execute the declaration (Form 1).
34   Serve notice of making on occupiers (not minor
      tenants) and owners and lessees who returned claim
      forms after Item 30 (use Form 3).
35   After 28 days, land and right to enter it vest.
36   Serve notice to treat and 14-day notice of entry on
      minor tenants.

Checklist of Compensation and Benefits under the Land Compensation Act 1973

A *Where land acquired*
  1 Owner-occupier
  2 Lessee
  3 Tenant
B *Where no land acquired*
C *Farmers*
  1 Owner-occupier
  2 Landlord
  3 Tenant

A (1) OWNER-OCCUPIER WHOSE INTEREST IS ACQUIRED
  Market value
  Disturbance compensation
  Compensation for severance and injurious affection if part only taken

  PLUS

s 29	Home loss payment if occupier for five years.

s 52	90 per cent advance of compensation—on date of dispossession and within three months of claim.

	If asked to sell part only
s 58	Wider right to insist on purchase of whole.
s 44	When left with severed part, 'before' and 'after' valuation for injurious affection compensation.
s 20	Noise insulation measures if excessive noise from traffic on new road.

s 46	Trader or businessman aged 60 or more and property not exceeding rateable value £18,000— may claim on basis of total extinguishment of business.

s 45	House adapted for disabled owner or occupier—compensation on basis of equivalent reinstatement.

A (2) LESSEE WHOSE INTEREST IS ACQUIRED [following notice to treat or notice under s 20 of the Compulsory Purchase Act 1965]

Compensation for loss of interest

Disturbance compensation for loss of profits, removal expenses etc.

Compensation for severance and injurious affection if part only taken.

PLUS

s 52	90 per cent advance of compensation on dispossession and within three months of claim.
s 47	Business tenant's compensation has regard to tenant's right to apply for new tenancy.
s 46	Business tenant over 60 may get compensation based on extinguishment of business.
s 45	Disabled tenant in adapted home can get comparable modifications.
s 29	Home loss payment if occupied five years.
s 39	Right to rehousing from housing authority if cannot get alternative accommodation on reasonable terms.
s 41	Qualifies for 'interest only' loan if he has a lease with three years or more to run and wants to buy a new home.
s 43	If buying alternative accommodation, may get reasonable incidental expenses.
s 58	If asked to sell part only Wider right to insist on purchase of whole.
s 44	When left with severed part, 'before' and 'after' valuation for injurious affected compensation.
s 20	Noise insulation measures if excessive noise from traffic on new road.

A (3) TENANT REQUIRED TO GIVE UP POSSESSION BY NOTICE OF ENTRY [yearly, monthly, weekly or statutory tenant]

s 29	Home loss payment if occupier for five years.
s 39	Right to be rehoused if cannot get alternative accommodation on reasonable terms.
s 38	Removal expenses.
s 38 s 46	Trade loss (assessed on basis of total extinguishment if aged 60 or over).
s 38	If disabled (or with disabled member of family) can get alterations in new premises comparable to any alterations in old which were grant assisted or eligible for grant.

B LAND NOT ACQUIRED—OWNER, LESSEE OR OCCUPIER

s 3 Compensation for depreciation by noise, fumes, lights, etc, if he is
owner of a house
owner-occupier of a farm
owner-occupier of a business property with rateable value not
exceeding £18,000
(owner includes lessee with three years or more of lease to run).
Must wait one year to see effects of use of the road, aerodrome or
other public works. And may then claim—unless he sells within the
year when he need not wait to claim.
No compensation for intensified use of existing roads or aerodromes.
Major carriageway or runway alterations to other public works are
included.
Claim must exceed £50.

s 20 Noise insulation against excessive traffic noise from new roads.

s 22 Authority may offer to buy property if future enjoyment is seriously
affected.

s 28 Hotel expenses to allow move during construction works if
authority agree.

C (1) OWNER-OCCUPIER FARMER
Market price
Disturbance compensation
Compensation for severance and injurious affection if part only
taken.

PLUS

s 29 Home loss payment on farmhouse if occupied for five years.

s 34 Farm loss payment to cover temporary loss of yield on new farm
which he begins to farm in three years.

s 63 Can require authority who want part of farm only to take the whole.

s 52 90 per cent advance of compensation on date of dispossession and
within three months of claim.

s 20 Noise insulation for farmhouse if excessive noise from new road.

s 3 If there is depreciation caused by nuisance from new roads, etc, he
can claim compensation one year after start of use even if no land
was taken.

C (2) Landlord of farm

s 48   Market value of reversion but discounting vacant possession value if only obtainable by virtue of the compulsory acquisition.

s 53   Can make authority who want part only of the farm take the whole, if remainder is not a viable farm unit. Otherwise may claim for severance and injurious affection.

s 54   If tenant has made authority take all the holding, landlord gets tenancy of remainder not needed for scheme back on reasonable terms.

s 52   90 per cent advance of compensation—on date of dispossession and within three months of claim.

s 20   Noise insulation for farmhouse against excessive noise from new roads, even if tenant does not agree.

C (3) Tenant farmer
Either
        Continues farming for balance of year plus 12 months on notice to quit under agricultural holdings law.

Or
        Receives value of unexpired interest terminated by notice of entry and based on his security of tenure under agricultural holdings legislation.

And
        Disturbance loss (one year's rent normal minimum).
        Tenant's right, ie, value of improvements.
        Four times the rent tax free.

        Plus

s 29   Home loss payment on farmhouse if occupied for five years.

s 55   Can make authority who want part of farm take the whole if remainder is not a viable farm unit.

s 20   Noise insulation for farmhouse for excessive noise from new roads.

Appendix 4

Compulsory Purchase by Non-Ministerial Acquiring Authorities (Inquiries Procedure) Rules 1990 (SI 1990 No 512)

Citation and commencement

1 These Rules may be cited as the Compulsory Purchase by Non-Ministerial Acquiring Authorities (Inquiries Procedure) Rules 1990, and shall come into force on 31 March 1990.

Interpretation

2 In these Rules, unless the context otherwise requires, references to sections and Parts are references to sections and Parts of the Acquisition of Land Act 1981, and—

'acquiring authority' means a local authority or any person (other than a Minister) who may be authorised to purchase land compulsorily and who has made and submitted an order to the Secretary of State for confirmation in accordance with Part II;

'assessor' means a person appointed by the Secretary of State to sit with an inspector at an inquiry or re-opened inquiry to advise the inspector on such matters arising as the Secretary of State may specify;

'clearance area order' means a compulsory purchase order made pursuant to section 290 of the Housing Act 1985;

'document' includes a photograph, map or plan;

'inquiry' means a local inquiry in relation to which these Rules apply;

'inspector' means a person appointed by the Secretary of State to hold an inquiry or a re-opened inquiry;

'land' means the land to which the order relates or, where a right over land is proposed to be acquired, the land over which such a right would be exercised;

'official body' means a Minister of the Crown or a government department;

'official case' means written statement by an official body setting out in detail its case in support of an order;

'official representation' means a written representation made by an official body in support of an order;

'order' means a compulsory purchase order as defined in section 7, or a compulsory rights order made pursuant to section 4 of the Opencast Coal Act 1958,

'outline statement' means a written statement of the principal submissions which a person proposes to put forward at an inquiry;

'pre-inquiry meeting' means a meeting held before an inquiry to consider what may be done with a view to securing that the inquiry is conducted efficiently and expeditiously, and where two or more such meetings are held references to the conclusion of a pre-inquiry meeting are references to the conclusion of the final meeting;

'relevant date' means the date of the Secretary of State's notice to the acquiring authority under rule 4(a); and 'relevant notice' means that notice;

'statement of case' means a written statement containing full particulars of the case which a person proposes to put forward at the inquiry (including, where that person is the acquiring authority, the reasons for making the order), together with copies of any documents referred to in such statement, or the relevant extracts therefrom, and a list of any documents to which that person intends to refer or which he intends to put in evidence;

'statement of matters' means a statement by the Secretary of State of the matters which appear to him to be likely to be relevant to his consideration of the order in question;

'statutory objector' means any objector to whom the Secretary of State is obliged by virtue of section 13(2) to afford an opportunity to be heard; and

'the 1976 Rules' means the Compulsory Purchase by Public Authorities (Inquiries Procedure) Rules 1976.

Application of Rules

3–(1) Subject to paragraphs (2) to (4), and to the provisions of rule 22(1) in respect of clearance area orders, these Rules shall apply in relation to any inquiry which is caused by the Secretary of State to be held in England or Wales pursuant to section 5, and which concerns an order made by an acquiring authority.

(2) The following paragraphs of this rule apply where a public authority (as defined in rule 3 of the 1976 Rules) has, prior to the date on which these Rules come into force ('the commencement date') submitted a compulsory purchase order to the Secretary of State for confirmation, and on that date no decision as to confirmation has been issued.

(3) Where at the commencement date a local inquiry has been opened but the inspector has not yet reported, the 1976 Rules shall continue to regulate the procedure until immediately before he reports, but these Rules shall apply to the making of the report and all subsequent procedures.

(4) Where at the commencement date a local inquiry has not been opened, the 1976 Rules shall continue to apply until the inquiry is opened, but these Rules shall apply thereafter.

Preliminary action to be taken by the Secretary of State

4 Where the Secretary of State intends to cause an inquiry to be held, he shall, not later than 14 days after either the expiry of the time within which objections to the order may be made, or the submission of the order to the Secretary of State for confirmation (whichever is the later), give written notice—

    (*a*) to the acquiring authority and to each statutory objector of that intention; and

    (*b*) to the acquiring authority of the substance of each objection made by a statutory objector, and, so far as practicable, of the substance of any other objections.

Preliminary action — acquiring authorities and official bodies

5 Where an acquiring authority proposes to rely, in its submissions at the inquiry, on an official representation, it shall within 7 days of receipt either of that representation or of the relevant notice (whichever is the later) send notification to the official body concerned that an inquiry is to be held; and within 14 days of receipt of such notification, the official body shall (unless it has already done so) supply to the acquiring authority an official case.

Procedure where Secretary of State causes pre-inquiry meeting to be held

6–(1) The Secretary of State may cause a pre-inquiry meeting to be held if it appears to him desirable and where he does so the following paragraphs apply.

(2) The Secretary of State shall serve with the relevant notice a notification of his intention to cause a meeting to be held and a statement of matters.

(3) Where an official representation or an official case has been made—

    (*a*) its text shall be included in the statement of matters served under paragraph (2); and

    (*b*) a copy of that statement shall be served on the official body concerned.

(4) The acquiring authority shall cause to be published in a newspaper circulating in the locality in which the land is situated a notice of the Secretary of State's intention to cause a meeting to be held.

(5) The notice published pursuant to paragraph (4) shall include the text of the statement of matters.

(6) The acquiring authority shall, not later than 8 weeks after the relevant date, serve on the Secretary of State and on each statutory objector an outline statement.

(7) The acquiring authority shall include the text of any official representation or official case in the outline statement, and shall, not later than 8 weeks after the relevant date, serve a copy of the statement on the official body concerned.

(8) The Secretary of State may by notice in writing require—

    (*a*) any statutory objector; and

    (*b*) any other person who has notified him of any intention or wishes to appear at the inquiry—

within 4 weeks of the date of such notice to serve on him, on the acquiring authority and on any other person specified in such notice, an outline statement.

(9) The meeting (or, where there is more than one, the first meeting) shall be held not later than 16 weeks after the relevant date.

(10) The Secretary of State shall give not less than 21 days written notice of the meeting to the acquiring authority, each statutory objector, and any other person whose presence at the meeting seems to him to be desirable; and he may require the acquiring authority to take, in relation to notification of the meeting, one or more of the steps mentioned in rule 11(5) and (6) in relation to notification of the inquiry.

(11) The inspector shall preside at the meeting and shall determine the matters to be discussed and the procedure to be followed; and he may require any person present at the meeting who, in his opinion, is behaving in a disruptive manner to leave and may refuse to permit that person to return or to attend any further meeting, or may permit him to return or attend only on such conditions as he may specify.

(12) Where a meeting has been held pursuant to paragraph (1), the inspector may hold a further meeting; and he shall arrange for such notice to be given of a further meeting as appears to him necessary; and paragraph (11) shall apply to such a meeting.

Service of statements of case, etc

7–(1) The acquiring authority shall, at least 28 days before the date fixed for the inquiry and not later than—
   (a) 6 weeks after the relevant date; or
   (b) where a pre-inquiry meeting is held pursuant to rule 6, 4 weeks after the conclusion of that meeting—
serve a statement of case on the Secretary of State and on each statutory objector.

(2) The acquiring authority shall, unless it has done so in an outline statement served pursuant to rule 6(6), include in its statement of case the text of any official case or official representation, and shall supply a copy of the statement to the relevant official body concerned within the relevant period for service of a statement of case under paragraph (1).

(3) The Secretary of State may by notice in writing require—
   (a) any statutory objector; or
   (b) any other person who has notified him of an intention or a wish to appear at the inquiry—
within 4 weeks of the date of such notice to serve a statement of case on him, on the acquiring authority and on any other person specified in such notice.

(4) The Secretary of State shall supply a copy of the acquiring authority's statement of case to any person who is not a statutory objector but has been required to serve a statement of case under paragraph (3).

(5) The Secretary of State or an inspector may require any person who has served a statement of case in accordance with this rule to provide such further information about the matters contained in the statement as he may specify.

(6) Unless a statement of matters has already been served pursuant to rule

6(2), the Secretary of State may, within 12 weeks from the relevant date, serve such a statement on the acquiring authority, each statutory objector and on any person from whom he has required a statement of case.

(7) The acquiring authority shall afford to any person who so requests a reasonable opportunity to inspect and, where practicable, takes copies of any statement or document which, or a copy of which, has been served on or by it in accordance with any of the preceding paragraphs of this rule; and shall specify in the statement served in accordance with paragraph (1) the time and place at which the opportunity will be afforded.

Further power or inspector to hold pre-inquiry meetings

8–(1) Where no pre-inquiry meeting is held pursuant to rule 6, an inspector may hold one if he thinks it desirable.

(2) An inspector shall arrange for not less than 14 days' written notice of a meeting he proposes to hold under paragraph (1) to be given to the acquiring authority, each statutory objector, any other person known at the date of the notice to be entitled to appear at the inquiry, and any other person whose presence at the meeting appears to him to be desirable.

(3) Rule 6(11) shall apply to a meeting held under this rule.

Inquiry timetable

9 Where a pre-inquiry meeting is held pursuant to rule 6 an inspector shall, and in any other case may, arrange a timetable for the proceedings at, or at part of, the inquiry and may at any time vary the timetable.

Notification of appointment of assessor

10 Where the Secretary of State appoints an assessor, he shall notify every person entitled to appear at the inquiry of the name of the assessor and of the matters on which he is to advise the inspector.

Date and notification of inquiry

11–(1) The date fixed by the Secretary of State for the holding of an inquiry shall be—

    (*a*) not later than 22 weeks after the relevant date; or

    (*b*) in a case where a pre-inquiry meeting is held pursuant to rule 6, not later than 8 weeks after the conclusion of that meeting; or

    (*c*) where the Secretary of State is satisfied that in all the circumstances of the case it is impracticable to hold the inquiry within the applicable period mentioned in (*a*) or (*b*), the earliest practicable date after the end of that period.

(2) Unless the Secretary of State agrees a lesser period of notice with the acquiring authority and each statutory objector, he shall give not less than 42 days written notice of the date, time and place fixed by him for the holding of an inquiry to every person mentioned in rule 12(1).

(3) The Secretary of State may vary the date fixed for the holding of an

inquiry whether or not the date as varied is within the applicable period mentioned in paragraph (1); and paragraph (2) shall apply to a variation of a date as it applies to the date originally fixed.

(4) The Secretary of State may also vary the time or place for the holding of an inquiry and shall give such notice of any such variation as appears to him to be reasonable.

(5) Unless the Secretary of State otherwise directs, the acquiring authority shall, not later than 14 days before the date fixed for the holding of an inquiry, post a notice of the inquiry in a conspicuous place near to the land and also in one or more places where public notices are usually posted in the locality.

(6) If the Secretary of State so directs, the acquiring authority shall, not later than 14 days before the date fixed for the holding of the inquiry, publish in one or more of the newspapers circulating in the locality in which the land is situated a notice of the inquiry.

(7) Any notice of inquiry posted or published pursuant to paragraph (5) or (6) shall contain a clear statement of the date, time and place of the inquiry, and of the powers under which the order has been made, together with a sufficient description of the land to identify approximately its location without reference to the map referred to in the order.

Appearances at inquiry

12–(1) The persons entitled to appear at an inquiry are:
- (*a*) any statutory objector;
- (*b*) the acquiring authority,
- (*c*) any other person who has served an outline statement under rule 6 or a statement of case under rule 7.

(2) Nothing in paragraph (1) shall prevent the inspector from permitting any other person to appear at an inquiry, and such permission shall not be unreasonably withheld.

(3) Any person entitled or permitted to appear may do so on his own behalf or be represented by counsel, solicitor or any other person.

(4) An inspector may allow one or more persons to appear on behalf of some or all of any persons having a similar interest in the matter under inquiry.

Representatives of official bodies at inquiry

13–(1) An official body shall arrange for its representative to attend the inquiry if it has—
- (*a*) made an official case pursuant to rule 5; and
- (*b*) received, not later than 14 days before the date fixed for the holding of an inquiry, a written request for such attendance from the acquiring authority or from a statutory objector.

(2) A person attending an inquiry as a representative in pursuance of this rule shall state the reasons in support of the official case in question and shall give evidence and be subject to cross-examination to the same extent as any other witness.

(3) Nothing in paragraph (2) shall require a representative of an official

body to answer any question which in the opinion of the inspector is directed to the merits of government policy.

Statement of evidence

14–(1) The Secretary of State may by notice in writing require any person who—

    (*a*) is entitled to appear at an inquiry; and

    (*b*) proposes to give, or call another person to give, evidence thereat by reading a written statement—

to serve a copy of that statement of evidence on the inspector, such service to be effected not later than 3 weeks before the date on which the person entitled to appear is due to give evidence in accordance with the timetable arranged pursuant to rule 9 or, if there is no such timetable, 3 weeks before the date fixed for the holding of the inquiry.

(2) An inspector may by notice in writing require any person who has served on him a copy statement pursuant to paragraph (1) to supply to him, within such period as he specifies, a written summary of the contents of the statement.

(3) Where the acquiring authority sends a copy of a statement of evidence or a summary to an inspector in accordance with paragraph (1) or (2), it shall at the same time send a copy to every other person mentioned in rule 12(1); and where any such person sends a copy statement or summary to the inspector he shall at the same time send a copy to the acquiring authority.

(4) Where the inspector has required a written summary of evidence in accordance with paragraph (2), the person giving that evidence at the inquiry shall do so only by reading the written summary, unless permitted by the inspector to do otherwise.

(5) Any person required by this rule to send a copy of a statement of evidence to any other person shall send with it a copy of the whole, or the relevant part, of any documents referred to in it, unless copies of the documents or parts of documents in question have already been made available to that person pursuant to rule 7.

Procedure at inquiry

15–(1) Except as otherwise provided in these Rules, the inspector shall determine the procedure at an inquiry.

(2) Unless in any particular case the inspector with the consent of the acquiring authority otherwise determines, the authority shall begin and shall have the right of final reply; and the other persons entitled or permitted to appear shall be heard in such order as the inspector may determine.

(3) A person entitled to appear at an inquiry shall be entitled to call evidence, and the acquiring authority and the statutory objectors shall be entitled to cross-examine persons giving evidence, but, subject to paragraphs (2), (4), (5) and (7), the calling of evidence and the cross-examination of persons giving evidence shall otherwise be at the inspector's discretion.

(4) The inspector may refuse to permit—

(*a*) the giving or production of evidence,

(*b*) the cross-examination of persons giving evidence, or

(*c*) the presentation of any other matter,

which he considers to be irrelevant or repetitious; but where he refuses to permit the giving of oral evidence, the person wishing to give the evidence may submit to him any evidence or other matter in writing before the close of the inquiry.

(5) Where a person gives evidence at an inquiry by reading a summary of his evidence in accordance with rule 14(4), the statement of evidence referred to in rule 14(1) shall, unless the person required to supply the summary notifies the inspector that he now wishes to rely on the contents of that summary only, be treated as tendered in evidence, and the person whose evidence the statement contains shall then be subject to cross-examination on it to the same extent as if it were evidence he had given orally.

(6) The inspector may direct that facilities shall be afforded to any person appearing at an inquiry to take or obtain copies of documentary evidence open to public inspection.

(7) The inspector may require any person appearing or present at an inquiry who, in his opinion, is behaving in a disruptive manner to leave and may refuse to permit that person to return, or may permit him to return only on such conditions as he may specify; but any such person may submit to him any evidence or other matter in writing before the close of the inquiry.

(8) The inspector may allow any person to alter or add to a statement of case served under rule 7 so far as may be necessary for the purposes of the inquiry; but he shall (if necessary by adjourning the inquiry) give every other person entitled to appear who is appearing at the inquiry an adequate opportunity of considering any fresh matter or document.

(9) The inspector may proceed with an inquiry in the absence of any person entitled to appear at it.

(10) The inspector may take into account any written representation or evidence or any other document received by him from any person before an inquiry opens or during the inquiry provided that he discloses it at the inquiry.

(11) The inspector may from time to time adjourn an inquiry and, if the date, time and place of the adjourned inquiry are announced at the inquiry before the adjournment, no further notice shall be required.

Site inspections

16–(1) The inspector may make an unaccompanied inspection of the land before or during an inquiry without giving notice of his intention to the persons entitled to appear at the inquiry.

(2) The inspector may, during an inquiry or after its close, inspect the land in the company of a representative of the acquiring authority and any statutory objector; and he shall make such an inspection if so requested by that authority or by any such objector before or during an inquiry.

(3) In all cases where the inspector intends to make an inspection of the kind referred to in paragraph (2) he shall announce during the inquiry the date and time at which he proposes to make it.

(4) The inspector shall not be bound to defer an inspection of the kind referred to in paragraph (2) where any person mentioned in that paragraph is not present at the time appointed.

Procedure after inquiry

17–(1) After the close of an inquiry, the inspector shall make a report in writing to the Secretary of State which shall include his conclusions and his recommendations or his reasons for not making any recommendations.

(2) Where an assessor has been appointed, he may, after the close of the inquiry, make a report in writing to the inspector in respect of the matters on which he was appointed to advise.

(3) Where an assessor makes a report in accordance with paragraph (2), the inspector shall append it to his own report and shall state in his own report how far he agrees or disagrees with the assessor's report and, where he disagrees with the assessor, his reasons for that disagreement.

(4) If, after the close of an inquiry, the Secretary of State—

  (a) differs from the inspector on any matter of fact mentioned in, or appearing to him to be material to, a conclusion reached by the inspector, or

  (b) takes into consideration any new evidence or new matter of fact, (not being a matter of government policy)—

and is for that reason disposed to disagree with a recommendation made by the inspector, he shall not come to a decision which is at variance with that recommendation without first notifying the persons entitled to appear at the inquiry who appeared at it of his disagreement and the reasons for it; and affording them an opportunity of making written representations to him within 21 days of the date of the notification, or (if the Secretary of State has taken into consideration any new evidence or new matter of fact, not being a matter of government policy) of asking within that period for the re-opening of the inquiry.

(5) The Secretary of State may, as he thinks fit, cause an inquiry to be re-opened to afford an opportunity for persons to be heard on such matters relating to the order as he may specify, and he shall do so if asked by the acquiring authority or by a statutory objector in the circumstances and within the period mentioned in paragraph (4); and where an inquiry is re-opened (whether by the same or a different inspector)—

  (a) the Secretary of State shall send to the persons entitled to appear at the inquiry who appeared at it a written statement of the specified matters; and

  (b) paragraphs (2) to (7) of rule 11 shall apply as if references to an inquiry were references to a re-opened inquiry, but with the substitution in paragraph (2) of '28 days' for '42 days'.

Notification of decision

18–(1) The Secretary of State shall notify his decision on the order and his reasons therefor in writing to—

(*a*) the acquiring authority;

(*b*) each statutory objector;

(*c*) any person entitled to appear at the inquiry who did appear thereat; and

(*d*) any other person who, having appeared at the inquiry, has asked to be notified of the decision.

(2) Where a copy of the inspector's report is not sent with the notification of the decision, the notification shall be accompanied by a copy of his conclusions and of any recommendations made by him; and if a person entitled to be notified of the decision has not received a copy of that report, he shall be supplied with a copy of it on written application made to the Secretary of State within 4 weeks of the date of the decision.

(3) In this rule 'report' includes any assessor's report appended to the inspector's report but does not include any other documents so appended; but any person who has received a copy of the report may apply to the Secretary of State in writing, within 6 weeks of the publication of the notice of confirmation pursuant to section 15, for an opportunity of inspecting any such documents and the Secretary of State shall afford him that opportunity.

Allowing further time

19 The Secretary of State may at any time in any particular case allow further time for the taking of any step which is to be taken by virtue of these Rules, and references in these Rules to a day by which, or a period within which, any step is to be taken shall be construed accordingly.

Service of notices by post

20 Notices or documents required or authorised to be served or sent under any of the provisions of these Rules may be sent by post.

Revocation of previous Rules

21 Subject to rule 3, the 1976 Rules are hereby revoked.

Clearance area orders

22–(1) Notwithstanding the provisions of rule 3, these Rules shall apply in relation to an inquiry concerning a clearance area order only where that order is made on or after the coming into force of paragraphs 72 and 73 of Schedule 9 to the Local Government and Housing Act 1989.

(2) Where a building is included in such an order on the ground that it is unfit for human habitation, the statement of case served by the acquiring authority pursuant to rule 7(1) shall contain their principal reasons for being satisfied that the building is so unfit.

Appendix 5

Draft Agreement for Sale Providing for Reference to Lands Tribunal if Compensation not Settled by Agreement

[See p 35]

NOTE—This agreement recites that a notice to treat is deemed to have been served on the date of the agreement. This will not, however, stabilise values as at this date. Provided that the authority intend to take possession at an early date, no problem should arise. The value will then be assessed as at the date of taking possession. If however, a longer period may elapse before the land may be needed, the parties should consider and provide for a date as at which market value is to be assessed. As to the problems which may arise under an agreement of this sort in regard to the date for assessing compensation see *Marchment and others* (*Execs*) v *Hampshire County Council* (1979) 43 P & CR 436.

   1 I/WE
of
agree to sell to the   Council (hereinafter called 'the Council')
my/our interest in   at a price to be agreed or failing
agreement to be settled by the Lands Tribunal under the Lands Tribunal Act 1949 in the same manner as if the necessary steps for acquiring such interest compulsorily had been taken under the   Act   and the Acquisition of Land Act 1981 and a Notice to Treat had been served on the date of this Agreement.

   2 It is agreed that I/We shall not by virtue of this agreement be obliged to give any other title or convey any other estate than would have been the case if the land/premises had been acquired under a Compulsory Purchase Order made under the Acquisition of Land Act 1981.

   3 The Council may take possession of the said land/premises immediately/on the   and may execute such works thereon and use the land/premises for all such purposes as they may require.

   3A The Council shall on taking possession execute within   months the works described in the Schedule hereto for the benefit of my/our adjoining land.

4 Interest is to be paid on the purchase price as agreed or awarded at the statutory rate for the time being in force (less tax) from the date of such entry until the completion of the purchase provided that no interest shall be payable whilst my/our tenant continues to pay rent to me/us in respect of the said land/premises.

5 The Statutory or other Forms of Conditions of Sale shall not apply to this Agreement
or:
The Law Society's Contract for Sale (1984 Revision) or the National Conditions of Sale 1980, 20th ed, as amended and annexed to this agreement shall form part hereof and apply hereto.

6 The Council upon completion of the purchase shall pay the sum of   in respect of my/our Solicitors' costs in connection with this Agreement and in addition will pay my/our Solicitors' costs for deducing title and perusing and completing the Conveyance and (unless the price is fixed by arbitration) my/our Surveyors' fees on the basis of Scale 5 (a) of the Schedule of Professional Charges of the Royal Institution of Chartered Surveyors.

7 My/our interest in the property is
Dated this   day of   199

Signed................................

The Council hereby accepts the above offer.
Signed on behalf of the Council.

....
Solicitor to the Council

Date.............................. 199.............

Schedule of accommodation works

Index